Mussolini's Gadfly
ROBERTO FARINACCI

Mussolini's Gadfly

ROBERTO FARINACCI

—◦●◦—

HARRY FORNARI

1971
VANDERBILT UNIVERSITY PRESS
Nashville

Printed in the United States of America by
Kingsport Press, Kingsport, Tennessee

71, 919

TO MISA

CONTENTS

ILLUSTRATIONS

ix

PREFACE

ITALIAN FASCISM, both as a political doctrine and as a form of government, officially came to an end a quarter of a century ago. Since then, there have been some scholarly studies of the history of Italy during the Fascist regime and of certain prominent episodes of the regime itself. With a strange disregard for the truism that history is made by the actions of individuals, however, historians have produced no biographies of the many oligarchs who created Fascism and kept it in power for more than two decades, with the single exception of the acknowledged founder and ruler of Italian Fascism, Benito Mussolini. About Mussolini much has indeed been written, but even for him a definitive biography is only halfway completed. In any event, Mussolini obviously did not originate and sustain Fascism single-handed. He was not even an archetypal Fascist, for the man who best answered that description, although less well known than some others, was the one who most completely exemplified the Fascist drive to power through any and all violent means: Roberto Farinacci.

Throughout his activist career, which began shortly before World War I and ended at the hands of partisan executioners in April 1945, Farinacci was a firebrand determined to make his views prevail at any cost. From 1919 on, in fact, he was "more Fascist than the Duce," as Mussolini was called, with histrionic aping of ancient Roman grandeur. Indeed, Mussolini, for all his bombast, was not a heroic figure, but a fraud who selfishly based his policies and actions primarily on the shifting guidelines of cynical opportunism. Farinacci, just as egocentrically, spoke and acted with unwavering adherence to the totalitarian tenets of Fascism, trying, all the while, to steer Mussolini and, through him, the Fascist government unto the same orthodox course.

To begin to fill the biographical vacuum which exists in the historiography of Fascism, it is therefore the purpose of this study to provide a full and accurate history of Farinacci's life and career, making use primarily of documentary evidence which is now abundantly available. The U.S. National Archives in Washington, D.C., are in possession of microfilm copies of voluminous Italian government files, taken by the Germans after their occupation of Rome in September 1943 and captured by the Allies at war's end. The files of Mussolini's private secretariat are in this collection, and they comprise thousands of letters, telegrams, police reports, and other documents, specifically relating to Roberto Farinacci, from the early 1920s right down to 1945. The Italian State Archives in Rome also have substantial collections of Farinacci's own records; and complete files of Farinacci's newspapers, from *La Squilla*, begun in 1914, to the final issue of *Il Regime Fascista* on April 25, 1945, are preserved in Cremona.

From these sources, it will be shown how, behind the monolithic façade of Fascism, there always raged, albeit with varying intensity, a struggle between Mussolini's aspirations to pretentious respectability and Farinacci's sectarian intransigence; how, given the existence of such a struggle, it was generally necessary for Mussolini to maintain a stance sufficiently truculent not to alienate his most factious supporters and, eventually, to act in accordance with the aggressive totalitarian spirit; and finally how Farinacci's goading of Mussolini played an indirect but instrumental part in dragging the Fascist government to its end and Italy through a tragic and costly interlude.

It is axiomatic that no historian can describe events and personalities of his own time and maintain complete immunity to the influence of his own experiences and convictions. The author of this study claims no exception to such a rule; but he has nevertheless made a conscientious effort to obtain and present all the factual evidence, in the belief that the facts alone will provide an eloquent indictment of Fascism and in the hope that the study will make a modest contribution to historical knowledge and understanding—for, as Marc Bloch wrote, "When all is said and done, a single word, understanding, is the beacon light of our studies."

HARRY FORNARI

Great Neck, New York
July 1970

ACKNOWLEDGMENTS

Since it would be impossible to list and thank individually the many persons in the United States and in Italy who at one time or another have lent some measure of support or advice to my historical studies, I should like to express to them all collectively my sincere appreciation.

Some names, however, stand out in the mind and in the heart and mentioning them is not only a dutiful but a particularly pleasant task.

First, the former Executive Officer of the History Doctoral Program at the City University of New York, Dean Hyman Kublin, and his successors, Professors Howard L. Adelson and Allen McConnell, all of whom have been most generous and understanding with me.

My research has been aided immeasurably by the co-operation of Dr. Angelo Daccò, Director of the Civic Library of Cremona; Dr. Richard Logsdon, formerly Director of Libraries at Columbia University; Professor Leopoldo Sandri, Superintendent of the Italian State Archives in Rome; and Dr. Richard Bauer of the U.S. National Archives in Washington, D.C. Valuable help with background material has also been freely given by Professor Renzo De Felice of the University of Rome.

A special word of praise goes to Lesley Ashford and Pat Timpanaro, who bravely and efficiently typed and retyped a growing mountain of pages.

Professor Keith Eubank, Chairman of the History Department at Queens College, was at all times lavish with guidance and advice, and he was also instrumental in correcting mistakes of method and style: my gratitude for his help is deep and heartfelt.

I wish to thank Laura Fermi, widow of "the architect of the nuclear age," and herself a noted specialist in the history of Italian Fascism, for her perceptive comments and helpful suggestions.

My thanks also go to the staff of Vanderbilt University Press for continuing support and wise counsel, particularly to Martha Strayhorn, who edited the manuscript with unfailing grace and the sharpest critical eye.

Finally, and in dedication to her of this effort as of all past and future ones, I wish to mention my wife, Maria Luisa Fornari, without whose intelligent encouragement and loving forbearance this work would not have been possible.

H. F.

Mussolini's Gadfly
ROBERTO FARINACCI

I

FIRST
SPARKS OF A
FIREBRAND

"HE WHO behaves like a sheep," says an old Italian proverb, "is bound to get eaten by a wolf."

Few episodes in history illustrate the truth of this bit of popular wisdom more clearly than the rise of Fascism in Italy during the immediate aftermath of World War I, and the subsequent take-over and engulfment of all Italian life and institutions by a totalitarian Fascist regime with the fearful acquiescence or cowering co-operation of vast segments of the Italian population. And few figures in history give a clearer picture of the methods and techniques used by "wolves" to subdue "sheep" than that of the man who throughout his life was identified as the standard-bearer of Fascism's most intransigent faction: Roberto Farinacci.

Farinacci's origins were humble. His father was an indigent public servant, born in Naples while that city was still under Bourbon rule. Michele Farinacci had joined the Italian police force in his early twenties and served his apprenticeship in several cities of Tuscany. He had gone back to Naples in 1885 to choose a bride and there had married Amelia Scognamiglio, a pretty brunette whose physical charms were enhanced by a dowry consisting of some cash and a few apartments, the rental of which handily supplemented his meager police pay.

A six-footer with broad shoulders and an equally ample waistline, ruddy complexion, and jet-black handlebar moustaches, Michele Farinacci was a striking figure of a man, usually wearing a broad-brimmed black hat and carrying a knobby walking stick. He was a conscientious functionary, well liked by his superiors, so that a few years after his marriage he advanced to the rank of *Commissario di Pubblica Sicurezza*.[1]

Meanwhile two children were born to the Farinaccis, Giuseppe and Mario. The beautiful Amelia was well advanced in her third pregnancy when Michele was once more transferred and the family moved to Isernia, a small town in the Molise region of central Italy. There, on October 16, 1892, Amelia gave birth to another son, who was named Roberto after his maternal grandfather.

No notable events marked young Roberto's infancy and boyhood, except the birth of two more brothers, Ettore and Armando, and a sister, Amalia. Then, in 1900, the Farinacci family again had to pull up roots and move to Michele's new post at Tortona, in cold and unfamiliar Piedmont. There Roberto, who had begun grade school at Isernia, continued for the next eight years in a half-hearted attempt to keep up with his more conscientious older brothers and to obtain a formal education. His lack of success, however, resulted in his being twice compelled to repeat the year's courses, so that, by 1908, when again the family moved, this time to Cremona, fifty miles south of Milan, Roberto was only in the ninth grade. The violent temper which was to become his most obvious characteristic in later years was already beginning to assert itself, and the youth of sixteen, sporting a black moustache and looking older than his age, found it unbearable to sit day after day in class with a group of fourteen-year-olds in short pants, listening to lectures that held no interest for him.

His decision to drop out of school and get a job met with little

1. Literally, "Commissioner of Public Safety," a high-sounding title which is, however, merely the equivalent of "Precinct Commander." The subdivision of Italy into regions (Piedmont, Lombardy, Tuscany, etc.) is a purely geographical expedient; the administrative and juridical local units are the ninety-odd provinces, each formed of a city or large town and its hinterland, and each headed by a prefect directly responsible to the central government in Rome. Under the general authority of the prefect, the police functions in each city are exercised by a *Questore*, who in turn assigns a *Commissario* and a number of plainclothesmen to each borough or section of the city and to each neighboring town. Only during the last few years, as a result of local agitation, have there begun to be exceptions made to this centralizing system, by giving Sicily, the Tyrol, and most recently Calabria, a measure of administrative autonomy.

or no opposition from his parents. Probably his father, the good police functionary, felt relieved at the thought of having one less mouth to feed. Consequently, in the fall of 1909, Roberto obtained the position of assistant telegraph operator with the Italian State Railways. He was assigned to the railroad station in nearby Piacenza; but after a few months, his father, through friends in the administration, was able to have him transferred back to Cremona. After a short period of service in the freight dispatcher's office, Roberto moved to the job of telegraph operator, a position he was to hold for most of his twelve years as a railwayman. Around this same time, as befitted an ambitious young man with a quick, sharp tongue and no fear of jumping into debates or fights, Roberto Farinacci began to take an active part in politics.

Since the proclamation of the Kingdom of Italy in 1861, the liberals had dominated the Italian political scene, because, although not united in a single formally organized party, they had, through a continually shifting combination of "Right" and "Left" groupings, enjoyed on the whole an overwhelming majority of the seats in Parliament. By the turn of the century, however, socialism and radicalism had spread throughout the country and had achieved a fairly substantial and disproportionately vocal representation in the Chamber of Deputies. The growth of socialism was, of course, both cause and effect of the organization of labor unions, which in the early 1900s in Italy began to reach impressive proportions, accompanied, as was to be expected, by widespread unrest and strikes sparked by political as well as economic motives. Cremona's Deputy, Leonida Bissolati, in the forefront of the socialist agitation since 1895, was the founder of the Socialist Party newspaper *Avanti!* and leader of the party's "reformist" faction.[2]

Roberto Farinacci, by inclination, would probably have joined

2. At the Italian Socialist Party Congress in 1902, the struggle which had been already in progress for several years resulted in the splitting of the party into two opposing factions: the Revolutionaries, led by Costantino Lazzari, who pursued a doctrinary Marxist program of class struggle; and the Reformists, who accepted and supported Bissolati's goal of inserting the proletarian masses into the existing political system, and eventually achieving their participation in the government.

the Revolutionary Socialists or perhaps the Anarchists, had he not come under the spell of Bissolati, whose charismatic figure and fiery speeches quickly made him the idol of the young activist. Bissolati, in turn, found in Farinacci a useful helper, always ready to represent the Reformists in the almost daily street-corner debates with the Revolutionaries and with the Clericals, and even more in the free-for-alls which frequently interrupted or culminated the debates.

Since politics and unionism in Italy were as much interconnected then as now, Farinacci soon became involved in labor disputes as an agricultural union organizer.

Cremona's location in the heart of the Po Valley made it a focal point of the struggle between tenant farmers and agricultural day laborers. In the early 1900s, these two groups began to organize into co-operatives, each aiming to extract from the other the greatest possible economic advantage. In 1910, a heated controversy arose over the ownership and use of threshing machines, and young Roberto Farinacci participated actively in the debates and negotiations which ensued.[3]

Also at the end of 1910, shortly after his eighteenth birthday, Farinacci was married. His bride, Anita Bertolazzi, was a pretty brunette of the same age, the daughter of an ardent socialist who owned an ice cream parlor. The dark, handsome Roberto had swept her off her feet with his aggressive manner, and when it appeared obvious that any further delay would prove embarrassing, a wedding was hastily arranged. The young couple moved in with the bride's family, and, in the spring of 1911, Anita Farinacci gave birth to a son, Franco.

The spring of 1911 brought certain political developments which affected Farinacci to some extent and, more directly, affected the man with whom Farinacci's entire future life and career would become passionately and irrevocably intertwined, Benito Mussolini.

There was, at this time, a sharpening of the conflict between the two factions, the Revolutionaries and the Reformists, within the

3. L. Preti, *Le Lotte agrarie nella valle padana* (Turin: Einaudi, 1955), p. 255.

Socialist Party. At the end of March, the Luzzatti Cabinet fell, and King Victor Emmanuel called Leonida Bissolati, among others, to the Quirinale Palace to discuss the composition of a new cabinet.[4] Having been asked by Giovanni Giolitti, the new Premier, to join the cabinet, Bissolati refused, expressing "invincible repugnance" for the work of a Minister; but he stated that outside the government he could do much to bring about the serious reforms needed to give a solid base to Giolitti's task.[5]

The mere fact of having had contact with the monarch, however, brought Bissolati under attack by one of the most extreme Revolutionaries, Benito Mussolini. Mussolini, who was to become Italy's first dictator in modern times, had been born in 1883 in Romagna, the hotbed of Italian socialism. The son of a blacksmith and a schoolteacher, Mussolini had himself been a teacher for a brief period but had soon moved on to a variety of odd jobs, including a stint as a bricklayer. A two-year stay in Switzerland had brought him into contact with international socialism, and on his return to Italy in 1904 he had begun the journalistic career and active participation in politics which were ultimately to pave the way for his power grab eighteen years later.

As leader of the Socialists in Romagna, Mussolini now thundered against Bissolati's action, demanding his expulsion from the party. Violent debates followed throughout northern Italy, and Farinacci did his share of haranguing in defense of his Reformist mentor. The immediate outcome of the polemic was the withdrawal of Mussolini and his followers from the party into a splinter group which continued to assail the Reformists at every opportunity. A major topic of argument was provided during the summer of 1911 by the rising agitation for the occupation of Tripolitania. The most ardent advocates of this colonial adventure were the members of the newly organized Nationalist Movement, which was avowedly against Liberalism, Democracy, Freemasonry, and Socialism, and whose concern with national pride found ex-

4. I. Bonomi, L. *Bissolati e il movimento socialista in Italia* (Turin: Einaudi, 1955), p. 255.

5. Bissolati to Giolitti, March 27, 1911, Italian Central State Archives, Rome (hereinafter referred to as ICSA), Bissolati Fund, Env. 1, Folder 2.

pression at this time in the desire to channel Italian emigrants to conquered colonies rather than to foreign countries.[6]

Squarely in opposition stood Mussolini and his Romagnoli Socialists, while the Socialist party was lukewarmly opposed and Bissolati and the Reformist faction were willing to go along with the government's decisions.

When, at the end of September 1911, the Italian ultimatum was sent to Turkey, Mussolini made a violent speech opposing the imminent war and calling for a general strike. The strike took place only in Romagna, and Mussolini was arrested two weeks later and eventually sentenced to five months in jail for inciting to riot. His prestige, however, was greatly enhanced, as was to become only too apparent at the Socialist Party Congress which was held in Reggio Emilia in July 1912. Three months earlier, soon after his release from jail, he had led his group back into the fold of the party, which was now even more troubled by the split of the Reformist group into "left" and "right" factions. At the Reggio Emilia Congress, Mussolini delivered the keynote speech and, by a strong majority vote, ultimately obtained the expulsion from the party of the "right" reformist leaders, Bissolati and Ivanoe Bonomi. This victory propelled Mussolini from the position of a mere provincial chieftain within the Socialist party to that of a national leader, and it was to result a few months later in his being made editor in chief of *Avanti!*.[7]

Another result of the Reggio Emilia Congress, however, was the formal organization by Bissolati and his followers of the Reformist Socialist party and the emergence of Roberto Farinacci as one of the leaders of this party at Cremona. Farinacci began to write from time to time for *L'Eco del Popolo*, Cremona's Socialist weekly, which, after wavering for a few months, had come out

6. As part of their expansionistic platform, the Nationalists were also in the forefront of Irredentism, clamoring for the "liberation" of those Alpine and Adriatic regions which, although ethnically predominantly Italian, were parts of the Austro-Hungarian Empire. The Nationalists later became leading supporters of intervention in World War I and of Italy's territorial claims at the Versailles Peace Conference, and, at a very early stage in the organization of the Fascist party, they merged with it.

7. Gaudens Megaro, *Mussolini in the Making* (Boston and New York: Houghton Mifflin Co., 1938), pp. 44–50.

supporting Bissolati and calling for unity in the Socialist ranks.[8]

Also in this period, owing to his increasing political activity, Farinacci entered into a close relationship with Alessandro Groppali, an older Socialist lawyer and university professor, who, in later years, became for a while Farinacci's law partner and financial adviser. From Groppali, Farinacci acquired a smattering of culture, which, superimposed on his naturally aggressive delivery, made him more popular than ever as a partisan orator. Often he neglected his railroad job, but invariably his colleagues, some out of friendship and some out of fear, covered up for him and actually did his work. He was thus able to make frequent trips to Rome to see Bissolati (as a railroad employee, he enjoyed the use of a free pass) and to roam the countryside organizing the farm workers into the Reformist Socialist party and launching vitriolic attacks against the Catholic labor organizations led by the Deputy of nearby Soresina, Guido Miglioli.

Towards the end of 1913, Farinacci, the better to give vent to his anti-clerical views, founded a students' club in Cremona, the *Circolo Laico "Roberto Ardigò,"*[9] whose meetings consisted primarily of lectures and discussions on atheism and attacks on organized religion. This move helped to increase his following among Cremonese Socialists, but Farinacci was still, undeniably, in the shadow of Bissolati. Through the spring and summer of 1914, Farinacci continued to alternate his halfhearted work in the railroad station with the more satisfying political speechmaking. Articles written by him, some unsigned and some under the pseudonym "Bob," continued to appear in *Eco del Popolo,* which was, as in the past, engaged in endless polemics with the Liberal weekly *La Provincia* and the Clerical *Azione.*

Then came Sarajevo; and the emergence of new issues opened new vistas and fields of activity for Roberto Farinacci, penniless railwayman and politician, not yet twenty-two, but already possessed of a wife, a child, some notoriety, and insatiable ambition.

8. *L'Eco del Popolo* (Cremona), May 10, 1913.
9. *L'Eco del Popolo* (Cremona), December 20, 1913.

II

FARINACCI
IN THE TRENCHES AND
ON THE STUMP

ITALY HAD been since 1882 a member of the Triple Alliance with Germany and Austria-Hungary. Originally conceived by Italy as protection against any French attempt to restore the temporal power of the Papacy, by Austria-Hungary as a guarantee of Italian neutrality in the event of war with Russia, and by Bismarck as an attempt to control the other two restless nations through yet another strand in his diplomatic web, the Triple Alliance had subsequently undergone numerous modifications prompted by the shifting policies and alignments of European diplomacy and politics over more than three decades. Furthermore, in 1902, although subscribing the quinquennial renewal of the Triple Alliance after obtaining from Austria-Hungary in a secret protocol a free hand in Lybia, and from Germany the release from the obligation to send troops to the Rhine in the event of war, Italy had concluded a secret agreement with France promising to remain neutral if France were the object of direct or indirect aggression by one or more powers, or if she went to war as a result of a direct provocation.

Regardless of diplomatic entanglements, in any event, Italian public opinion in 1914 was shaped primarily by attitudes and prejudices of long standing: Austria-Hungary, repeatedly fought during the *Risorgimento* and the wars of independence, was the traditional enemy, while France, in spite of occasional family quarrels, was Italy's "Latin sister," and England was the object of respectful envy and admiration.

It came as no surprise, therefore, that on August 2, 1914, five days after Austria had declared war on Serbia, and the day after

Germany had invaded Luxemburg, the Italian government declared that Italy would remain neutral, since she had not been consulted by the other members of the Triple Alliance before going to war, and since the war appeared to be one of aggression while the Triple Alliance was of a defensive nature. And, as could also be expected, the outbreak of war and the Italian declaration of neutrality sparked violent dissension among Italian political leaders and vast segments of the population.

The Nationalists, at the outset, favored intervention on the side of Germany. The Clericals, following the veiled Austrophile leanings of the Vatican, supported neutrality, as did, for different doctrinaire reasons, the official Socialist party. As editor of *Avanti!*, Mussolini initially took a strong antiwar position, and in fact published a manifesto advocating a referendum against the war. After a few months, however, his attitude began to change; and suddenly, on November 15, he quit his post and began publishing *Il Popolo d'Italia*, clamoring for Italy's intervention on the side of the Allied Powers. The funds for his new venture were supplied in part by Italian industrialists and in part by the French government.[1]

The Reformist Socialists, taking as their goal the liberation from Austrian rule of the northeastern regions surrounding Trento and Trieste and stressing the innate hostility between Latin and Teutonic civilizations, were from the start in the forefront of the movement that favored Italian intervention against the Central Powers.

A meeting was held in Milan at the end of October 1914 to co-ordinate interventionist efforts in Lombardy, and it was decided there to start in each city a publication devoted to the aim of bringing Italy into the war against the Central Empires. At Cremona, the task of organizing this publishing effort fell to a committee of five members, among them Roberto Farinacci; and on November 18, 1914, the first issue of *La Squilla* (*The Clarion*) was printed.

The masthead of this four-page newspaper clearly identified it as a "Socialist Weekly" and as the official newspaper of the Pro-

1. Luigi Salvatorelli e Giovanni Mira, *Storia d' Italia nel periodo fascista* (Turin: Giulio Einaudi editore, 1964), pp. 43–51.

vincial Federation of Autonomous Socialist Groups and the Reformist Group of Cremona. Flanking the title were two mottoes, one by Marx and the other by Mazzini.[2] Angelo Fulgoni appeared as publisher, but it was common knowledge in Cremona that the driving force behind the paper, and the interventionist movement as well, was Roberto Farinacci. Perhaps to give the impression that the paper had many contributors, Farinacci used the pseudonyms *L'Osservatore* (Observer) and *Noi* (We). The leading editorial in the first issue, entitled "A Crisis in History and a Crisis in One's Conscience," called on all patriots to rally against the "eternal enemies," Austria and Germany, and to answer the call of the *squilla* (clarion). On page 2, a brief note signed "Observer" pointed out that "all the Socialists have not prevented Europe from exploding into war, but the best part of socialism is that which loves the Motherland."[3]

In an obvious effort to spread circulation and to win readers and supporters throughout the countryside, the rest of the paper was filled with bits of local news from the smaller towns and villages surrounding Cremona. This was truly essential, for Cremona, in spite of its millenary history, was not a large city. Founded by the Romans *circa* 218 B.C. as an outpost against the Gauls, it became one of the first Italian city-states through the expulsion of its count-bishop in 1022. Nevertheless, Cremona had remained relatively small and unimportant through the centuries—a large town rather than a true city, with its main claim to fame being the inimitable string instruments produced there in the seventeenth century by Amati, Stradivari, and Guarneri. Now, in 1915, Cremona was indeed the capital of the province; but its population was a mere 40,646, while the other 132 towns and villages in the province had a total of 312,933 inhabitants.[4]

2. The quotation from the Father of Socialism read: "There is never a political movement which is not at the same time a social one." The apostle of Italian republicanism was quoted as saying: "Principles are the only foundations."

3. *La Squilla* (Cremona), November 18, 1914. Since the outbreak of war, *L'Eco del Popolo* had reverted to the strict party line of the Revolutionary Socialists.

4. *Calendario Generale del Regno d'Italia pel 1915*, Compiled by the Ministry of Interior (Rome, 1915).

Roberto Farinacci, therefore, well aware of the need to reach and captivate the rural population, endeavored from the beginning to devote ample space in *La Squilla* to the petty issues which interested the farmers. His articles and notes, even when unsigned, could be easily recognized because of their vituperative style and the abundance of expletives and pejorative adjectives; Farinacci, in other words, wrote as he spoke. He also began a practice which would always characterize his writings, the use of the first person plural pronoun; those who knew him maintain that this was meant more as a *pluralis majestatis* than as the editorial "we."[5]

Propaganda favoring Italy's entry into the war was never missing from the pages of *La Squilla* as publication continued, but more and more prominence was given to polemics against other parties' newspapers over local issues and local political personalities and, above all, to attacks on the official Socialist party and its activities in the province of Cremona. This first editorial effort by Farinacci was, it must be recognized, an uphill battle, because the vast majority of the population was under the influence of the official Socialists, and the one area where the Socialists were less strong, the rich farmland around Soresina, was closely controlled by the Clerical Syndicalists led by Guido Miglioli.

In an effort to stir up enthusiasm for the interventionist cause, therefore, the Reformist Socialists joined together with the Republicans and the Rightist Liberals in holding a series of rallies. The first, highlighted by an impassioned cry for help by the Belgian patriot and diplomat Jules Destree, was well attended; but it was with the second rally, held at the Ponchielli Theatre on December 29, 1914, that the interventionist movement of Cremona asserted itself as a strong political force. The principal speaker was Cesare Battisti, the irredentist leader from Trento who was to join the Italian Alpine Corps upon Italy's entry into the war, and who in July of 1916 would be captured and hanged by the Austrians as a deserter. His speech at the rally, as reported by

5. The first instance of this mannerism appears in the fifth issue of *La Squilla*, where, replying to accusations of mud-slinging made by *L'Eco del Popolo*, Farinacci wrote: "We repeat that our moral superiority over you is beyond question." *La Squilla* (Cremona), December 16, 1914.

Farinacci in *La Squilla*, could hardly have been more inflammatory, again and again denouncing Austrian persecution of the Italian population of the Trentino region and closing with a call to all Italians to rise in arms to liberate their oppressed brethren. Such a speech, which neglected the welfare of faraway Belgium or abstruse aspects of international politics but stressed the pitiful plight of "*Italia irredenta*," could not fail to strike a sensitive chord, and it was received by the audience with wild enthusiasm.

Farinacci, as one of the organizers, shared in the rally's success. In the next issue of *La Squilla*, he boasted that his newspaper had reached a circulation of 2,000 copies, and characteristically concluded: "Tomorrow is ours."[6]

As 1915 opened, the lineup of the opposing factions in the province of Cremona became increasingly clear, with Farinacci's paper and the Liberal *La Provincia*, a daily supported by landowners and industrialists, jointly accusing the Clericals of collusion with the official Socialists in advocating neutrality.[7] It was a stinging charge, prompting the Clerical *Azione* to reply that while it would always fight Socialism, as long as "the laws and all sense of public and private honesty" were trampled on, it would fight alongside free men, "no matter what their banner."[8]

That there was some substance to the accusation of collusion, however, seemed clear in mid-February, when a public rally, called by the interventionists of Cremona in the *Piazza del Municipio*, was disrupted by joint action of Socialist and Clerical groups, and ended in fist fights and clubbings. Spurred, by reaction, into greater effort, Roberto Farinacci intensified his propaganda and recruiting of supporters, and soon afterwards he was able to claim a membership of 1,200 for the interventionist movement in the city of Cremona alone.[9]

The growth of the interventionist forces seems confirmed by the fact that in the next violent confrontation, following a prowar rally at the Eden Theatre on April 10, the Socialist and Clerical assailants were routed with quite a few broken heads and

6. *Ibid.*, December 30, 1914.
7. *Ibid.*, January 6, 1915.
8. *Azione* (Cremona), January 31, 1915.
9. *La Squilla* (Cremona), April 3, 1915.

bloody noses. A gloating Farinacci described the encounter in detail, adding: "Let's hope they've learned their lesson."[10]

About this time, Farinacci became the Cremona correspondent for *Il Popolo d'Italia*, and thus came in contact with Mussolini. At first, it was merely a nodding acquaintance, but, as the months passed, a closer relationship developed. In fact, when *Azione* accused Mussolini of cowardice, Farinacci came to his defense, writing: "We, who do not campaign for Mussolini because we do not share his revolutionary conception, yet admire him. He had the courage to leave a good position in the Party because of his convictions."[11]

Meanwhile, the Italian government, on the basis of article VII of the Triple Alliance, had asked Austria for territorial compensations as counterpart to her own expansion into the Balkans and had been rebuffed. Turning to the *Entente* powers, Italian Foreign Minister Sydney Sonnino opened negotiations aimed at bringing Italy into the war on their side, and on April 26, 1915, secretly concluded with them the Treaty of London which, in return for Italy's intervention, promised her the Alpine and Adriatic regions now ruled by Austria, including northern Dalmatia, as well as other territorial gains in Asia Minor and in Africa.

The interventionist agitation reached a feverish pitch, until, on May 3, Italy denounced the Triple Alliance and, twenty days later, declared war on Austria-Hungary.[12]

On May 29, Leonida Bissolati enlisted and left at once for the front, but Farinacci remained in Cremona through the summer and fall, making patriotic speeches and printing violent attacks on the Socialist municipal administration and on his growing list of political opponents. Because his writing had become more vituperative than ever, in June *La Squilla* was made the target of three suits for libel, and its publisher, Angelo Fulgoni, received a suspended sentence. Possibly because of this, Fulgoni withdrew and was replaced as publisher by another figurehead, Riccardo Bona.

10. *Ibid.*, April 17, 1915.
11. *Ibid.*, August 28, 1915.
12. Italy declared war on Turkey in June 1915, but did not take this step against Germany until more than a year later, on August 27, 1916.

Farinacci's failure to join the army at once, however, could not be ascribed to cowardice. He had been exempted from serving his statutory term of duty in 1910 because he was a railroad worker. When he tried to volunteer in 1915, he was rejected as being a state employee in an essential occupation. *L'Eco del Popolo* naturally took him to task for his apparent failure to practice what he preached, and Farinacci printed side by side his application to join the army as a volunteer and the official notice of rejection.[13]

Either through his continuing efforts to enlist or because of a change in official policy, however, a few days later Farinacci did join the army; and on December 4, 1915, he reported for duty with the 3rd Regiment of Telegraph Engineers in Florence.[14]

After a brief training period, Farinacci's outfit was assigned to the war zone, arriving there on April 16, 1916. Nine days later, Farinacci was promoted to corporal in the 3rd Company, with which he moved to the front lines near *Passo di Rolle*, in the Dolomites. He remained in this area for almost a year, showing great courage and disregard of physical danger. At one time, he volunteered to remain in a forward position continuously for four months, while most of his comrades were relieved every fifteen days. On another occasion, with an officer, he brought to safety several wounded soldiers during an enemy bombardment. He also served on detached duty with the *Bersaglieri* on a peak in the *Colbricon* range, at an altitude of more than 8,000 feet, and there he was slightly wounded.[15] He was later awarded the Military Cross.[16]

While in the army, Farinacci managed to maintain contacts with his political friends in Cremona and from time to time wrote brief pieces for *La Squilla*. Even though its original aim of interventionist propaganda had been accomplished, *La Squilla* had continued publication in support of the war effort and as mouth-

13. *La Squilla* (Cremona), November 20, 1915.

14. Military District of Cremona, Archives, Index No. 25930.

15. Testimony of Angelo Jacoponi at trial for defamation on charges brought by Farinacci against *L'Eco del Popolo*. *La Squilla* (Cremona), December 1, 1917.

16. Military District of Cremona, Archives, Index No. 25930.

piece of the Reformist Socialists against the official Socialists and the Clericals.

Early in 1917, however, the Italian government realized that the railroad service was being poorly run by inexperienced personnel, and decided to call back from the front all railwaymen who had been drafted into the army. Accordingly, on March 29, 1917, Corporal Farinacci was sent on indefinite leave and ordered to resume his duties with the State Railways in Cremona. Once home, he plunged with greater passion than ever in the political struggle, intensifying his attacks on the opposition both in the columns of *La Squilla* and in frequent street debates. His polemics were no longer limited to local opponents: he did not hesitate to inveigh against the official Socialists of Milan, who had met the representatives of the Moscow Soviet, Josif Petrovich Goldenberg and Vladimir Mihailovich Smirnoff, with cries of "Long live Lenin, down with Kerensky." "Revolutionary Russia," Farinacci wrote on this occasion, "wants first of all the destruction of German militarism and imperialism. The Leninists are a negligible and tiny minority. A separate peace would be a crime against democracy throughout the world."[17]

One of the opposition newspapers, smarting under his intemperate diatribes, retorted with accusations of cowardice, claiming that Farinacci had found in the army a safe niche in the rear echelons. Farinacci sued for defamation of character and, some months later, was vindicated when the Court gave judgment in his favor.

He also began to get involved in practical matters, such as the negotiation of the Farming Agreement between agricultural workers and landowners. This was an annual contract, which fixed working conditions as well as rates of pay. Bargaining had generally been conducted for the workers by the Socialist Chamber of Labor, except in the Soresina area which was controlled by the Clericals and their White Leagues. Now a third force appeared on the scene, propelled by the joint efforts of all interventionist groups, the Independent Farmers Leagues. At the

17. *La Squilla* (Cremona), August 18, 1917.

first congress of these organizations, held in Cremona on April 28, 1917, Farinacci was named to head a committee for the revision of the Farming Agreement. As part of this work, he toured the province holding meetings and rallies in order to bring more and more farmers within the ranks of the Independent Leagues. It was a chance to come into contact with large masses of people and to make himself better known. Farinacci did not miss the opportunity; nor did he slacken his activity in support of the war. A Patriotic League had been formed in Cremona early in 1917; and on his return, Farinacci joined it, soon emerging as its leader. Besides his weekly tirades in *La Squilla*, Farinacci spoke almost daily in Cremona or in the countryside, aiming his most intemperate attacks at the Clerical Deputy of the Soresina District, Guido Miglioli, and at the Socialist mayor of Cremona, Mario Garibotti.

Early in the fall of 1917, Farinacci's organizing efforts were rewarded when the Farm Agreement prepared by the Federation of Independent Farmers Leagues was accepted by a large number of landowners. Soon after, however, the rout of the Italian army at Caporetto threw a pall of gloom on the country and infused new energy into the Socialist and Clerical groups who had been vocally opposing the war.

After the Italian retreat was finally halted on the banks of the Piave River, supporters of the war began looking aggressively among military and political leaders for scapegoats upon whom to pin responsibility for the disaster. General Luigi Cadorna, who was removed from the post of commander in chief of the Italian forces, quickly became a byword as a symbol of defeat. And Guido Miglioli, Deputy from Soresina, was singled out as one of the principal exponents in the Chamber of Deputies of the antiwar feeling which was equated with lack of patriotism. On December 13, 1917, as he was walking on a street in Rome, Miglioli was set upon by a group of fanatic interventionists who beat him and spat on him. Two weeks later, during a public session of the Provincial Council of Cremona, which it was known that Miglioli would attend, Farinacci and his followers packed the gallery and successfully disrupted the meeting, going as far as stoning the hapless Deputy as he escaped from the hall. In his own way, Farinacci described the incident. ([On December 27, 1917 [he testified later], I arrived in Cremona and was informed that the Provincial Council intended to pass a motion of sympathy for Miglioli, deploring the actions of our Roman friends who had beaten and spat upon the most obscene defeatist in Italy. We attended the meeting, and first heard Councilman Lanfranchi deliver a speech in praise of our army on the Piave, which was loudly applauded. At that moment Miglioli entered the hall, the man on whom must fall the responsibility for Caporetto, and he joined in the applause. We could not let this provocation go unanswered, and we shouted at him: "German, sold-out, traitor, coward, sodomite, the Germans are at the Piave because of you." I took part in this demonstration, and I am proud of what I did against that bum on whose head the maledictions of all Italy must fall. . . . We did too little to him. . . . The man who has spread so much poison in the Soresina district, inciting women to sabotage the war, telling soldiers to drop their arms, urging the people to rise like in Russia, deserved more, he deserved to be forever put out of circulation.[18]

Even though Farinacci thus admitted the truth of the charges brought against him, the Italian army's success in arresting the Austro-German onslaught and, even more, the fact of having the enemy inside Italy served to create among the population a wave of patriotic feeling in which all excesses of the war's supporters could be condoned and even praised. It was not surprising, therefore, that the charges of hooliganism brought by Miglioli against Farinacci for the incident of December 27, 1917, were dismissed, when trial was held the following March 18, by the judge finding that "no crime [had] been committed." In June 1918, Miglioli's appeal was also rejected by a higher court.

Emboldened by his acquittal on April 20, 1918, Farinacci published an open letter advocating "that the example of Rome be followed in Cremona, and that the dishonorable sodomite of Soresina be removed from circulation."[19]

18. Testimony of Roberto Farinacci at trial on charges brought against Farinacci and La Squilla by Miglioli. (La Squilla (Cremona), June 1, 1918.)
19. La Squilla (Cremona), April 20, 1918.

This time it was Miglioli's secretary, Giulio Speranzini, who preferred charges against *La Squilla*. The resulting controversy was widely reported in the national press, thus first bringing Farinacci's name before a wider public. In fact, contributions to defray the cost of the defense came to *La Squilla* from many parts of Italy, as did a message from Mussolini inviting "the friends of Cremona to pursue with vigor the struggle for the final liquidation of one of the most obscene representatives of black defeatism."[20]

By now, Roberto Farinacci was undeniably a major power on the Cremona political scene, as well known in the city as in the countryside. Those who were close to him at the time remember him as undefatigable, always on the move between the *Tipografia Sociale* where *La Squilla* was published and the railroad station where he had to put in sporadic appearances if only to justify collecting the salary which was still his only source of income.[21] He was always in the forefront of any street fracas, holding rallies in the villages around Cremona or presiding at meetings of the *Lega Patriottica* or the *Societá Giordano Bruno* (an anticlerical group which had replaced the *Circolo Ardigò*) or the Independent Farmers League. His temper was as violent as ever and his speech more than ever intemperate and interspersed with obscenities. So unpredictable and frenetic were his comings and goings that his family saw little of him. The sweet and docile Anita appeared reconciled to remaining quietly in the background, raising the child and just waiting for her Roberto to come home when it suited him. From all accounts, incidentally, Farinacci had already embarked at this time on the career of marital infidelity which he was to pursue throughout his life. In a provincial city

20. Paolo Pantaleo, *Il Fascismo Cremonese* (Cremona: Societá Editoriale "Cremona Nuova," 1931), p. 30. The trial was not held until November 27, 1918, and in the euphoric atmosphere of the victory just won, the Court dismissed the charges, again with the verdict that "no crime [had] been committed."

21. In the summer of 1918, reporting the appointment of Farinacci as chief of the telegraph office in the Cremona railroad station, the opposition press pointedly called attention to his manifold political activity which must greatly reduce the efficiency of his railroad work. (*L'Eco del Popolo* (Cremona), August 17, 1918.)

like Cremona, secrets were obviously difficult or impossible to keep; nevertheless, it does not appear that Farinacci ever made any attempt at concealment of his casual adventures. The good Anita may have cried privately but she maintained a dignified posture in public.

Meanwhile, the Italian war effort gained momentum, while the Hapsburg strength continued to dwindle. The last Italian offensive in October 1918 broke through the enemy lines into the Vittorio Veneto plateau and converted the Austrian retreat into a rout, culminating in the armistice of November 4. Thus the curtain fell on the last act of a European tragedy, and immediately rose again on the first act of an Italian one.

III

THE
TROUBLED
PEACE

LESS THAN two weeks after World War I ended with the victory of the Allies, the Italian Chamber of Deputies held its first peacetime session in three and one-half years. At once it was obvious that the debates would be dominated by two opposing political views rather than by the amorphous liberal majority. Champions of these opposing views were the Socialists and the Nationalists: the former demanded the resumption of the political struggle but with more radical aims, while the latter advocated the abolition of this struggle through a national totalitarian regime.[1]

As early as December 12, 1918, the official Socialist party published a program which proposed as its objective the institution of a Socialist Republic and the dictatorship of the proletariat. Almost simultaneously, the Nationalist movement launched an appeal to all "men of good faith," except "defeatists," to join in a holy crusade against "bolshevism." Meanwhile, new political forces were coming to the fore. On January 18, 1919, there was formed in Rome a new political party, the Popular party, which was based on principles of Christian democracy and had the unofficial backing of the Vatican. At the beginning of 1919, also, the vast masses of demobilized soldiers formally organized the National Association of War Veterans, with the distribution of land to farm workers as its main program. And the same month of January 1919 saw the founding of an organization which was

1. Salvatorelli e Mira, *Storia d'Italia*, pp. 16ff.

shortly to provide the bulk of Mussolini's early supporters and street-fighters, the Association of Italian Arditi.[2]

At Cremona, as in many other areas of northern Italy, municipal administrations were in the hands of the official Socialists, both in the provincial capital and in a large number of neighboring towns and villages. Peculiar to the province of Cremona— primarily because of the syndicalist activities of Guido Miglioli in the Soresina district—was an unofficial working alliance between Socialists and Populars. Against these groupings, which were drawing strength from the end of the war and the return of demobilized soldiers, stood a motley crew of Reformist Socialists and Nationalists, members of one or more of three interventionist and "antibolshevik" organizations which Roberto Farinacci had joined and of which he had quickly become a leader: the Lega Patriottica, the Rinnovamento (literally, Renewal), and the Fascio Antibolscevico.[3]

The competition and frequent clashes between all these groups throughout Italy caused growing unrest which had primarily economic origins. Italy, never a rich country, had sought and received ample loans from the Allies to sustain her war effort, but the end of hostilities had also put an end to this flow of financing. Food supplies were scarce, especially for city dwellers, and Italy, although victorious on the battlefield, found itself in economic straits almost as dire as those of the defeated countries.

2. The Arditi (literally, the "daring ones") had been elite assault troops, similar to the future Commandos, who had distinguished themselves during the war as much for bravery in combat as for rowdiness and lack of discipline.

3. The fascio (literally, bundle), was the armful of rods bound to an ax which, as the tools of punishment, the lictor bore when preceding the consul in ancient Rome. The rods and ax had been used as the emblem of Mazzini's Roman Republic in 1849; and the Sicilian rebels in the 1890s had taken the time-honored name of a workers' group: Fascio. The name fascio, in the sense of grouping, had also been used by the interventionists led by Filippo Corridoni and by Mussolini in the organization of the "Interventionist Fasci of Revolutionary Action" in 1915, by the Nationalists and the Liberals who had set up the "Parliamentary Fascio for National Defense" in the Italian parliament first in 1914 and again after the Caporetto debacle in 1917, and also by the Futurist followers of F. T. Marinetti, who, in 1917, had joined in the "Political Futurist Fasci."

During the war, the rich had gotten richer and the poor had gotten poorer. The worst off were the small bourgeoisie, the farmers, public employees, and industrial workers. At the end of the war, those farmers and workers who had been able to raise their standards of living through the scarcity of labor and through war salaries wanted to keep those advantages and to increase them; and those who had seen nothing but blood and toil during the war wanted to get some compensation from the nation.

These large masses of disgruntled farmers, workers, and unemployed veterans were the prize over which argued and fought the activist members of the more extreme political currents. At the outset it appeared that the official Socialists, as the longer established and better organized representatives of the laboring classes, would gain control of them.

The ascendancy of the official Socialists was aided by the decline of the Reformists, owing to Leonida Bissolati's virtual disappearance from the political scene. The Reformist leader, who had fought bravely in the front lines and had been gravely wounded in 1916, had subsequently served as minister without portfolio under the premiership of Paolo Boselli, and as Minister for War Pensions in the Orlando Cabinet. On December 31, 1918, he had resigned from his post, claiming that Italy's territorial demands were incompatible with his principles. On January 11, 1919, under the auspices of the Friends of the League of Nations, Bissolati was to speak at a rally at La Scala in Milan, to explain the reasons for his withdrawal from the government and his opposition to the government's expansionist policy. In Milan that day, it was widely rumored that acute disturbances would mark the rally. In fact, Farinacci, at Cremona, considered for a time driving to Milan with a band of supporters to defend Bissolati, but in the end did not go because the truck he had tried to obtain for transportation could not be used. That evening at La Scala, large groups of hecklers, led by Mussolini and F. T. Marinetti, shouted Bissolati down until he gave up trying to make himself heard. It was a turning point in Mussolini's career which once again put him in the national limelight.

Mussolini had been in the forefront of the interventionist movement since his defection from Revolutionary Socialism in

November 1914. On August 31, 1915, he had been called to the colors, and had served at the front in the *Bersaglieri* until February of 1917, when he was seriously wounded by the explosion of a mortar shell. After a long but successful recovery, he had gone back in August 1917 to Milan, to the editorship of *Il Popolo d'Italia*. After Caporetto, Mussolini had been most aggressive in attacking neutralists and "defeatists," accusing the Socialists and the Clericals of treason and the government of ineptitude.

Il Popolo d'Italia, since its first issue, had borne the subtitle "Socialist Daily." On August 1, 1918, however, this caption was replaced by another, "Daily Newspaper of Fighters and Producers." As has been aptly noted, the switch represented an astute tactical maneuver aimed at providing Mussolini with a number of new options. By the summer of 1918, the end of the war was in sight. The official Socialist party was stronger than ever, and to them Mussolini was a traitor and an outcast. The Nationalists had strong contacts in the ruling political and industrial circles. The Clericals, while accepting the war, had maintained their basic pacifist attitude, and thus the backing of the Church. Even the Reformist Socialists, while ardently in favor of the war, had not severed all ties with Socialism and Democracy. Mussolini instead was alone, and he decided to lay the groundwork for a future offensive which would gain him a large following. By eliminating any reference to Socialism in his newspaper's masthead, he gave himself freedom to assume any more suitable political coloring; the new reference in the masthead to "fighters" made him the champion of returning veterans; and the claim to represent "producers" was ambiguous enough to permit him to appeal to farmers and workers as well as to landowners and industrialists who, after all, were also engaged in "production."[4]

Throughout the rest of 1918, Mussolini continued his agitation in the columns of his newspaper and in public speeches, now supporting the aspirations of the working masses, now justifying the "antibolshevik" resistance of the employers. At war's end, he supported the League of Nations, and when U.S. President Woodrow Wilson visited Milan on January 5, 1919, Mussolini gave vir-

4. Salvatorelli e Mira, *Storia d'Italia*, pp. 52–53.

tually the entire issue of *Il Popolo d'Italia* over to praise for "the People's Prophet." At the same time, however, he launched the attack on Bissolati which was to culminate in the tumultuous meeting at La Scala on January 11, basing his vituperation on Bissolati's opposition to Italy's territorial claims. "Imperialism," wrote Mussolini, "is the eternal and immutable law of life."[5]

Roberto Farinacci, who had continued to work as correspondent from Cremona for Mussolini's newspaper, had not, however, so far cut his ties to Socialism.[6]

Now attracted by Mussolini's demagogic leadership and aware of his rising stature on the political scene, Farinacci decided to abandon Bissolati and jump on Mussolini's bandwagon, and he published an article boasting that *La Squilla*, which had been "born even earlier than its big brother, *Il Popolo d'Italia*," and which had been in the forefront of interventionism, would no longer be the organ of the Reformist Socialists.[7] Farinacci multiplied his attacks on the official Socialists and the Clericals—now represented by the newly formed Popular party—analyzing scornfully the latter's program of social reform and accusing its members of being "nothing but priests."[8]

The attacks against Farinacci also naturally continued, with both *L'Eco del Popolo* and *L'Azione* publishing exposés accusing him of having misappropriated railroad funds and of having suborned a witness against him in the administrative inquest that had followed.[9] It is obviously impossible to determine now where the truth of the matter lay; it is significant, however, that all Farinacci could retort was that the judicial authorities had not found sufficient grounds to proceed against him.[10]

While Farinacci was intensifying his political and journalistic

5. *Il Popolo d'Italia* (Milan), January 1, 1919.
6. The whole of Farinacci's writings in *La Squilla* until the end of 1918 belies the claim he made in 1933: "We, who in 1914 abandoned Socialism to follow Benito Mussolini . . ." (Roberto Farinacci, *Squadrismo—Dal mio diario della vigilia, 1919–1922* (Rome: Edizioni Ardita, 1933), p. 11.)
7. *La Squilla* (Cremona), January 14, 1919.
8. *Ibid.*, February 8, 1919.
9. *L'Eco del Popolo* (Cremona), January 11, 1919; *L'Azione* (Cremona), January 16, 1919.
10. *La Squilla* (Cremona), February 8, 1919.

activity in Cremona, agitation by farmers and industrial workers was spreading throughout Italy. The farmers were demanding the distribution of land, and the industrial workers wanted increased wages and participation in management. The claims of the working classes were advanced by various labor organizations, each with a distinct political coloring. Strongest by far was the General Confederation of Labor, fully controlled by the official Socialists, against which stood the Italian Workers' Union, which was run by interventionist syndicalists in alliance with the Republican party. The latter union had among its members most of the two thousand workers who, on March 15, 1919, after vainly demanding a number of concessions, such as collective bargaining, the eight-hour day, and a minimum wage, from the management of the Franchi-Gregorini Foundry at Dalmine, near Milan, struck and took over the plant, in the very first instance of a sit-in strike in the history of Italian syndicalism. On March 17, the intervention of fifteen hundred soldiers forced the evacuation of the factory; but on March 20, Mussolini went to Dalmine and addressed the strikers, promising them support for their just demands, but exhorting them to rise above the selfish interest of their class and to strive for the betterment of the entire nation.[11]

It was an obvious maneuver to build a following among the masses, drawing them away from doctrinaire Socialism. The lesson was not lost on Farinacci, who, on March 21, appeared at Grontardo at a rally called by the Socialist Chamber of Labor and tried to solicit farmers to join the Independent Farmers Leagues by promising support for an eight-hour day for farm laborers. The organizers of the rally, however, prevented him from participating in a debate with the Socialist speakers, an affront which Farinacci swore would not happen again.[12] Two days later, with two Cremonese followers, Oreste Mainardi and Leonardo Cottarelli, Farinacci went to Milan to attend the meeting called by Mussolini for the founding of the *Fasci di Combattimento*.[13]

11. *Il Popolo d'Italia* (Milan), March 21, 1919.
12. *La Squilla* (Cremona), March 22, 1919.
13. Farinacci's wife was at this time in the last stages of her second pregnancy, and while her husband was with Mussolini in Milan on March 23, 1919, she gave birth to a daughter, Adriana, whom Farinacci first saw on his return to Cremona.

The first announcement of the meeting had appeared in *Il Popolo d'Italia* on March 1, and it had been followed on March 9 by an article signed by Mussolini stating that on March 23 he would found, not a party, but a movement, in fact "an antiparty, namely, the *Fasci di Combattimento*, which will fight against two dangers: the opposition to change of the Right, and the destructiveness of the Left." "We must," he concluded, "save the peace from sabotage, which may come from the top or from the bottom, from the imbecility of the government or from the ignorance of [Socialist] party members."

It was obvious that Mussolini, realizing at last the hopelessness of any attempt to rejoin the Socialist camp (his recent offensive against Bissolati might have been aimed at replacing him at the head of the Reformists, but it had not achieved that result) and recognizing also the need to create for himself a formal following which could constitute a basis for dealing with other parties from a less isolated position, now strove to rally to himself all those who, regardless of party affiliation or economic class, had supported interventionism and were opposed to Leninist socialism. Mussolini made this even more clear when, after boasting of the great number of acceptances and promises of support he claimed to have received from all parts of Italy, he wrote: (*If one examines the platforms of the various parties, old and new . . . they resemble each other. In some parts they are identical. What differentiates parties is not the platform: it is the starting point and the finish line. . . . Our starting point is the nation, the war, the victory. In other words, we start from interventionism. This divides us irreparably . . . from official Socialism . . . we claim the right and accept the duty of transforming, if necessary even with revolutionary methods, Italian life. Whoever would paint us as conservatives or reactionaries . . . is a big idiot. We interventionists are the only ones in Italy who have the right to speak of revolution. . . . We have already made our revolution, in May 1915. The revolution which continued under the name of war during forty months is not over. . . . Which are the basic principles of our future action? We want the material and spiritual rise of all Italian citizens (not only of those who call themselves proletarians) and the greatness of our people in the world. As to the means, we have no rigid principles, we will use whichever are necessary: legal means, and so-called illegal ones.*[14] In spite of Mussolini's boast, the group which Farinacci joined on March 23 in the hall of the Commerce and Industry Association at Piazza San Sepolcro in Milan consisted of only about seventy men and a few women. The meeting lasted all day, marked by violent speeches against "the government of deserters" betraying Italy at Versailles and against the "bolshevik" violence erupting throughout Italy. The participants approved a number of resolutions reaffirming their patriotism and their opposition to all "defeatists." They heard Mussolini, contradicting his recent disdain of programmatic postulates, recite a program which offered something to the extremists of all parties, from the abolition of the monarchy to the limitation of state functions, from the distribution of lands to the farmers and of profits to the industrial workers to the abolition of the draft and the prohibition of arms manufacture. He also, however, courted the bourgeoisie, by pointing out that workers must be made to realize the difficulties and responsibilities of management and ownership, and that the state must be prevented from interfering with the creation of wealth. Able politician that he was, Mussolini that same night underscored in his newspaper the flexibility of his program, stressing that the new movement could "afford the luxury to be aristocratic and democratic, conservative and progressive, reactionary and revolutionary, legal and illegal, according to the circumstances of time, place, and situation."[15] And in an interview granted to an independent newspaper a few days later, he even more specifically hedged by stating: "Platforms can be iron cages. . . . We have no republican plank and no monarchical plank; we have no planks for Catholicism, for Socialism, or against Socialism. We are pragmatists, solvers of problems, doers."[16]

For all of Mussolini's gyrations, the meeting at Piazza San Sepolcro created no great impression either in the Italian press or in the government, which, beset by political troubles at Ver-

14. *Il Popolo d'Italia* (Milan), March 18, 1919.
15. *Il Popolo d'Italia* (Milan), March 23, 1919.
16. *Il Giornale d'Italia* (Rome), March 26, 1919.

sailles and economic troubles at home, regarded the new movement as merely an additional and not too sharp thorn in its side. The mass of the population was not immediately aware of the founding of the *Fasci di Combattimento*, and those who read about it in their newspapers put it down as one more of the splinter groups then mushrooming in Italy. In the minds of a few, however, Roberto Farinacci among them, the meeting of March 23 marked "a declaration of war . . . the decision to put an end at any cost to the ideas and the men of the parliamentary system."[17]

That evening, Farinacci and a few others met with the leader of the Milanese *Arditi*, Ferruccio Vecchi, and joining hands over the blade of a dagger swore "to act again to defend Italy, this time from its internal enemies, and to be ready to kill and to die."[18] Under the false banner of patriotism, war was indeed declared, a civil war which would only end three and one-half years later with the victory of the apostles of violence and the enslavement of the Italian nation.

17. Roberto Farinacci, *Storia della Rivoluzione Fascista* (Cremona: Società Editoriale "Cremona Nuova," 1939), I, 136–137.
18. Farinacci, *Squadrismo*, p. 19.

IV

ON THE
GROUND FLOOR
OF FASCISM

As soon as Farinacci returned from Milan to Cremona, he set out to organize there a local branch of the new Fascist movement, a *Fascio di Combattimento*. On March 29, he published Mussolini's program, adding, by way of comment, that the first and principal enemy was "bolshevism."[1] His next step was to recruit a nucleus of followers, which he did by simply telling all members of the *Lega Patriottica* and of the *Società Giordano Bruno* that they would henceforth be instead members of the *Fascio*. Most of the younger men, about fifty altogether, agreed to this transfer and, on April 11, the *Fascio di Combattimento* of Cremona was officially organized, under the leadership of Roberto Farinacci as its political secretary.[2]

Fasci were also being organized at this time in many other Italian cities, on the premise that Fascism was still only a movement joining together in common aspirations and for joint action members of various political parties, from the Republicans to the Radicals and to the Reformist Socialists, as well as individuals with no party affiliation. The activist arm of the *Fascio* was the *squadra d'azione* (literally, "action squad"), whose members wore the black shirts and black fezzes which, during the war, had been

1. *La Squilla* (Cremona), March 29, 1919. In the same issue, Farinacci also published an item which may have been merely the fruit of his imagination, since no corroboration can be found anywhere, namely, that Mussolini had agreed to be a candidate for Parliament from the district of Cremona in opposition to Guido Miglioli.

2. The older organizations, left without their most active members, withered and soon disappeared from the scene.

the uniform of the elite shock troops, the *Arditi*. The *squadristi* also adopted the *Arditi's* insignia, silver skulls and crossbones. Many of the *squadristi* were indeed former *Arditi*, who saw in Fascism an opportunity to renew their wartime experiences of adventure and violence. Although Farinacci had not been an *Ardito*, his temperament fitted him perfectly to be a *squadrista*. At this time, he began to carry a pistol, which he wore stuck in a garter under his left trouser leg, so that it would not be found if he were searched, while by just bending over he could grasp it with his right hand and be ready to shoot.[3]

Continuing the fight against the Socialist and Popular syndicalists in the countryside and taking advantage of his growing notoriety, Farinacci on May 10 had himself elected to the presidency of the Federation of Independent Farmers Leagues of the province of Cremona and began agitating for a revision of the Farming Agreement granting better terms to agricultural laborers. The Fascists, at this point, were still striving to attract the masses by advocating social and economic reforms, and they were making even wilder promises than the official Socialists from whose programs the Fascists in reality differed only in their attitude toward the war, toward Italy's international expansionism, and toward bolshevism. In practice, however, the Socialists were strongly organized and could resort to strikes to support their demands, while the Fascists, still numerically weak, could only make their influence felt by joining with the Nationalists and other supporters of "law and order" in opposing the Socialist-led strikes and in the process often starting bloody riots. An incident representing a prime example of these tactics took place in Milan on April 15, 1919, when the Socialists called a general strike and, as a result, a mob of Fascists and *Arditi* attacked the office of *Avanti!*, burning it and destroying the printing presses.[4] One soldier and three workers were killed and thirty-nine were wounded in what could be considered the baptism of fire for the *squadristi*.

The economic situation, meanwhile, was worsening. Inflation

3. Manlio Cancogni, *Storia dello Squadrismo* (Milan: Longanesi & Co., 1959), p. 24.
4. ICSA, Ministry of Interior Fund, Reports of Police Directorate (1919), Env. 40, Folder 2.

so plagued Italy that a paper *lira*, worth eighty-one *centesimi* in gold at the beginning of 1919, was only worth sixty-one by the end of June.[5] In the month of May alone, there were 316 strikes throughout Italy.

Strikes were soon to plague Cremona, where Farinacci was actively and successfully proselytizing among the railroad workers, many of whom, attracted by the Fascists' appeal to patriotism, joined the *Fascio* and also organized themselves in a syndicate opposing the Socialist local union. A showdown between the two groups came on July 20 and 21, 1919, when the Confederation of Labor called a general strike throughout Italy. Farinacci devoted virtually an entire issue of his newspaper to articles opposing the strike,[6] and his followers were in fact able to prevent disruption of public services in Cremona.

The summer of 1919 also provided Farinacci with another opportunity for advancement which he was quick to grasp, in order to raise himself socially and enter a profession. Admission to a university normally required eight years of study in a *Gymnasium* and a *Lyceum*, culminating in a very hard comprehensive examination in all subjects, including Latin, Greek, philosophy, history, Italian, and a number of scientific subjects. A special law was now enacted permitting returning veterans, regardless of previous schooling, to obtain the diploma which opened the doors to university study and professional careers by merely passing examinations in history and in Italian language and literature. With a little cramming and his usual aggressiveness, plus some pressure on the examiners by his good friend and mentor Professor Alessandro Groppali, Farinacci got his diploma and enrolled in the Faculty of Law at the University of Modena.[7]

5. Salvatorelli e Mira, *Storia d'Italia*, p. 124. A gold lira was worth at the time U.S. $0.158.

6. *La Squilla* (Cremona), July 19, 1919.

7. In Italy, then as now, attendance at most university courses is not required. Examinations are often perfunctory, and a passing grade of 18⁄30ths is generally obtainable with little or no preparation. After four years of enrollment, the defense of a dissertation almost automatically gives the student his parchment and the title of *Dottore*. For an account of the way in which Farinacci got around the dissertation hurdle, see pp. 75–76.

During this period, Farinacci also contracted one of his most notorious and most durable extramarital liaisons. Maria Antonioli was working as a typist in a lawyer's office in Sesto Cremonese when Farinacci first met her. Short, pale, she could not be called pretty; but she was young, ambitious, and attracted to the young firebrand who was obviously a rising public figure. Farinacci, in turn, was completely devoid of moral scruples or restraint, and in short order the two became lovers. Eventually, Maria Antonioli became Farinacci's private secretary and, after his rise to power, she was a most influential adviser and a force to be reckoned with in Cremona.

Besides his organizing work for the *Fascio* and his amorous escapades, Farinacci was deeply involved at this time in the nationalist agitation concerning Dalmatia.

As noted earlier, the Italian government's price for bringing Italy into the war on the side of the Allies had been spelled out in April 1915 in the Treaty of London. After Russia's collapse in 1917, the Bolsheviks published the text of the treaty, and "it was at once assailed, not only in Great Britain, America, and France, but also in the Italian Chamber. It was described as a document of shameless imperialism."[8] The United States, of course, was not a party to the Treaty of London and, once the Peace Conference opened at Versailles, President Woodrow Wilson made it clear that he refused to acknowledge the terms of a treaty such as this, which violated his insistence on the principle of self-determination for all peoples. After all, in his speech of January 8, 1918, Wilson had proclaimed as the ninth of his fourteen points that "A readjustment of the frontiers of Italy should be effected along clearly recognizable lines of nationality."[9] And *(Italy was by the Treaty of London promised territories which would place under her domination some 1,300,000 Jugoslavs, some 230,000 Germans, the whole Greek population of the Dodecanese, the Turks and Greeks of Adalia, all that was left of the Albanians, and vague areas in Africa. It was not, therefore, a treaty which was in*

---

8. Harold Nicolson, *Peacemaking, 1919* (New York: Grosset & Dunlap, 1965), p. 162.
9. *Ibid.*, p. 40.

any consonance with the principle of self-determination or the doctrine of the Fourteen Points.[10]

The haggling over the loot due Italy for her participation in the conflict thus repeatedly hampered the already muddled proceedings at Versailles and was the cause of considerable rioting in many Italian cities through the spring and summer of 1919, with the Nationalists and Fascists clamoring for territorial expansion, and the Socialists opposing it as violating their doctrines of international brotherhood.

The focal point of Italian nationalist demands, besides various areas on the Adriatic coastline of Dalmatia, was the north-Adriatic city of Fiume, which the Italians wanted even though, under Article 5 of the Treaty of London, it should have gone to Croatia. The principle of self-determination, it must be pointed out, was not easy to apply in this area, where the cities are Italian and the countryside is Slav. At Fiume, in particular, the Italian-speaking majority was clamoring for annexation to Italy.

Suddenly, on September 12, the Italian poet and Nationalist leader Gabriele D'Annunzio occupied Fiume with a few hundred volunteers, and the turmoil between the opposing factions rose to new heights throughout Italy. Mussolini, after some initial hesitation, jumped on the bandwagon and launched in the columns of *Il Popolo d'Italia* an appeal for contributions to help D'Annunzio's expedition, raising, in less than a month, more than three million lire.[11] While much of this money did reach D'Annunzio, considerable sums were used by Mussolini himself to finance his newspaper and to pay and arm his own bands during the electoral campaign which took place two months later.[12]

In Cremona, as was to be expected, the new development provided Roberto Farinacci with a pretext for a bloody confrontation. On September 15, while the Socialists were holding a rally in the Verdi Theatre, deploring D'Annunzio's Nationalist raid, a mob of about fifty Fascists led by Farinacci moved from the *Fascio* head-

10. *Ibid.*, p. 161.
11. Renzo De Felice, *Mussolini il rivoluzionario* (Turin: Giulio Einaudi editore, 1965), p. 560.
12. *Ibid.*, pp. 583–586.

quarters in Vicolo Santa Croce towards the theatre. The police, forewarned, barred the way and, in the melee that ensued, several Fascists and policemen were beaten up. In the end, Farinacci and a few other Fascists were arrested and spent the night in jail. The episode did not fail to impress Mussolini, who had Farinacci made a member of the Central Committee of the *Fasci di Combattimento*, thus raising him to a position of leadership in the movement which let him participate in the making of its policies.

Three weeks later, the first Congress of the *Fasci di Combattimento* took place in Florence, and Farinacci attended with a few followers. Little was accomplished, besides the passage of numerous orders of the day attacking the government. But the presence of such a concentration of Fascists provoked their opponents into a number of violent clashes, culminating in a gunfight on the Piazza Vittorio Emanuele in the evening of October 19. There Farinacci, if one is to believe him, "led the counterattack, pistol in hand, and chased away the subversives."[13]

Back in Cremona, Farinacci was soon confronted with a hard decision. On October 29, the Chamber of Deputies was dissolved, and new elections were announced for the middle of November. Farinacci would have liked to put forward his own candidacy, but the Central Secretariat of the *Fasci*, realistically recognizing the numerical weakness of its adherents, decided to support fusion slates everywhere and to present Fascist candidates only in Milan. The province of Cremona was entitled to five seats in the Chamber of Deputies, and the contest was between the official Socialists, the Populars, and a fusion slate of Republicans, Liberals, and Reformist Socialists, headed by Leonida Bissolati. Despite the attacks against Bissolati by Mussolini and his followers the previous January, Farinacci was now instructed by the Secretary General of the *Fasci* to campaign for Bissolati's slate, on the grounds that although some of Bissolati's political views were distasteful to the Fascists, yet he was a fighter and "a supporter of the war against both the red and the black defeatists.[14]

13. Farinacci, *Squadrismo*, p. 24.
14. Umberto Pasella to Farinacci, October 25, 1919, ICSA, *Mostra della Rivoluzione Fascista* Fund, Env. 101.

Farinacci reluctantly agreed, and early in November he began touring the countryside, holding electoral rallies which almost without exception degenerated into shouting matches and often free-for-alls. A particularly violent clash took place on November 9 at Piadena, where Farinacci succeeded in provoking a Socialist mob with his insults. Soon he and his bodyguards were surrounded by angry Socialists. They were saved by the timely arrival of a truckload of Fascists, who began clubbing the Socialist farmers and broke through to rescue Farinacci.

Two days later, Farinacci, aided by a few *squadristi*, disrupted a Socialist rally at Robecco with a successful hit-and-run raid. On November 12, he tried to repeat the performance at Sesto Cremonese, but this time, finding the opposition ready, he was forced to seek refuge in a friend's house and then escape through a back window, making his way back to Cremona through the fields.[15]

All in all, it was a hectic period, but Farinacci seemed to thrive on the verbal and physical violence which was never missing wherever he appeared, since he generally deliberately created it. The results of all this agitation, however, were far from encouraging for the Fascists. At Cremona, Bissolati alone of the fusion candidates was elected to the Chamber of Deputies, while the Socialists elected Giuseppe Garibotti and Costantino Lazzari, and the Populars returned to Parliament Pietro Cazzamalli and Guido Miglioli. The Fascists won no seats at all in the new Parliament; and in Milan, they received 4,795 votes against 170,000 for the official Socialists and 74,000 for the Populars.

As soon as the electoral results were known, new disorders erupted, particularly in Milan, where, on November 17, a bomb was thrown among a group of Socialists. The next day, the police searched the headquarters of the *Arditi* and of the *Fascio*, as well as the offices of *Il Popolo d'Italia*, and found in all three places explosives and firearms. Ferruccio Vecchi, F. T. Marinetti, and several others were arrested, as was Mussolini who, however, was released the next day. Farinacci, on learning of Mussolini's arrest, left Cremona for Milan, but he was arrested on arrival, kept in jail overnight, and sent back to Cremona.

15. Farinacci, *Squadrismo*, pp. 26–31.

The Fascist movement was clearly at a low ebb in the last months of 1919, and it lost large numbers of adherents. In contrast, the over-all electoral results constituted a great victory for the official Socialist party and for the Popular party, the first winning 156 seats and the second 100. The old liberals no longer had a majority, since they only had 252 seats out of 509.[16]

The Socialists, however, did not know how to exploit their victory, because they steadfastly refused to coalesce with other parties, while they lacked sufficient strength to form a government themselves. The Populars, on the other hand, were shrewdly bargaining to obtain concessions from the government in return for their support. The opposition's failure to take immediate advantage of its electoral victory gave the surviving Fascist nucleus time to analyze its mistakes and devise a new strategy, namely, a decided shift to the right, aimed at obtaining the support of the middle class by promising to protect it from the proletariat.

At Cremona, Farinacci stopped publication of *La Squilla*, and on January 5, 1920, came out with the first issue of *La Voce del Popolo Sovrano* (The Voice of the Sovereign People), written by the same staff and printed in the same shop, but now purporting to represent "all the sane and healthy forces of the nation" and liberally filled with advertisements for National Debt Bonds and for the products of a large pharmaceutical firm, Manzoni & Co., of Milan.

An early test of the new direction of the Fascist movement came during the same month of January 1920, when railroad workers throughout Italy called a strike for higher wages. Farinacci, the founder and leader of the Fascist Railwaymen's Syndicate, opposed the strike, as did Mussolini, thus beginning to appeal to the bourgeoisie who would later justify and support the Fascist dictator because "he made the trains run on time." On the very first day of the strike, Mussolini stigmatized the action as "an enormous crime against the nation,"[17] while at Cremona, according to Farinacci, 500 railroad workers, or a vast majority of the total force, remained at their post, giving proof of their "sense of

---

16. Salvatorelli e Mira, *Storia d'Italia*, pp. 113–114.
17. *Il Popolo d'Italia* (Milan), January 20, 1920.

responsibility towards society."[18] The strike, however, was generally successful; and after ten days, the government, headed by Francesco Saverio Nitti, granted virtually all of the railwaymen's demands.

The continuing inflation created an atmosphere of uncertainty which greatly contributed to the rising unrest. By the end of December 1919, a paper *lira* was only worth thirty-seven *centesimi* in gold, and the government, which in July 1919 had begun spending 200 million *lire* a month to support the price of bread, by the end of the year was disbursing twice as much monthly for this purpose.

The first half of 1920, therefore, saw workers seizing factories and farm laborers taking possession of the land in growing numbers and on an increasingly vast scale, while riots broke out throughout Italy. More and more, during the early part of 1920, new types of individuals began to stream into the Fascist ranks: students, shopkeepers, professional men, army and navy officers, government employees, men with confused political ideas and often with none at all, but all opposed to "bolshevism" and, at least nominally, all advocates of "law and order."

The younger and most daring of these new converts went to reinforce the ranks of the *squadre d'azione*. Armed with bludgeons and wooden clubs, which they called "manganelli," daggers, and assorted firearms, and travelling in surplus army trucks, the *squadristi* organized "punitive expeditions" against "Bolshevik" groups and individuals, with considerable bloodshed, especially among their opponents, since the *squadristi* were generally careful to have numerical preponderance. In the fighting between Fascists and Socialists, there were 145 dead and 440 wounded among the Socialists in the twelve months ending in April 1920.[19]

While the rank and file argued and fought, however, the Fascist leadership was seeking to consolidate its new rightist orientation. A typical example of the Fascist tactics was given in a report submitted to Prime Minister Francesco Saverio Nitti by his Chief of Cabinet, Giovanni Flores, stating that a reserve army general had

18. *La Voce del Popolo Sovrano* (Cremona), January 26, 1920.
19. *Avanti!* (Milan), April 30, 1920.

visited several factories near Milan, "offering to the industrialists the protection of the *Fasci di Combattimento* by means of the intervention of *squadre d'azione* in the event of strikes or disorders." "This offer," Flores went on, "was accompanied by a request for money, which the industrialists generally accepted, paying to the *Fasci* several thousand *lire*."[20] It was thus with a new lease on life, thanks to increasing financial support and rising membership, that the second Fascist Congress was held in Milan on May 24, 1920. Roberto Farinacci was again named to the Central Executive Committee, and Mussolini was able to report the existence of 118 Fasci with a total of 27,430 members.[21]

Back in Cremona, Farinacci was soon confronted with a test which required all his resources of demagogy and violence. At the beginning of June, eight railroad cars loaded with artillery and ammunition arrived at Cremona's yards, en route to Albania. Claiming this shipment of war material to be a provocation to the international proletariat, the Cremonese Socialist railwaymen refused to handle the cars or to permit their being moved from Cremona. Urged on by Farinacci, the Fascist station master, Luigi Bergonzoni, made several vain attempts to have the cars hitched to outgoing trains, but the Socialist workers refused to obey any of his orders and demanded his removal. After several days of inconclusive negotiations, on June 12, the police intervened and made it possible for the military shipment to go through, whereupon the Socialist Railway Syndicate called for a strike which soon extended to all of Lombardy and to the neighboring Emilia region. With his Fascist railwaymen, Farinacci attempted to maintain service, but this time the opposition was much stronger. In fact, other Socialist unions came out in support of the railwaymen, and on June 26 a general strike was declared. Bloody street fights and attacks on individuals took place in and around Cremona. In one instance, Farinacci, confronting a group of strikers with his omnipresent pistol, was stoned and bled profusely from a head wound. In the end, however, as time passed

20. Flores to Nitti, April 19, 1920. Quoted in Renzo De Felice, *Mussolini il Rivoluzionario*, p. 592.
21. *Il Popolo d'Italia* (Milan), May 25, 1920.

and people lost interest, the strike fizzled out, and the resumption of traffic was claimed by Farinacci as a great personal victory.[22] During the same period, Farinacci took an extremely active part in the phenomenon which marked the summer of 1920 in Italy, and which was in fact a determining factor in the sudden and powerful emergence of Fascism as a national force: the struggle between owners and workers in the farmlands of the northern regions.[23] The key to this development may be found in the fact that, after the war, a vast number of landowners in the Po Valley, afraid of the proletarian agitation, disposed of their holdings to their former tenants and sharecroppers. When these new proprietors decided to defend their rights and property against the Socialists and "Bolsheviks," an alliance was automatically made between the landowners and the Fascist leaders who were endeavoring to re-orient their movement to the right and to gain the support of the bourgeoisie.

Farinacci expressed the new Fascist views in detail in an editorial entitled "The Principle of Fascist Action," in which he stressed that Fascism did not want to be just another political party, but, rather, a movement which would "support and recognize the great role of the working bourgeoisie, a precious and indispensable element."[24]

Translating his words into action, Farinacci led raids against striking farm workers, especially in the Soresina area, where the followers of Guido Miglioli were successfully preventing the harvest and disrupting the operations of dairy farms. Bloody confrontations took place when groups of "free farmers" organized by Farinacci attempted to gather wheat in the fields and milk

22. *La Voce del Popolo Sovrano* (Cremona), July 5, 1920.

23. Another phenomenon typical of this period was the consolidation in power of the *rasses*, as local Fascist leaders were disparagingly nicknamed by reference to the provincial governors in the Abyssinian feudal structure. Most major Italian cities became the bailiwick of a *ras*: Farinacci in Cremona, Italo Balbo in Ferrara, Dino Grandi in Imola, Giuseppe Marsich in Venice, Cesare Maria De Vecchi in Turin, and Dino Perrone-Compagni in Florence were the most notorious, but many others came to the fore in each region, each building around himself a following of *squadristi*, minor politicians, disgruntled war veterans, and local businessmen and industrialists.

24. *La Voce del Popolo Sovrano* (Cremona), July 26, 1920.

cattle in the barns of Fascist landowners. With each incident, the tension mounted and the agitation multiplied. The violence employed by the Fascists in these struggles, furthermore, generally met with the complacent acquiescence of the local authorities, whose sympathies were naturally with the middle class and against the proletarians. The government in Rome, now led by the grand old man of Italian liberalism, Giovanni Giolitti, paid lip service to the need to maintain law and order, but in reality felt that the Fascist strong-arm methods were useful in containing the tide of workers' unrest. Police and military units, in fact, often sided with the *squadristi* against strikers and demonstrators.

At the height of the turmoil, when each day saw new seizures of factories by the workers in the cities and new clashes between farmers and strike-breakers in the country, Farinacci, on September 5, 1920, held a convention of the *Fasci* of the entire Lombardy region in Cremona. He prevailed on Mussolini to attend, and in fact drove him from Milan to Cremona at night, bluffing his way through a roadblock manned by Socialist strikers.[25]

As a counter demonstration, on the same day, the Socialist Chamber of Labor organized a rally demanding recognition of Soviet Russia, but the police succeeded in preventing a clash between the Socialists and the Fascists on their way to the convention hall.

Mussolini's speech to the Fascist delegates received wide publicity and drew more and larger segments of the middle class towards Fascism. "I am," he said, "reactionary and revolutionary, depending on circumstances. I am, to put it better, a catalyst. . . . If I see the people rushing towards an abyss, I am not a reactionary if I stop them, even if I have to use violence.[26]

Farinacci in turn reviewed the growth of the Fascist movement in Cremona, calling for increased efforts and the use of any means to accomplish the total defeat of the Socialist and Popular forces.

In the evening, the Fascist delegates left Cremona, but not before a number of scuffles and fist fights had broken out between them and the Socialists who had concluded their own rally. The

25. Farinacci, *Squadrismo*, p. 58.
26. *La Provincia* (Cremona), September 7, 1920.

next day, the atmosphere was still heated, and again clashes took place between Fascists and Socialists. In the early evening, two young Fascists, Guido Anselmino and Mario Franzetti, were dragged out of the Caffé Roma and severely beaten by five Socialists. Farinacci then decided to retaliate, and, surrounded by a strong band of well-armed *squadristi*, he moved towards the Piazza Roma where a Socialist crowd was milling around. Partisan versions naturally differ as to who fired the first shot;[27] in any event, a pitched battle was soon joined, and when the police finally succeeded in restoring order, two dead Fascists and two dead Socialists, as well as several wounded from both sides, lay on the pavement.

Farinacci, who had suffered only some cuts and bruises in what soon became known as the "Piazza Roma Massacre," was escorted home from the scene by a few friendly army officers. Later that night, he was arrested and taken to jail, where he remained until September 10—four days—when he was released because ballistic tests had failed to show that any of the fatal bullets had come from his pistol. ([*As soon as I am out of jail* [he wrote in his diary] I run to Piazza Roma to address the Fascists who had come from Milan and other towns for the funeral of Luciano Priori and Vittorio Podesta [the two Fascist dead of the September 6 incident]. I receive much applause and a great ovation. Then I accompany the Milanese Fascists to their train, and on the way back from the station I have my Fascists give a good beating to all the subversives we meet on the street. Most of the social-communists have gone into hiding. My release from jail has caught them off-stride.*[28]

In a pretense of impartiality, the authorities issued injunctions against the leaders of the warring factions, requiring their commitment to abstain from violence, but Farinacci, while acknowledging the injunction, publicly proclaimed his contempt for it and his determination to use any means to achieve his goals. "Your injunction," he wrote in an editorial addressed to the prefect of

27. *Il Popolo d'Italia* (Milan), September 7, 1920; *L'Eco del Popolo* (Cremona), September 11, 1920.

28. Farinacci, *Squadrismo*, p. 71. This passage is fully typical of Farinacci's style, and reflects quite faithfully his egocentric and self-glorifying personality.

Cremona, "makes not the slightest difference. We who will always be in the right cannot allow ourselves to be intimidated by your orders."[29]

All through the rest of 1920 and the spring of 1921, Farinacci continued to organize branches of the *Fascio* in the towns and villages of the Cremonese countryside and bound these *Fasci* in a Provincial Federation of which he got himself elected Secretary General. The Fascists found themselves pitted not only against the Socialist unions, but also against the Populars, who, under the leadership of Guido Miglioli, showed a brand of activism in the province of Cremona unique among the members of their party. The result was a series of violent confrontations, which invariably resulted in the destruction of property and often resulted in loss of lives. A typical example of these clashes, naturally seen and reported from his partisan viewpoint, was described by Farinacci himself in his diary under the date of April 8, 1921. *The founding of the Fascio at Rivarolo del Re has caused serious consequences. The Socialists, to retaliate, have cut the vines in the fields of our first members, destroying the harvest of about 60,000 kilos of grapes. To pay them back at once, I organize a punitive expedition, and after sunset, together with several squadre of Fascists from Cremona, I invade Rivarolo, break down the door of the Socialist Co-operative, and take possession of their roster so as to have the names of all our enemies. Then I have all the furniture moved out into the square, and set fire to it. The Socialists begin shooting at us from the windows and we return their fire forcing them to close the shutters. We take the clerk as a hostage, and make him lead us to the homes of the Socialist leaders, who are seized and punished on the spot. . . . The same night we go to neighboring villages, and there too we drag the Socialist and Communist leaders from their homes.*[30]

With the beginning of 1921, Farinacci's newspaper became the official organ of the Fascist Federation of the Province of Cremona, and changed its title to *La Voce del Fascismo Cremonese*.

At this time, Farinacci resigned from his railroad job, to which

29. *La Voce del Popolo Sovrano* (Cremona), December 20, 1920.
30. Farinacci, *Squadrismo*, pp. 75–76.

he no longer even pretended to devote any time or effort. Ostensibly he now had no source of income, but obviously his close relationship with a number of landowners and businessmen, whose interests he actively defended with his *squadristi*, allowed him to support his family well and never lack for pocket money.

Farinacci's chance to move onto the national scene came in May 1921, when the Fascist leadership, with the tacit acquiescence of Prime Minister Giovanni Giolitti, was invited to present candidates for election to the Parliamentary Chamber of Deputies jointly with the other nationalist parties. To represent Cremona, the Fascists naturally named Farinacci, and after a hectic and often bloody campaign, he was elected as deputy on May 14, together with Mussolini and thirty-three other Fascist candidates. From that day on, even if in name only, he would be the Honorable Farinacci. Having joined the Fascist movement on the ground floor, he had succeeded in starting his ascent to the big time.

V

THE FASCIST
CONQUEST
OF POWER

No ONE really expected that Farinacci the deputy would behave any differently from Farinacci the *squadrista*, and this view was confirmed on the very first day of his attendance in the Chamber of Deputies.

A Communist leader, Francesco Misiano, had been convicted during World War I as a deserter but had been freed by the amnesty which had followed the armistice and had now been elected to the Chamber of Deputies. On the morning of June 13, 1921, Farinacci and the other Fascist deputies met and decided that Misiano should not be allowed to sit in Parliament. In the early afternoon, when the Communist deputy arrived to take his seat in the Chamber, he was attacked in the cloakroom by Farinacci, by Cesare Maria De Vecchi, by the *ras* of Trieste, Francesco Giunta, and several others. The hapless Misiano tried to defend himself, but Farinacci, pistol in hand, kept at bay other leftist deputies who were coming to Misiano's aid and, with the other Fascists, literally kicked Misiano down the corridor and out of the main entrance, all the while shouting, "Out with deserters! We won't tolerate this insult to the glorious dead of the war and of our revolution!"[1]

The incident immediately created a storm of protests in the Chamber, and the leftist deputies sought the intervention of Prime Minister Giovanni Giolitti. The Prime Minister, however, was intent, as usual, on trying to use the Fascists as cat's-paws, and

1. Farinacci, *Squadrismo*, pp. 89–93; *Il Giornale d'Italia* (Rome), June 13, 1921.

he refused to become involved. In the end, no action was taken against Farinacci or his followers, either by Giolitti or by Ivanoe Bonomi, who replaced Giolitti as Prime Minister on June 23. The Fascist deputies, who sat in the Chamber on the extreme right, next to the Conservatives and to the Nationalists,[2] were among the most vociferous of the deputies, creating frequent disturbances in the debates and often engaging in fist-fights with their opponents in the corridors and even in the Chamber. Also, obviously encouraged by the first success of their movement at the polls, the most intransigent among the Fascist leaders, with Farinacci in the forefront, mounted more and more frequent and bloody attacks on their home grounds against their adversaries of whatever party or group, to intimidate them all and establish their own supremacy. Throughout Italy, and especially in Farinacci's province of Cremona, there were hundreds upon hundreds of attacks by *squadristi* upon Chambers of Labor, as union halls were called, Socialist meeting rooms, newspapers, farms, and individual homes. Burnings and lootings became commonplace, as well as beatings and shootings, the forced ingestion of castor oil, and many cases of rape, torture, and murder.[3] These "punitive expeditions" succeeded to a large extent in establishing Fascist control of many towns and villages, whose Socialist administrators resigned or fled. Public opinion, generally not fully aware of all the facts, reacted by demanding action to restore law and order.

In an effort to quell the continuing unrest and violence, the President of the Chamber of Deputies, Enrico De Nicola, began negotiations between the leaders of the extremist parties. Benito Mussolini, who already had his eye on entering the government and wanted therefore to create for himself an image of respectability, was in favor of such a "peace pact," but he found himself strongly opposed by Farinacci and several other *rasses*, who thrived on violence and refused to deal with their enemies other than with a bludgeon or a gun. In fact, as early as July 23, Farinacci resigned from membership in the Central Committee of the *Fasci*,

2. Renzo De Felice, *Mussolini il Fascista* (Turin: Giulio Einaudi editore, 1966–68), I, 92.
3. Salvatorelli e Mira, *Storia d'Italia*, pp. 176–182.

addressing to it a letter which attacked the pacifist attitude of the Committee and proclaimed the need to fight to the end against Socialists and Communists.[4] Mussolini, however, continued to negotiate with the Socialist leadership, and finally on August 2, 1921, an agreement was signed by leaders of the Fascists, the Socialists, and the leftist General Confederation of Workers. The parties undertook to prevail on their members to abstain from violence and intimidation, and to restore any property which had been seized. Eventual violations of the agreement were to be examined and judged by impartial arbitrators.[5]

The reaction of the *squadristi* leaders was immediate and loud. The *ras* of Imola, Dino Grandi (the same who twenty-four years later would be instrumental in causing Mussolini's downfall), published an editorial sharply rejecting the "peace pact,"[6] and Farinacci similarly thundered against any compromise with the opposition, printing the full text of his letter of resignation from the Central Committee.[7] Farinacci and Grandi then called a meeting of representatives of the *Fasci* of the entire Po Valley, at Bologna on August 16. After a heated discussion, the vast majority of the delegates approved a motion stigmatizing the "peace pact" and requesting that the National Council of the *Fasci* be called into session at once to consider the matter and decide on future policy, obviously expecting that the "peace pact" would be disavowed. Faced with such an open rebellion, Mussolini gambled on being able to regain the ascendancy over his divided followers by threatening to withdraw from the movement, and on August 18 he announced his resignation from the Central Committee of the *Fasci*, stating that he "hoped" to be able to "remain just a member of the Milan *Fascio*."[8] Only a week later, however, he began advocating the transformation of the Fascist movement into a political party, and calling for a Fascist Constitutional Convention in the fall.[9]

4. Farinacci, *Squadrismo*, pp. 94–96. The letter was not made public until two weeks later, after the "peace pact" had been concluded.

5. *Il Popolo d'Italia* (Milan), August 3, 1921.

6. *L'Assalto* (Bologna), August 6, 1921.

7. *La Voce del Fascismo Cremonese* (Cremona), August 8, 1921.

8. *Il Popolo d'Italia* (Milan), August 18, 1921.

9. *Ibid.*, August 23, 1921.

When the National Council of the *Fasci* met in Florence on August 26, it was at once clear that a compromise would be found, because Farinacci, several of the other extremist leaders, and Mussolini, all of whom had resigned, were absent. The "peace pact" was neither denounced nor ratified; each *Fascio* was left free to follow the judgment of its leaders; and the resignations of Mussolini, Farinacci, and some others were not accepted. Farinacci agreed to withdraw his letter of resignation, while Mussolini did not, preferring to bide his time until the Constitutional Congress. In the intervening months, Mussolini was able to consolidate his strength, reaching a compromise with the *ras* of Imola, Dino Grandi, who was really the only one of his opponents who might then have challenged Mussolini's leadership of Fascism. Farinacci, instead, continued unchecked in his efforts to organize "punitive expeditions" against the Socialists and the Populars in the Cremona hinterland. He personally led many of them, such as the one of September 7 at Pieve d'Olmo, to mark the anniversary of the "Piazza Roma Massacre."

The Fascist Constitutional Congress met in Rome on November 7, 1921, and little was said any more about the "peace pact." By now, it seemed, there were in existence 2,200 *Fasci* with 320,000 members. The movement was converted by the Congress into the National Fascist party, led by a Central Committee and a directorate. Farinacci, being out of favor with Mussolini, was not elected to either of the two ruling bodies, but he pretended not to recognize the obvious rebuff. In fact, he airily headlined the report of the Congress's proceedings "The Views of Cremonese Fascism Have Triumphed,"[10] and he shortly afterwards published a photograph showing him together with Mussolini reviewing a contingent of *squadristi*.[11]

Concentrating on building up his power in the province of Cremona, Farinacci more and more took up the cause of the landowners who were refusing to recognize the terms of the "Lodo Bianchi," an arbitral decision rendered by a Socialist expert, Giovanni Bianchi, covering farm salaries and working conditions in Lombardy. Bianchi's decision was also supported by the

10. *La Voce del Fascismo Cremonese* (Cremona), November 15, 1921.
11. *Ibid.*, November 21, 1921.

Popular followers of Guido Miglioli. Farinacci instead advocated a form of sharecropping which would have left the workers completely at the mercy of the owners, and he went as far as drafting a master agreement which was, as could be expected, turned down by the workers' leagues.

Another setback for Farinacci came at the beginning of December 1921, when the *Questore* of Cremona, Emilio Wenzel, who had been working hand in glove with Farinacci in restraining the police from interfering with the activities of the *squadristi*, was transferred to Gorizia.[12]

Farinacci, however, soon reached a gentlemen's agreement with the new *Questore*, and continued with his *squadristi* to terrorize the Cremonese countryside. The most shocking episode of this bloody period took place in mid-December, when *squadristi* cornered the Socialist vice-president of the Cremona Provincial Council, Attilio Boldori, and beat him to death. Farinacci aggressively defended the murder, claiming that it was justified because Boldori had been personally responsible for the "Piazza Roma Massacre," and he finally had the effrontery to blame Boldori for having "a skull too weak to withstand the Fascist *manganelli* (wooden clubs)."[13]

As 1922 began, the Fascist antiproletarian offensive gained momentum, supported as it now was, not only by the landowners and the industrialists, but also to an increasing degree by the urban middle class. On January 25, 1922, a Fascist convention at

12. Wenzel also helped Farinacci to mastermind the legal defense of those Fascists who had been arrested, writing Farinacci, for instance, that "if your protegé were to be tried now, he could not possibly get away with less than seven months in jail . . . while if he obtains a postponement he will go scot free because of the forthcoming amnesty." (Wenzel to Farinacci, October 10, 1921, ICSA, Farinacci Fund, "1921," Env. 2.) Wenzel's pro-Fascist activities, however, were too brazen, and Miglioli obtained his removal. Wenzel appealed to Farinacci for help in no uncertain terms, but in vain. (Wenzel to Farinacci, December 2, 1921, *Ibid.*)

13. *La Voce del Fascismo Cremonese* (Cremona), December 13, 1921. Boldori's killing bears a marked resemblance to that of Matteotti in 1924, at which time Farinacci also advanced the claim that Matteotti had died of a hemorrhage because his lungs were too weak to absorb a single blow in the chest from one of his abductors.

Bologna organized the National Confederation of Syndicalist Corporations, which comprised syndicates of both employers and workers. Farinacci took a leading part in the proceedings, which laid the groundwork for the eventual take-over of the labor movement after the Fascist conquest of power.

The general unrest increased further, and on February 1, the Bonomi Ministry fell. After four days of fruitless consultations by King Victor Emmanuel with a great number of political leaders, a cabinet of technicians was formed under the presidency of a rightist Liberal, Luigi Facta. When the new ministers appeared before him to take the oath of office, Victor Emmanuel remarked that this was the twentieth crisis of his reign, or an average of one a year.[14]

Farinacci, meanwhile, realized that a weekly newspaper was no longer sufficient to represent and advance the Fascist goals in Cremona. Consequently, on March 1, 1922, he began to publish a daily, called *Cremona Nuova*, a four-page paper whose circulation was of course limited to Cremona and its suburbs. It was clearly aimed at the middle class, since it advertised such luxuries as automobiles and home heating furnaces, as well as the services of Rome banks and stockbrokers. Using the new paper as a platform of propaganda and intimidation and at the same time intensifying the activities of his *squadristi*, Farinacci now launched a full-scale campaign to gain control of the political and economic organizations in the province of Cremona. Principal targets, at the outset, were the municipal administrations of the many towns and villages, which until then had been almost exclusively controlled by the Socialists. In some cases, as in the villages of Ca' d'Andrea and Spineda, the *squadristi* simply forced the incumbent mayors and councilmen to resign and replaced them with Fascist officials.[15] Elsewhere, as at Volongo, Voltido, Gussolo, and other towns, where administrative elections were held, the intervention of the *squadristi* at the polls brought about the victory of the Fascist candidates.[16]

14. Salvatorelli e Mira, *Storia d'Italia*, p. 220.
15. *La Voce Fascismo Cremonese* (Cremona), February 13, 1922.
16. *Cremona Nuova* (Cremona), March 8, 1922.

At the same time, at Farinacci's urging, most landowners and many businessmen joined in organizing the Provincial Federation of Employers' Syndicates, which specifically stipulated in its by-laws that any disputes arising between workers and employers would be settled by the Secretary General of the Provincial Federation of the *Fasci*, namely, Farinacci.

Frightened by the violence which obviously made the casting of free ballots impossible, the central government in Rome on March 18 suspended *sine die* the remaining administrative elections in the Province of Cremona.[17] The same day, Farinacci held a rally in the Verdi Theatre, inveighing against the government and urging his followers to disrupt the activities of the Socialist administrations still in office and to refuse to pay taxes as long as these administrations remained in power.[18]

As could be expected, the appeal to a tax strike fell on willing ears, and the vast majority of Cremonese taxpayers did in fact refuse to pay taxes, spurred on by Farinacci's purple prose in *Cremona Nuova*. Scarcely a day passed without a new exposé in the Fascist newspaper, alleging corruption and malfeasance by this or that member of the Socialist City and Provincial Councils.

In a last effort to turn back the Fascist tide, the Socialist and Popular leaders of Cremona now officially joined forces, but this agreement to act in common was not ratified by the central directorates of the two parties. A month thus passed, during which more municipal administrations in the countryside were taken over by the Fascists, while the taxpayers' strike continued in full force.

The prefect of Cremona, Pietro Guadagnini, in desperation, issued a manifesto appealing to the population's "sense of civic duty," to which Farinacci answered with insulting comments, defying the prefect to order the arrest of the delinquent taxpayers.[19]

The next day, April 20, Farinacci addressed a mammoth rally

17. *Il Popolo d'Italia* (Milan), March 18, 1922.
18. *Cremona Nuova* (Cremona), March 22, 1922.
19. *Ibid.*, April 19, 1922.

on the Piazza Roma, repeating his attacks against the provincial and municipal administrations of Cremona and concluding with an open threat: "If the government does not have the strength to dissolve the present city council, we will replace this government which no longer represents the will of the nation."[20]

The Minister of the Interior then appointed a high functionary, Mario Zanon, to conduct an investigation of the public administration of Cremona, but the Fascist-led tax strike continued until May 12, when the prefect agreed to several concessions, including the waiver of penalties and the promise to ask the government for the dissolution of the city council. On this basis, Farinacci ended the strike, with the avowed intention of resuming it if the city council had not been removed by June 15.

Meanwhile, the activities of the *squadristi* continued unabated, marked by a particularly bloody episode on May 7 in Cremona itself. The occasion was the belated celebration of May Day by the Socialists, after the prefect of Cremona had first forbidden all demonstrations on May 1. Farinacci had publicly announced that he would allow the celebration provided no red flags were displayed, and he could address the Socialist marchers to explain to them the fallacies of Marxism and the beauty of Fascism.[21]

Farinacci had also issued orders to several thousand *squadristi* from the countryside to concentrate in Cremona on the morning of May 1, and then the prefect had decreed the ban on all public meetings. In fact, the prefect had also issued a search warrant for the *Fascio* headquarters in Cremona and for Farinacci's own office, but the police had failed to find any arms or explosives.[22]

Under pressure from Popular leader Guido Miglioli, the prefect now authorized a demonstration to be held on May 7, but on the terms imposed by Farinacci, and strong police contingents were stationed throughout the city. In spite of these precautions, the opposing forces met at several spots along the route of the Social-

20. Pantaleo, *Il Fascismo Cremonese*, p. 131.
21. *Cremona Nuova* (Cremona), April 28, 1922.
22. "If they had lifted certain planks in the floor," wrote Farinacci in his diary, "they would have discovered a fair quantity of pistols, bombs, and ammunition." (Farinacci, *Squadrismo*, p. 108.)

ist procession, and numerous clashes and firefights took place, resulting in a large number of wounded on both sides.[23]

Obviously, however, the defeat and demoralization of the leftist labor unions and co-operatives could not be an end in itself. In fact, the Fascist leadership aimed at creating and exploiting situations which would force the central government to deal with it and grant its most extreme demands.

Accordingly, on May 12, 60,000 Fascists, led by Italo Balbo, *ras* of Ferrara, occupied Ferrara and succeeded in obtaining from the national government a vast program of public works to relieve unemployment. On May 20, the same tactic was successfully applied at Rovigo; and at the end of the month, Bologna was taken over by Fascist mobs, who obtained from Rome the removal of the prefect.

At Cremona, Farinacci decided to begin his take-over of the governing bodies by first destroying the Provincial Council. At the head of a large group of Fascists, he invaded the gallery of the council meeting hall on the morning of May 16, and began clamoring to be allowed to address the council. The police were called and, after a hard fight, they succeeded in ejecting all the Fascists except Farinacci and the secretary of the Cremonese *Fascio*, Luigi Balestreri, whom they perhaps at first considered too important to manhandle. The president of the council then tried to open the session, but again Farinacci began shouting insults at the councilmen. Finally, he was carried out, managing, on the way, to kick out several windows. As soon as he was put down on the square outside of the meeting hall, Farinacci again ran into the building and began haranguing the councilmen, so that the meeting was adjourned to the afternoon. When the session resumed,

23. As an example of the *squadristi's* indiscriminate violence, the president of the Cremona branch of the National Association of Tubercolotic War Veterans wrote to Farinacci as Secretary of the Provincial Fascist Federation, complaining that three of his members had been "set upon and beaten by a group of about sixty Fascists," while another had also been beaten by a group of *squadristi* because he was wearing "not a red bandanna, but a blue one [the colors of the Nationalists]." (Gino Rossini to Farinacci, May 16, 1922, ICSA, Farinacci Fund, "1922," Env. 1.)

the Fascists were again in the galleries, and again they fought the police who tried to eject them. In desperation, the president of the Provincial Council adjourned the meeting, and the councilmen withdrew, leaving Farinacci and his *squadristi* masters of the field.[24] The Provincial Council never met again until after the March on Rome nearly six months later, by which time it would be controlled by the Fascists and presided over by Farinacci himself.

Within two weeks, however, the Socialist and Popular deputies succeeded in dealing a blow to Farinacci when the Chamber of Deputies voted not to ratify the election of Farinacci and two other Fascist deputies, Dino Grandi and Giuseppe Bottai, because they had not yet reached the required minimum age of 30.[25] Farinacci's seat was given to his runner-up, the Liberal leader Ettore Sacchi, whom Farinacci never forgave for accepting the Chamber's decision. Stripped of his official position in Parliament, Farinacci now redoubled his efforts to bring the municipal administrations in the province of Cremona under Fascist control. Helped by the armed might of the *squadristi* and by the financial support of the landowners, he did in fact take over an additional number of town halls during the month of June. As the next logical step, he then set his sights on the City Council of Cremona itself.

The opportunity arose at the beginning of July 1922. The weather was hot; many of the opposition leaders were away on vacation; and, in fact, on July 3, not a single councilman happened to be in Cremona. Farinacci was well aware of this situation, and early in the afternoon he presented himself, with two bodyguards, at the city hall, asking to see the mayor or one of the councilmen. When told by the mayor's secretary that there was no one who could receive him, Farinacci forced his way into the mayor's office, sat down at the desk, and wrote to the prefect of Cremona: "For the dignity of Cremona, I feel the right and the duty to appoint myself acting mayor of the city, until you will replace me with a Special Commissioner." One Fascist was sent to take the letter to

24. Farinacci, *Squadrismo*, pp. 114–119.
25. *Cremona Nuova* (Cremona), June 1, 1922.

the prefect, while the other ran to spread the news and to call on the Cremonese *squadristi* to assemble in the city hall square. The poor prefect, faced with an unprecedented situation, appealed to Rome for instructions. He was advised to begin criminal proceedings against Farinacci, but at the same time he must use his discretion in dealing with the crisis. After repeatedly but vainly asking Farinacci to leave peacefully, the prefect ordered the police to clear the city hall square. Farinacci then ordered his cohorts to move to the Prefecture square, and to lay siege to the prefect in his own office. At 9:00 P.M., the prefect capitulated, and appointed as Special Commissioner for the City of Cremona the same Mario Zanon who had been investigating the city's public administration, a man who had already proved himself sympathetic to the Fascist cause.[26]

When news of the events of Cremona reached Rome, the Chamber of Deputies was thrown into an uproar. Spurred on by the leftist Cremonese deputies, a majority of the deputies asked the government to reinstate the Socialist City Council. They pressed Prime Minister Luigi Facta until he was forced to act on July 13 in order to avoid the fall of his ministry. As a first step, Facta recalled Zanon to Rome. He then ordered the removal of the *Questore*, as well as an investigation into the failure of the police to put down the disorders.[27]

Immediately Farinacci issued a proclamation to the citizens of Cremona: "We accept the challenge of the government, determined to oppose all our strength and all our high resolve to the cowardice and weakness of the central authorities, who once more, because of their miserable calculations of parliamentary opportunism, violate justice and the free will of the people."[28] Simultaneously, he called his *squadristi* to action, and formed them into two columns, one of which he led to sack the Chamber of Labor, while the other invaded and burned down the printing shop of *L'Eco del Popolo*. As a result, numerous clashes occurred between the Fascists and the police who were trying to stop them, with

26. Farinacci, *Squadrismo*, pp. 124–131.
27. *Il Giornale d'Italia* (Rome), July 14, 1922.
28. *Cremona Nuova* (Cremona), July 14, 1922.

several dozens being wounded on both sides. The next day, contingents of regular army troops moved into Cremona to try to restore order, but Farinacci mobilized more than four thousand Fascists from the entire province. Now the situation in the city appeared stalemated. Bullheaded as ever, Farinacci launched a surprise attack, on July 15, using a flying wedge of *squadristi* which broke through the police lines and confronted the prefect of Cremona in his own office. Again, the hapless functionary, rather than order the police and the troops to shoot to kill, collapsed and surrendered the city to the Fascists. Farinacci then led a victory parade which ended up in the sacking of the home of Popular deputy Guido Miglioli.

The national government in Rome, faced with a real threat of civil war, in turn capitulated; and on July 17, 1922, Prime Minister Luigi Facta published a Royal Decree officially dissolving the Cremona City Council.[29] Farinacci, wallowing in the turmoil, would have liked to maintain the city as an armed camp; but on the same day, he received the visit of one of Mussolini's lieutenants, Attilio Teruzzi, who delivered to him a proclamation praising the *squadristi* and inviting them to return home, together with a letter from Mussolini asking Farinacci to "suspend the action because the goals are achieved" and "not to force the situation so as not to be put in an untenable position." "The word of Mussolini," Farinacci wrote in his diary, "can not be discussed. I order the immediate demobilization of the Fascists, and in a few hours the city regains its normal appearance."[30] Whatever the meaning of "normal," one fact was incontrovertible: with Fascist members or sympathizers occupying virtually all posts in the administration, the city of Cremona was firmly in the grasp of Farinacci and his followers.

During the following days, other similar outbreaks took place in a number of cities throughout Italy, and violence in the countryside reached new heights. To protest the illegality of Fascist activities, the Labor Alliance, which represented the Socialists and the Populars, called a general strike on July 31, 1922, whereupon

29. *Il Giornale d'Italia* (Rome), July 13–17, 1922.
30. Farinacci, *Squadrismo*, pp. 134–139.

the Fascists issued an ultimatum demanding the end of the strike within forty-eight hours.[31]

Without waiting for the strike to end, however, the Fascists intervened in many cities in the operation of public utilities and transportation services, and their action provoked bloody clashes with the strikers. On August 2, the Labor Alliance announced that the strike would end the following day, but the Fascists, sensing the weakening of the opposition, redoubled their reprisals against the "red" workers' organizations and extended their seizures of municipal administrations. Farinacci, having the situation at Cremona well in hand, joined the Fascist leadership in Milan, where he was instrumental in organizing the storming and the occupation of the city hall. For the second time, he led the looting and burning of the *Avanti!* offices, as he had done three years earlier.

With the workers thus cowed by Fascist aggression, the general strike was a failure, and the leftist labor organizations were, at least temporarily, out of the political arena. According to Mussolini, "In August 1922, after the final defeat of the Labor Alliance . . . only two forces are left on the Italian political scene: the demo-liberal government, and the armed organization of Fascism."[32] The remaining enemy, then, was the "demo-liberal" government, for whose conquest the Fascists now set out to plan their final moves.

The moment was indeed a critical one, both for the Italian nation and for the Fascist party. The Italian economy, which had never recovered from the consequences of World War I, was now also suffering from the repercussions of the 1921–22 world depression and was in very poor condition. Unemployment was mounting, and the government was resorting to currency printing on a large scale. On the political front, while the caretaker Facta government tried to keep the state in operation with halfhearted

31. The Fascist proclamation specified: "The antinational parties have challenged Fascism and the nation. . . . We give the State forty-eight hours to assert its authority . . . after which Fascism will feel free to act and will replace the State whose impotence will have been proved once more." (*Il Popolo d'Italia* (Milan), August 1, 1922.)

32. Benito Mussolini, "Preludi della Marcia su Roma," *Gerarchia*, October 1927, quoted in De Felice, *Mussolini il Fascista*, I, 281.

measures, the traditional leftist and rightist parties jockeyed for position, becoming, in the process, torn and splintered by factional struggles. Public opinion, among the middle class and in the ruling industrial and financial circles, frightened by the specter of "bolshevism," was definitely in favor of the inclusion of Fascist representatives in a new government. Conditions were so bad that a number of former premiers—Giovanni Giolitti, Francesco Saverio Nitti, Vittorio Emanuele Orlando, Antonio Salandra— stood ready to deal with Mussolini in the tacit hope of neutralizing the Fascist contingent once it had become part of the establishment. The army was, in general, sympathetic to the Fascists, who claimed to be motivated by patriotism, and a large number of officers and even some generals had in fact openly sided with them. Even members of the royal family, such as the Queen and the Duke of Aosta, were known to be Fascist sympathizers.

On August 13, 1922, the Central Committee of the Fascist party met in Milan. Farinacci, although not a member, was allowed to attend, and he actually ended up by taking a leading part in the discussion and deliberations. It soon became clear, at the August 13 meeting, that the Fascist party was split into two factions having opposite tendencies: one, which had as its main advocates Dino Grandi, Giacomo Acerbo, and Massimo Rocca, could be defined as "legalistic," favoring as it did Fascist participation in a coalition government and the tapering off of *squadrista* activity; the other, represented by Farinacci, Italo Balbo, and Michele Bianchi, was avowedly "insurrectional."[33]

Mussolini, able politician that he was, did not openly side with either group, while the Central Committee made two decisions which reflected the views of both factions. To satisfy the "legalistic" faction, the Central Committee issued a manifesto calling for new national elections to be held in November. The Committee placated the "insurrectional" faction by organizing the

33. Addressing the Fascist Central Committee, Farinacci had still spoken of alternative solutions: "We must here and now solve the dilemma: to conquer power, either by legal means or by illegal ones." (*Il Popolo d'Italia* [Milan], August 14, 1922.) His report of the meeting to his Cremonese followers, however, was headlined "We must conquer power at all costs!" (*Cremona Nuova* [Cremona], August 15, 1922.)

squadre d'azione into the Fascist militia, to be led, on a national scale, by a triumvirate composed of Italo Balbo, Cesare Maria De Vecchi, and an army general, Emilio De Bono. A month later, in fact, the militia was formally organized as a military body, and Articles of War applying to it were published.[34]

The Facta government took no action, and Mussolini commented to his future press secretary, Cesare Rossi: (*If there were in Italy a government worthy of the name it should send here this very day its policemen and carabinieri to disband us and take over our halls. It is inconceivable that an armed organization, complete with cadres and Articles of War, coexist in a state which has its own army and police force. Except that in Italy there is no state. It's no use, we must inevitably go to power. Otherwise the history of Italy becomes a farce.*[35]

Farinacci, meanwhile, spent the rest of August and most of September consolidating the Fascist stranglehold on the countryside around Cremona, holding rallies and organizing "punitive expeditions" and installing Fascist appointees in the remaining municipal administrations of the province, after forcing the resignations of the Socialist or Popular incumbents. At the same time, he took up the cudgels against the leftist deputies who represented Cremona in Parliament, proclaiming their "banishment" from Cremona and going as far as writing that "the 'dishonorable' Miglioli must be put out of circulation."[36]

The police, on orders from Rome, formally warned Farinacci that he would be held personally responsible if any harm came to Miglioli or to the Socialist deputies, but Farinacci increased his defiance. Since Miglioli happened to be in Cremona, Farinacci issued an ultimatum to the prefect to get Miglioli out of the city within forty-eight hours. He wrote in his diary: "I have decided. Dead or alive, Miglioli must leave Cremona."[37]

Once more, frightened by the *squadristi* milling around the prefecture palace, the prefect gave in and, on September 22,

34. Italo Balbo, *Diario 1922* (Milan: A. Mondadori, 1932), p. 141.

35. Cesare Rossi, *Trentatre vicende Mussoliniane* (Milan: Casa Editrice Ceschina, 1958), p. 122.

36. *Cremona Nuova* (Cremona), September 19, 1922.

37. Farinacci, *Squadrismo*, p. 145.

Guido Miglioli was spirited out of town under police guard, not to return until after the fall of Fascism twenty-three years later. It was thus as absolute master of both the city and the province of Cremona that Farinacci on September 24, 1922, received Mussolini at the city gates and, followed by a column of squadristi, escorted him to the City Hall square where the new flags of more than fifty Fascist groups were to be consecrated. Mussolini, after eulogizing Farinacci as a "magnificent leader" and "an old and faithful friend," made a strong speech attacking the government and the parliamentary opposition. He concluded: "It is from the victory of Vittorio Veneto . . . that we have begun our march, which will not stop until we have reached the supreme goal: Rome! And no obstacles . . . can stop us!" The crowd went wild, and took up the chant: "To Rome! To Rome!"[38]

A week later, Farinacci led the last major Fascist attack on the government's authority before the final surrender of the state to the Fascist onslaught. The Italian administration of Trento and the South Tyrol, almost four years after the expulsion of Austria from the area, still allowed a considerable measure of autonomy to the German-speaking minorities. Under the pretext of defending the "Italianity" of the population, more than seven thousand squadristi, led by Farinacci, Francesco Giunta, and two other Fascist chieftains, Alberto De Stefani and Achille Starace, riding in commandeered railroad trains, arrived suddenly on October 2, 1922, in Trento and Bolzano. There they occupied the city halls and prefectural palaces. While Giunta concentrated on Bolzano, Farinacci assumed over-all command in Trento. In both cities, the Fascist leaders removed the local authorities, whom they accused of being anti-Italian and pro-German, and imposed a number of measures of a nationalist character in the administration. The central government, after considering intervention, decided instead on October 10 to acquiesce in the reforms imposed by the squadristi.[39]

The importance of Farinacci's raid at Trento cannot be overestimated, because the attack was not aimed at leftist workers

38. Il Popolo d'Italia (Milan), September 25, 1922.
39. Farinacci, Squadrismo, pp. 155–178.

but directly at the representatives of the state, without any possible excuse of economic class struggle. Farinacci himself underscored the special nature of the attack, by pointing out, in an interview, that Fascism had won two victories at Trento: it had proven the strength of the militia and spotlighted the weakness of the state. "Our action," he stated, "has presented the government with a serious dilemma: either we are enemies of the institutions (and this would be difficult to prove), or we do what the state is unable to do."[40]

Goaded into action by the extremist Fascist leaders and gradually convinced that participation in a coalition ministry would not have satisfied the mass of his followers, Mussolini decided to play for the highest stakes. On October 16, 1922, he called the three commanders of the militia to Milan, where he outlined to them his intentions for the conquest of power. On October 20, Italo Balbo, Emilio De Bono, and Cesare Maria De Vecchi met in Florence with the leaders of the provincial organizations, among them Roberto Farinacci, and formulated a plan for insurrection consisting of five steps:

1. Mobilization and occupation of public buildings in the main cities.
2. Massing of Blackshirts at Santa Marinella, Perugia, Tivoli, Monterotondo, Volturno.[41]
3. An ultimatum to the Facta government, demanding that it turn over all powers to the Fascist leadership.
4. Entering Rome, and taking over all ministries. In case of repulse, falling back towards central Italy.
5. In such case, forming a Fascist government in a city in central Italy. Rallying all Blackshirts from the Po Valley, and resuming the attack on Rome until victory and possession be achieved.[42]

When the Fascist leaders met again on October 24 at Naples, it was decided that action should start on October 27. A quadrumvirate composed of the three militia commanders—Italo

40. *Il Giornale d'Italia* (Rome), October 10, 1922.
41. The first four are towns ringing Rome, each thirty to one hundred miles from the capital, while the Volturno is a river between Rome and Naples.
42. Balbo, *Diario*, p. 186.

Balbo, Cesare Maria De Vecchi, and Emilio De Bono—and Michele Bianchi was named to lead the columns which were to converge on Rome. In a brief speech to a cheering Neapolitan crowd, Mussolini openly declared his intention to blackmail the constitutional authorities: "Either they will give us the government, or we shall take it by descending on Rome: it is a question of days, maybe hours."[43]

Ostensibly, the Naples meeting had been called as a party congress to discuss the development of Fascism in the southern provinces, and Farinacci had been named vice-president of the congress. After a desultory session on October 25, however, it was decided to adjourn the congress and discuss the final details of the insurrection. Commanders were named for each of twelve zones embracing all of Italy. Farinacci was placed in charge of the provinces of Cremona and Mantova. He was ordered to begin his attack at 6:30 P.M. on October 27. Farinacci left with Mussolini and others for Rome on the evening of October 25, and the following day, while the future *Duce* went back to Milan to await the development of events, Farinacci took the night train for Cremona.

Arriving there at 11:00 A.M., he immediately organized his forces, assigning certain *squadre* to take over the telephone and telegraph central offices, others to occupy the prefectural palace and other public buildings, and still others to attack and disarm the police and *carabinieri*. Promptly at 6:30 P.M., the attack was launched, and within a few hours all the objectives were reached except the prefectural palace, whose massive doors had been found locked and barred. At this point, the prefect, on orders from Rome, turned his powers over to the commander of the Cremona army garrison. Consequently, when Farinacci's followers tried to storm the prefecture, they were met by strong resistance and suffered a number of casualties. Their losses were so great that it was necessary to postpone further action until morning and to call for reinforcements from the countryside. The next

43. Benito Mussolini, *Opera Omnia*, edited by Edoardo and Duilio Susmel (Florence: LaFenice, 1951–63) XVIII, 453; hereinafter referred to as *Mussolini*.

day, Farinacci was able to mass more than five thousand *squadristi* before the prefecture. Now faced with certain annihilation, the colonel commanding the troops surrendered to Farinacci.

Seating himself at the prefect's desk, the *ras* of Cremona began to issue proclamations, announcing to the population the assumption of all powers by the Fascist military command, ordering the banishment from Cremona of several well-known leftist leaders "for motives of public order" and ordering all public functionaries to remain at their posts or be arrested. He also arrested a number of "suspicious characters," holding them in a temporary prison set up in a nearby school. He personally went to the city jail to release a few Fascist prisoners.[44]

Meanwhile, because similar actions had taken place in many other Italian cities, the Facta government considered proclaiming a state of siege and ordering the army to move against the Fascist insurgents. In the early morning of October 28, a decree to this effect was actually prepared and telephoned or wired to all prefects, and in many cities, including Rome, hastily printed wall posters notified the population of the emergency rules. At 9:00 A.M., Prime Minister Luigi Facta submitted the decree to King Victor Emmanuel, who, despite earlier indications of agreement to a firm stand, now refused to sign it and thus caused the state of siege to be revoked. Victor Emmanuel then accepted Facta's resignation and unofficially entrusted the task of forming a new government to former Premier Antonio Salandra, who had the backing of the Nationalists and of many leaders of the Right and who was hopeful of taming the Fascists by doling out to them a few portfolios in his cabinet.

Among the Fascist leaders themselves there were some, such as Cesare Maria De Vecchi, who favored such a solution, while others, captained by Michele Bianchi, insisted that Mussolini must be the new Prime Minister. Mussolini all the while had prudently remained in Milan, from where, if it became advisable, he could easily have escaped into Switzerland. Now emboldened by the king's refusal to put down the insurrection by force and sensing that an all-or-nothing gamble would pay off, Mussolini

44. Farinacci, *Squadrismo*, pp. 171–185.

flatly rejected Salandra's overtures and refused even to come to Rome for discussions with him. Salandra was thus forced to decline the royal designation, and the king on October 29 called Mussolini to Rome.[45] The future *Duce* left Milan in a sleeping car and presented himself at the royal palace on the afternoon of October 30. Fascist bands had filtered into the suburbs of Rome since the twenty-eighth, but no incidents occurred because it was by now evident that no resistance would be offered.

On October 31, Mussolini presented his proposed cabinet to the king. It comprised three Fascists (Farinacci not among them), two Populars, two Democrats, one Liberal, one Independent, a general, and an admiral, while Mussolini kept for himself the portfolios of Foreign Affairs and Interior.[46]

With little marching, and virtually no fighting, the "March on Rome" was over.

45. De Felice, *Mussolini il fascista*, I, 356–374.
46. *Ibid.*, p. 386.

VI

FARINACCI'S DEBUT
AS CENSOR
OF FASCISM

FARINACCI's military dictatorship in Cremona was shortlived. While Mussolini was presenting his cabinet to the king in Rome, the Fascist Supreme Military Command issued a proclamation ordering the militia throughout Italy to suspend any further operations and exhorting all Fascists to co-operate with the authorities in restoring and maintaining law and order. Faced with such a direct injunction, the ras of Cremona had no choice but to obey; as a gesture of defiance, however, he turned even civil powers back to the commander of the army garrison, rather than to the prefect whose authority he had so often and so flagrantly nullified.[1]

The legalization of the Fascist insurrection, in any event, had no effect on Farinacci's habitual stance as the de facto ruler of Cremona or on his activities as the self-appointed censor of Fascist political purity. Only a week after the formation of the Fascist-led government, Farinacci scornfully reported in his newspaper that a number of provincial councilmen had informed the prefect of their intentions of resuming their posts. He commented: "Too bad that in our rising we did not give them half a liter of castor oil; but we're still in time if they insist. None of those we swept out must return to the provincial council."[2] He also published a circular issued by Mussolini to the prefects, ordering them to discontinue the banishment "of those who no longer engage in antinational action." But Farinacci boldly stated:

1. Farinacci, *Squadrismo*, p. 188.
2. *Cremona Nuova* (Cremona), November 8, 1922.

"This does not apply to Miglioli, Garibotti, etc. When they will cease to represent Cremona in Parliament, then we will apply Mussolini's circular."[3]

It was in fact during the Fascists' first experiences in government, a period from the "March on Rome" to the murder of Giacomo Matteotti, political secretary and spiritual leader of the Unitarian Socialist party, in June 1924, that the differences in outlook and tactics between Mussolini and Farinacci became clearer. Mussolini, older and more experienced, through a mixture of opportunism and bluster, had made full use of his most violent followers as well as of his middle-class sympathizers, to reach his immediate goal. Now he was intent on consolidating his power. This task required the re-establishment of relative quiet throughout the country, and the gradual infiltration of the organs of government by the Fascists on a nationwide scale, in order to create a strong Fascist state. The younger firebrand, instead, conceived the mission of Fascism as the prompt and forcible imposition on the nation of the policies formulated by a ruling elite. Instead of being one of several parties co-operating in the administration of the state, the National Fascist party, in Farinacci's view, should itself be the state, and the Fascist *squadristi* should be its military arm. Anyone holding opposing views should be silenced or banished.

Much as Mussolini might have liked to keep Farinacci out of the limelight, the *ras* of Cremona was not only irrepressible, but he had a considerable following among the more intransigent Fascist activists, of whom he in fact was the unofficial leader. It was for this reason, therefore, that while he succeeded in keeping Farinacci out of the government, Mussolini had to appoint him a member of the Grand Council of Fascism, which was created in December 1922 to replace the directorate and to be the highest consultative body of the Fascist party.

Both in the sessions of the Grand Council and in his daily editorials in *Cremona Nuova*, Farinacci now let no occasion pass to express his opposition to any conciliatory move towards non-

3. *Ibid.*

Fascists. At this stage in building his regime, Mussolini often had to comply with Farinacci's views, lest the intransigents' opposition cause disruptive rifts in the Fascist ranks.

A good example of Farinacci's influence was shown by the events of December 1922, which concerned the General Confederation of Labor. Some secret negotiations had taken place, under the auspices of Gabriele D'Annunzio, the poet and Nationalist leader, to join that group of leftist unions with the Fascist syndicates into a single, theoretically nonpolitical labor organization.[4] Mussolini had quietly encouraged this initiative, which in fact would have considerably enlarged the Fascist penetration of the labor movement. Farinacci, however, on learning of the negotiations, began attacking the very idea of a possible compromise, claiming that the only basis for labor unity was the absorption of all other unions by the Fascist syndicates and hinting that any other solution would provoke a serious schism within Fascism.[5]

Mussolini at the time was in London attending the War Reparations Conference. When he learned of Farinacci's stand, he realized the danger confronting him. He promptly cabled Farinacci to reassure the ras of Cremona that he agreed with his views on the Italian labor movement and that "any illusions to the contrary will be dispersed and those enemies who will not disarm will be inexorably and definitely crushed."[6]

Farinacci, both to boast of his influence and to make it impossible for Mussolini to change his mind, gave the cable wide circulation. On December 14, he boarded Mussolini's train at Milan to discuss the matter face to face on the way to Rome. The next day, gloatingly, he reported the meeting, commenting: "The Prime Minister agreed completely with the Hon. Farinacci who, with his article in *Cremona Nuova*, caused the known cable by the Hon. Mussolini, which cable eliminated any doubt or uncertainty and took away from the enemy any hope of infiltrating our ranks and encircling our party."[7]

Another important instance of Farinacci's interference with

4. De Felice, *Mussolini il Fascista*, I, 604–606.
5. *Cremona Nuova* (Cremona), December 7–10, 1922.
6. *Mussolini*, XIX, 383.
7. *Cremona Nuova* (Cremona), December 15, 1922.

Mussolini's plans—though this time unsuccessful—occurred in connection with the proposed electoral reform. Although he realized the need to obtain a secure parliamentary majority, Mussolini was, from the outset, well aware that he could never achieve this goal under the existing electoral law, which was based strictly on proportional representation. This system of electing deputies favored the minority parties, especially the Populars, whose membership was scattered throughout the country. A return to the old system of single-member constituencies would have been fatal for the Popular party, but at the same time it would have prevented the consolidation of a friendly parliamentary bloc which was Mussolini's goal. The Grand Council of Fascism, at Mussolini's urging, discussed the matter repeatedly during January 1923. It was soon clear that two opposing tendencies existed within the Fascist ranks regarding the electoral system. The first, represented by Michele Bianchi, one of the Quadrumvirs of the March on Rome, favored a mixed system in which the slate of candidates receiving more than one fourth of all votes cast would be entitled to two thirds of the seats in the Chamber of Deputies, while the remaining seats would be allotted proportionally among the minority slates.[8] The other faction, led by Farinacci, advocated instead a return to the single-member constituency. The *ras* of Cremona, in fact, made his views public in an open letter to Mussolini, pointing out that there was really no need to hold new elections because "the present Chamber, under the sword of Damocles of being dissolved whenever necessary, will always docilely bend to your will."[9] Nevertheless, on March 16, the Grand Council charged a committee of seven members, among them Bianchi and Farinacci, to prepare a project for an electoral reform within a month. When the committee reported with two widely different projects, however, one by Bianchi and the other by Farinacci, Mussolini preferred the former, as it was heavily

---

8. *Mussolini*, XIX, 72.

9. Farinacci to Mussolini, February 5, 1923, Italian Documents, National Archives, Washington, D.C., Microfilm Collection T. 586 (hereinafter referred to as: ID–NA T586), 034322–034328. The letter had already been published in *Cremona Nuova* on February 4.

loaded in favor of the Fascists; and complying with his wish, the Grand Council approved the Bianchi version by an overwhelming majority.[10] At the same session of the Grand Council, on April 25, 1923, Mussolini announced a revamping of this body, and as a result Roberto Farinacci's name was conspicuously absent from the new list of members.[11]

Thus Mussolini, angry at Farinacci, began to call his bluff, for, less than a month before, the *ras* of Cremona had threatened to resign his post of High Political Commissar in protest against "the attitude of some [of Mussolini's] closest collaborators."[12] The rebuff had some effect, and for a while Farinacci showed as much discipline as was possible for him. He even humbly asked for Mussolini's permission to attend a meeting of the Grand Council which was to discuss labor matters of special interest to him.[13] In fact, Mussolini now entrusted Farinacci with a special mission for which his intransigence made him particularly suited. During the preceding four years, a variety of petty criminals and confidence men had joined the Fascist party in vast numbers, with the influx being particularly heavy after the success of the Fascist insurrection. Because their presence constituted an obstacle to Mussolini's aspirations to respectability, Farinacci was instructed to "clean up" the fascist groups in Latium, which he did by expelling from the party some 40,000 "unworthy" individuals. So pleased was Mussolini that he wrote Farinacci a highly laudatory letter, adding: *(I believe it is necessary to apply the same methods of intelligent surgery also to a few other Italian regions. We must get rid of the ballast. We can, we must make a present to whoever wants them of 100[,000] or 200,000 Fascists who often show themselves beneath the oc-*

10. *Mussolini*, XIX, 207.

11. Attilio Tamaro, *Venti anni di Storia 1922–1943* (Rome: Editrice Tiber, 1953), I, 298.

12. Farinacci to Mussolini, March 28, 1923, ID–NA, T586, 031330–031333.

13. Farinacci to Mussolini, June 26, 1923, *Ibid.*, 030900–030901. By its by-laws, persons other than permanent members could attend meetings of the Grand Council only by Mussolini's invitation.

casion, and who, instead of helping, stupidly complicate the work of the Fascist government.[14]

The harmony between the two men, however, did not last much longer. Only a few days later, a new violent controversy between them was sparked by the reorganization of the Fascist militia. As has been noted, the militia had originally been meant to be simply a consolidation of the *squadre d'azione* on a nationwide scale under a unified command. The relatively bloodless nature of the October insurrection, however, had left the mass of the *squadristi* largely dissatisfied. As a result, the following months had witnessed a number of episodes of violence, ranging from beatings and dosings with castor oil to looting and murder, in which the *squadristi* vented their frustration on the more active and vocal members of the leftist parties. Mussolini, intent on widening the base of his support among the broadest possible strata of the population, had decided early in 1923 to reorganize the militia into a truly military body, Fascist in character, but at the orders of the government rather than of the party. The problem had been examined thoroughly by the Grand Council, and, according to the recollections of a participant,[15] there had been sharp dissension on this subject between Mussolini and Farinacci, with Farinacci insisting on the necessity of maintaining the *squadre* "in order to keep the country in line."

Now, on July 26, the Grand Council announced the creation of the Voluntary Militia for National Security. A few weeks later, it was further decreed that all militia officers had to pass examinations to be confirmed in their rank. At this, Farinacci exploded with a violent editorial denouncing the decision as one which would hybridize the character of the Fascist militia.[16] A month later, speaking in the Cremona Provincial Council, of which he had been elected president, Farinacci again took up the cudgels against the new militia organization, expanding his remarks into a sharp criticism of the government's action both in the political

14. Mussolini to Farinacci, August 15, 1923, ID–NA, T586, 030842.
15. Massimo Rocca, *Come il Fascismo divenne una dittatura* (Milan: Edizioni Librarie Italiane, 1952), p. 122.
16. *Cremona Nuova* (Cremona), August 16, 1923.

and in the syndical fields, threatening to start "a second wave" of aggression against those who "use Fascism rather than serve it" and announcing the impending resignation from the militia of himself and "a large number of other high officers."[17]

Mussolini, in turn, on learning of Farinacci's speech, sent him a scathing telegram, accusing him of "a serious breach of discipline" and ordering him and his followers "to meditate on the seriousness of the proposed gesture of tendering their resignations."[18] Farinacci, however, stuck to his guns. The same evening, the prefect telegraphed Mussolini that Farinacci and a group of consuls had insisted on submitting their resignations to militia headquarters in Milan, with a message asking to be replaced but stating that all their effort could not "prevent the disruption of the heroic Cremonese legions, born out of sacrifice, which had always wanted to serve that Fascism that we alone brought to victory."[19]

At this point, Mussolini had to act, to avoid a public scandal which would have shown dissension within the Fascist ranks. The very next day, through militia Commander in Chief Emilio De Bono, he informed Farinacci that his threatened resignations constituted "the crime of subornation and mutiny," and he sent a militia general to Cremona with orders to arrest Farinacci unless the resignations were withdrawn.[20]

Farinacci then backed down, but not before sending Mussolini and De Bono long telegrams querulously disclaiming any mutinous intentions and repeating his warnings against the deterioration of the Fascist character of the militia and of the government. The message to Mussolini, lamenting that his dignity had been offended, offered once more Farinacci's resignation from the party's Executive Board, an offer which Mussolini, however, again did not accept.[21]

17. *Ibid.*, September 18, 1923. Farinacci had been made a consul general in the militia, which was organized in Roman fashion into legions, under the command of consuls and centurions.

18. Mussolini to Prefect of Cremona, September 18, 1923, ICSA, Ministry of Interior Fund, Env. 5, Folder 45 (Cremona).

19. Prefect of Cremona to Mussolini, September 18, 1923. *Ibid.*

20. De Bono to Prefect of Cremona, September 19, 1923. *Ibid.*

21. Prefect of Cremona to Mussolini, September 19, 1923; Prefect of Cremona to De Bono, September 19, 1923. *Ibid.*

Another acrimonious controversy in which Farinacci played a leading role erupted immediately thereafter in the Fascist press, and resulted in another rebuff for Farinacci and his followers. It was, in fact, a quarrel secretly instigated and partly stage-managed by Mussolini, who aimed at reasserting absolute control over the party before the holding of new elections.

The Grand Council's scheme for electoral reform had been submitted by Mussolini to the Chamber of Deputies in June, in the form of a legislative proposal prepared by Undersecretary Giacomo Acerbo, from whom the new law would eventually take its name. There had also been contacts between the Fascist leadership and the Popular party, aimed at obtaining this party's support for the electoral reform. But the Popular spokesman, the future Premier Alcide De Gasperi, had made it clear that the reform as conceived by the Fascists was unacceptable, and he had advanced certain compromise proposals which Mussolini in turn had rejected.[22]

Consequently, the Fascist press, with Farinacci's *Cremona Nuova* in the forefront, had begun violent attacks against the Popular party, while *squadristi* engaged in widespread violence against Catholic groups and individuals. The Vatican, alarmed at the violence, had forced the priest who had been the party's founder and prime mover, Don Luigi Sturzo, to resign from the secretaryship of the Popular party. The Popular deputies, on whose votes hinged the possibility of an opposition victory which might have overthrown Mussolini's government, had entered the debate on the proposed law in a resigned and disconcerted mood.[23] Mussolini, sensing hesitation on the part of the most crucial segment of the opposition, addressed the Chamber on July 15 with what has aptly been defined "the most parliamentary speech he ever made,"[24] stating that nothing was further from his

22. De Felice, *Mussolini il Fascista*, I, 526.
23. Farinacci, with his usual brutal frankness, had written a few months earlier: "I, who am an atheist, realize the wisdom of Mussolini's policy toward the Vatican, because through that policy the Fascist government has emptied the Popular party of its Catholic contents." (*Cremona Nuova* [Cremona], March 12, 1923.)
24. Salvatorelli e Mira, *Storia d'Italia*, p. 291.

intentions than to abolish Parliament and asking for the opposition's collaboration in order to "reach the soul of the nation."[25] Many deputies who had planned to vote against the proposal had had second thoughts; and after a few days of inconclusive speech-making, they had approved the law by a vote of 223 to 123.[26] Thus Mussolini, always a master of opportunism, had managed to win an enormous success by dividing the opposition; but it was now essential that he obtain the widest possible consensus, not only in number of seats, which the provisions of the new law virtually assured, but also in the number of votes cast and in the quality of his candidates, so that he could confront those forces whose ultimate support was vital for him—the monarchy, the army, the industrial and financial world, the Church—from a solid base.[27] But the main obstacle to achieving this consensus was represented by the extremist, or intransigent, faction of the Fascist party itself, of which Farinacci was the most vociferous spokesman. As has been noted, for instance, while Mussolini intended to turn the militia into a regular military organization, the extremists would have preferred it to remain a revolutionary corps charged with maintaining Fascist ideals. Farinacci and his friends also looked upon the existing labor unions as bodies to be transformed into purely Fascist organizations, while Mussolini would have preferred, at least at this stage, not to antagonize the masses of international labor. Finally, and most crucial at this point, the extremists would have liked to include in the Fascist-backed majority slate only candidates subscribing to the principles of Fascism.

The ticklish situation was now resolved by Mussolini with a masterful tactical stroke. During the second half of September 1923, he encouraged the more moderate "revisionist" faction, led by Giuseppe Bottai and Massimo Rocca, to expound openly their ideas, which substantially advocated a full return to law and order and the independence of the state from the party, as well

25. Mussolini, XIX, 308–315.
26. Tamaro, Venti anni, I, 326.
27. De Felice, Mussolini il Fascista, I, 536.

as the end of the local dictatorships of the *rasses*.[28] Farinacci immediately thundered against these heretical views in the columns of *Cremona Nuova*,[29] but the revisionists, confident of being backed by Mussolini, stuck to their guns and renewed their attacks against the extremists, whom they accused of creating an anti-Fascist backlash throughout the nation with their intransigence and violent tactics. Rocca, in fact, went as far as hinting that it might be better to dissolve the Fascist party rather than to allow it to continue as a source of embarrassment to Mussolini's efforts at national pacification.[30] A showdown was inevitable. On September 27, the Executive Board of the Fascist party met and, under pressure of the extremists, expelled Rocca from the party. Mussolini then intervened, and, threatening to espouse publicly Rocca's cause, forced the Board to resign. When the Grand Council next met on October 12, Rocca's expulsion was revoked and replaced with a brief suspension. The Executive Board was abolished, and a temporary five-man National Directorate was named to rule the party. All polemics were prohibited, and Mussolini's supreme authority was re-established, while both extremists and revisionists were forced to lick their wounds in silence.

Farinacci took advantage of the lull to obtain his law degree. He had, after all, been registered at the University of Modena for the required four years, and, even without ever attending lectures, he had secured passing grades in the necessary number of courses. The faculty was extremely well disposed towards him because he had successfully exerted his political influence in staving off government measures which had threatened to close down some departments of the university. All he needed now was to submit and defend a dissertation. He had in fact prepared one, entitled "Dosing Subversives with Castor Oil on the Part of Fascists Cannot Be Considered an Act of Violence, but Must Be Deemed Simply an Insult or at Most a Slight Injury." The text of this magnum opus has not been preserved, but it probably was such that, with the

28. *Critica Fascista* (Rome), September 15, 1923; *Il Corriere Italiano* (Rome), September 16–25, 1923.
29. *Cremona Nuova* (Cremona), September 22–26, 1923.
30. *Il Corriere Italiano* (Rome), September 22, 1923.

best intentions, the Modena faculty could not have accepted it. At least, this must have been the considered judgment of Farinacci's old mentor and friend, Professor Alessandro Groppali, because the good professor dug up an old dissertation on "Natural Obligations" which had been submitted in 1921 by another candidate, a certain Marenghi, and Farinacci copied it verbatim and presented it as his own. With this ruse, on December 28, 1923, he was granted the degree of *Dottore in Legge* and embarked on a legal career which his political connections and influence peddling would eventually make exceedingly lucrative. The entire sordid story of Farinacci's stolen dissertation was unearthed in 1930, in the course of a secret investigation made by Senator Piero Alberici at the request of the Minister of Interior, after Professor Groppali, implicated in a financial scandal and resentful of Farinacci's failure to shield him, turned on his former protegé and partner and accused him of several fraudulent actions, including the apocryphal dissertation. No action could be taken against Farinacci on this count, however, because the use of nonoriginal dissertations was not formally prohibited by Italian law until April 1925.[31]

While Farinacci and his faction were temporarily subdued, Mussolini began casting about for support in the national elections expected to be held in the spring of 1924. In November, agreements in principle were reached with the main employers' organizations, the General Confederation of Industry and the Italian Federation of Agricultural Syndicates. During the same month, a pact of collaboration was concluded between the Fascist party and the National Association of War Veterans, and an increasing number of representative leaders from the "liberal" right wing came into the Fascist fold.[32] To strengthen his appeal to the country's nationalist masses, a diplomatic victory was also needed, and this Mussolini obtained by pushing through an agreement with Yugoslavia, signed in Rome on January 27, whereby the city

31. Report by Senator Piero Alberici, September 10, 1930, ID–NA, T586, 031352–031391.
32. *Mussolini*, XX, 340.

of Fiume became officially Italian, while the hinterland remained to Yugoslavia.[33]

By now, Farinacci was again chafing at the bit, trying to goad Mussolini into an open break with the Nationalist leader, Gabriele D'Annunzio.[34] Mussolini, however, remained firm in his program of general pacification. Speaking to a vast assembly of Fascist leaders in Rome on January 28, he openly defined his conception of the electoral slate he envisaged. Except for men of the extreme left, against whom he proposed to fight "with the old Blackshirted vigor," he offered to include in the Fascist majority slate "all men of all parties, or even of no party, who, because of their past during the war and after the war, or for their high skills as technicians or scholars, could usefully serve the nation."[35]

The following day, the National Council of the Fascist party appointed a five-man committee to select the candidates for the majority slate. This "Pentarchy," as it became known, after sifting through more than 3,000 prospective candidates, selected the 356 who would represent two thirds of the Chamber of Deputies. Of these only 200 were members of the Fascist party, while the rest were Liberals, Democrats, right-wing Populars and Independents.[36]

The publication of the *listone* caused much dissension within the Fascist ranks, since many felt that a number of deserving

33. This achievement resulted also in a personal honor, because two months later, to express gratitude for the annexation of the Dalmatian city, Victor Emmanuel decorated Mussolini with the collar of the Order of the Annunciation, which made him a "cousin" of the king.

34. Farinacci to Mussolini, January 24, 1924, ID–NA, T586, 034231. Ever since the Fiume raid in September 1919, relations between Mussolini and D'Annunzio had been strained, since the poet regarded Mussolini as an opportunistic upstart, while the Duce was resentful of D'Annunzio's fame and charismatic appeal, which might, if not properly contained, compete with Mussolini's own.

35. *Mussolini*, XX, 161.

36. Cesare Rossi, *Il Delitto Matteotti* (Milan: Casa Editrice Ceschina, 1965), p. 581. Rossi, who was one of the five members of the selection committee, has included in his book the names of the non-Fascist candidates in the *listone* (literally, big list), as the majority slate was soon called throughout Italy.

Fascist leaders had been left out. Farinacci, who had of course been included, was particularly vociferous in his criticism, and in turn he was sharply attacked by the more conformist Fascist press.[37]

The other parties, large and small, presented a total of twenty-one slates, so that the outcome of the elections might have been considered a foregone conclusion. Furthermore, Mussolini, for the reasons mentioned earlier, aimed at obtaining an "orderly" victory, and he did in fact issue repeated instructions to the local authorities for the prevention and suppression of electoral disorders.[38] Nevertheless, during February and March 1924, the electoral campaign was conducted in an atmosphere charged with violence and marked by thousands of Fascist-provoked incidents, including the destruction of opposition party headquarters, the disruption of electoral rallies, street fights, and armed attacks against individual opposition leaders. Hundreds of wounded and many dead, mostly among the Marxist parties, were counted in virtually all regions of Italy, with Farinacci's Cremona contributing its full share to the unrest and violence by which the Fascists successfully intimidated the opposition at the polls.[39]

The national elections for the Chamber of Deputies, held on April 6, 1924, saw a Fascist victory of unexpected proportions. More than seven million Italians, almost 64 percent of the eligible voters, went to the polls. The *listone* received 66.3 percent of the votes, while the Populars obtained 9.1 percent and the three Marxist parties a combined total of 14.6 percent.[40]

The Fascist government was now assured of a solid parliamentary majority, and even Farinacci had to admit that Mussolini's tactics had paid off.[41] The Twenty-seventh Legislature convened

37. Emilio Settimelli, who was considered an unofficial spokesman for Mussolini, on March 2 editorialized in Rome's *ABC*, praising the list of candidates and accusing Farinacci of not understanding Mussolini's greatness because of "vile cowardice and monumental stupidity" which caused him to "dishonor Italy and Fascism with his outbursts and bestiality." (ID–NA, T586, 034306.)

38. De Felice, *Mussolini il Fascista* I, 581–583.

39. Salvatorelli e Mira, *Storia d'Italia*, pp. 312–318.

40. De Felice, *Mussolini il Fascista*, I, 585.

41. *Cremona Nuova* (Cremona), April 10, 1924.

on May 24, and King Victor Emmanuel, in his speech from the throne, identified the national welfare with the activity of Fascism, praised the militia, and stressed that, while liberty should be preserved, license should be rejected and special interests should be subordinated to the general interests of the community.[42]

Less than a week later, the Secretary of the Unitarian Socialist party, Giacomo Matteotti, rose in the Chamber of Deputies to deliver the speech which was later called his "swan song." He thus involuntarily signed his own death sentence, set in motion the chain of events which threatened, for a time, to topple the Fascist regime, and provided the opportunity for Farinacci to rise to the peak of his influence and power.

42. Tamaro, Venti anni, I, 413.

VII

THE
MATTEOTTI
AFFAIR

WHEN GIACOMO MATTEOTTI died at 39, he had been a Socialist for a quarter of a century. The son of a well-to-do family from the Venetian countryside, he studied law at the University of Bologna, but devoted his entire activity to the political struggle and to the organization of farmers' co-operatives. No demagogue, he relied primarily on facts and figures to support his contentions, be they opposition to war, the need for workers to organize, or protest against Fascist misrule. Matteotti's qualities of cold courage, integrity, and fairness, as well as his opposition to rabble-rousing, made him unpopular with the more dogmatic Marxist politicians no less than with the Fascists. Elected to the Chamber of Deputies in 1919, in 1921, and again on April 6, 1924, he was the spiritual leader as well as the political secretary of the Unitarian Socialist party from its first appearance in the fall of 1922.[1] By the end of 1923, he had published anonymously a well-documented exposé of the first year of Fascist rule[2] and had strenuously opposed all efforts by the new Fascist government to win over the Socialist labor organizations or to come to an understanding with them.

Shortly before the last elections, he had written to Filippo Turati, dean of Italian Socialists: ([We must now assume a new

1. Farinacci and other Fascist journalists, in attacking Matteotti in the columns of their newspapers, always sneeringly referred to the *Partito Socialista Unitario* (P.S.U.) as "PUS."

2. An English translation made by E. W. Diekes was published in 1924, shortly after Matteotti's death, by the Independent Labour party in London under the title *The Fascisti Exposed*.

80

and different attitude towards the Fascist dictatorship: Our resistance to its arbitrary rule must become more active; we must
not yield on a single point; we must not abandon any position
without the sharpest and loudest protests. . . . Nobody can
delude himself that triumphant Fascism may lay down its arms
and spontaneously give back to Italy a regime of legality and freedom. . . . Therefore our party must rally only men determined
to practice a resistance without limitations, with firm discipline,
aiming at a single goal, liberty for the Italian people.[3]

It is in the light of this unlimited opposition that one must
view Matteotti's speech in the Chamber of Deputies on May
30, 1924.

A Fascist motion to ratify without debate the results of the
recent elections was on the floor, and after several other opposition deputies had spoken against such procedure, Matteotti denounced the systematic terrorism employed by the Fascists to
intimidate the voters during the campaign and at the polls.
Despite continuous and violent interruptions from the Fascist
benches, especially by Farinacci, Matteotti cited dates, names,
places, and specific irregularities, outright frauds, and acts of
violence, and he concluded by moving that the entire results of
the elections be invalidated and annulled.[4]

Matteotti's motion was of course voted down, and Mussolini,
turning to his press officer, Cesare Rossi, uttered the exclamation
which was to seal Matteotti's fate: "What's the Ceka[5] doing?
After such a speech, that man shouldn't be allowed to walk
around!"[6] A strong similarity exists between Henry II's irascible
remark unwittingly resulting in the murder of Thomas Becket,
and these words of Mussolini, which, possibly through a similarly
unintended interpretation, were probably a primary cause of the

3. Matteotti to Filippo Turati, quoted in De Felice, Mussolini il Fascista,
I, 617.
4. Stenographic minutes of the Acts of the Chamber of Deputies, May
30, 1924, reprinted in Frances Keene, editor, Neither Liberty Nor Bread (New
York and London: Harper & Brothers, 1940), pp. 45–57.
5. In late spring 1924, a small squad of Fascist "enforcers" was secretly
organized by some members of Mussolini's inner circle and dubbed the
Ceka, after the Soviet secret police.
6. Rossi, Il delitto Matteotti, p. 224.

assassination of Giacomo Matteotti. A vital difference, however, must be pointed out in the consequences of the two bloody deeds: in the earlier case, the Plantagenet king did penance and some benefits accrued to the populace from the Norman archbishop's martyrdom; in the more recent event, instead, the urge to survive pushed Mussolini to enforce extremely repressive measures which firmly established his Fascist dictatorship, and the entire Italian people were the ones who did penance for two long decades. According to Rossi, the statement that someone "shouldn't be allowed to walk around" was for Mussolini a fairly frequent one, to be understood as a deprecatory remark rather than as an order for liquidation.[7] Rossi himself, however, meeting a friend who was a newspaperman shortly afterward, told him excitedly: "To opponents like Matteotti, one can only answer with a gun."[8]

On June 3, Farinacci made a violent speech in the Chamber of Deputies, asking for emergency measures against the opposition press and leaders, including, for the latter, house arrest. He proposed that the government resume rule by decree, and, turning to the Left, threatened: "If you keep on provoking us, we won't limit ourselves to a few punches any more. Then we'll see what will happen here." As has been aptly stated,[9] the physical extermination of the opposition was indeed Farinacci's favorite threat and deepest aspiration.

In contrast, when Mussolini rose to deliver a major speech in the Chamber on June 7, he sounded almost conciliatory. He began by stating that the main thing was to know whether the feelings on both sides—feelings which were extremely violent and which showed that there had indeed been a revolution—would allow the Parliament to function. He hoped that they would if everybody would only be conscious of his own personal and political responsibility. But a dialogue could only be useful if it would result in a move from each side's positions. He defended the validity of the election and pointed out that, to a

7. *Ibid.*, p. 226.
8. Carlo Silvestri, *Matteotti, Mussolini e il dramma italiano* (Rome: Ruffolo, 1947), p. 40.
9. Salvatorelli e Mira, *Storia d'Italia*, p. 325.

certain extent, consensus was always necessarily based on force. Mussolini then spoke of liberty, claiming that it could not constitute the eternal gospel for the life of all peoples, but repeated that he wanted the Parliament to function, and that he would no longer govern by decree. He did not think he was infallible, not at all, he was a man, with all the faults and good qualities inherent in human nature. He was saying now, just as he had said twenty months earlier, that he did not seek anyone to join him, but he did not reject anyone who might want to do so, because the work of reconstructing the Motherland was still very difficult, long, and all efforts of good will had to be utilized. But in closing, he proclaimed that the Fascists who felt worthy of representing the Italian people had the duty and the right to keep on fighting to demolish the ideologies of the opposition in order to build up and increase the power of the Motherland.[10] Immediately afterwards, a vote of confidence was given to the government with three hundred and sixty-one in favor and one hundred and seven opposed.

Mussolini's speech, if examined carefully, was not so much an offer of reconciliation as a veiled injunction to submit, and the opposition well understood its meaning. The same could not be said for some foreign observers, who saw in the speech an olive branch to the opposition.[11]

Whether or not Mussolini's opportunist tactics might have succeeded in drawing some of the more moderate leftist organizations closer to the government will remain forever in the realm of conjecture, for in the early afternoon of June 10, 1924, while walking along the Tiber on his way to the Chamber of Deputies, Giacomo Matteotti was attacked by five men and forced into a closed car which took off at great speed in a northerly direction.[12]

10. *Mussolini*, XX, 204–221.

11. "It was the speech of a democratic leader . . . no hyperbole about Fascist rights." *The Times* (London), June 12, 1924.

12. Much has been written on the Matteotti Affair, and it is not the purpose of this work to delve into the details of the crime. Well-documented accounts will be found in Gaetano Salvemini, *The Fascist Dictatorship in Italy* (New York: Henry Holt & Co., 1927), Mario Del Giudice, *Cronistoria Del Processo Matteotti* (Palermo: La Cartografica, 1955); and G. Spagnuolo, *Ceka Fascista e delitto Matteotti* (Rome: Ruffolo, 1947). Del Giudice was

The men's names, as it was later ascertained, were Amerigo Dumini, Albino Volpi, Giuseppe Viola, Amleto Poveromo, and Augusto Malacria—names completely insignificant to the general public, but well known in Fascist circles as belonging to old-time *squadristi*.[13] They were members of the small squad of "enforcers" organized a few weeks earlier by the Administrative Secretary of the Fascist party, Giovanni Marinelli, and they were under the direct orders of Marinelli and of the Undersecretary of the Presidency of the Council of Ministers, Aldo Finzi. Farinacci was also well acquainted with them.

According to the testimony the five gave at their trial almost two years later, they had only meant to kidnap Matteotti in order to question him concerning the part played by Italian Socialists in the murder of the Secretary of the Paris *Fascio*, Nicola Bonservizi, on March 26, 1924. Once in the car, Matteotti had struggled and, being ill with tuberculosis, he had suffered a lung hemorrhage and had died.[14] The *squadristi*, thrown, they said, into a panic by this sudden turn of events, had driven about the countryside for hours and had finally buried the corpse in a wooded area called the Quartarella and had then headed back to Rome. Their leader, Amerigo Dumini, had returned the car to the editor of the Fascist *Corriere Italiano*, Filippo Filippelli, from whom he had borrowed it, and he had told Filippelli of the kidnapping and of Matteotti's accidental death, but he did not give

---

investigating magistrate for the first trial of Matteotti's killers in 1926, and Spagnuolo was public prosecutor at the second trial in 1947. Also of considerable interest, if taken with due caution, are the works of some protagonists, Cesare Rossi (cited above), and Amerigo Dumini, *Diciassette Colpi* (Milan: Longanesi, 1951), pp. 73–96.

13. Dumini had been one of the founders of the Florence *Fascio* in 1919. Volpi, who had done the same in Milan, had also been president of the *Arditi* Association, and in December 1921, while on trial for the murder of a Socialist worker, had been acquitted on the sworn testimony of Mussolini to the effect that another Fascist, now deceased, had committed the crime. (Gaetano Salvemini, "Nuova luce sull'affare Matteotti," *Il Ponte* XI, 3 [March 1955], 1–12.)

14. When the corpse of Matteotti was found, more than two months after his abduction, it was in such an advanced state of decomposition that it was impossible to determine the cause of death.

the location of the grave.[15] On the same night, another member of the Ceka, Aldo Putato, met Mussolini's private secretary, Arturo Fasciolo, in a cafe, where he related to him the gory tale and handed him Matteotti's blood-stained passport. Early the next morning, Fasciolo informed Mussolini, who ordered him to keep the matter quiet. Nevertheless, Fasciolo spoke about it to Rossi, assuming that the latter already knew and had in fact ordered the kidnapping, while instead, it later appeared, the order had been given by Marinelli without Rossi's knowledge.[16]

By June 11, Matteotti's disappearance was already causing considerable apprehension among his family and colleagues, one of whom notified the police. Then, on June 12, through the number on the license plates of Filippelli's car, jotted down by the doorman of a house near Matteotti's, the police were able to identify the car and trace it to Filippelli and through him to Dumini, a notorious *squadrista* closely connected with Mussolini's entourage. The identification of the car and its owner was reported to the Fascist chief of police, the Quadrumvir Emilio De Bono, who at once informed Mussolini. No longer able to ignore the matter, and in spite of having full knowledge of the facts, Mussolini that same evening told the Chamber of Deputies: ("I believe the Chamber is anxious for news of the Honorable Matteotti, who disappeared suddenly on Tuesday afternoon, when and where is not yet definitely known, but in circumstances which warrant the suspicion of a crime. Such a crime, if it had been committed, could not fail to arouse the horror and the indignation of the government and of Parliament. Mussolini claimed to have personally given orders to search for the missing deputy, and he assured the Chamber that the guilty ones would be arrested and brought to trial. "I hope," he concluded, "that the Honorable Matteotti may soon be able to resume his place in Parliament."[17]

At the end of the session, the opposition deputies (Unitarian Socialists, Extreme Socialists, Communists, Republicans, Popu-

15. Dumini, Diciassette colpi, pp. 79–84.
16. Rossi, Il delitto Matteotti, pp. 55–58.
17. Mussolini, XX, 326.

lars, Social Democrats) voted a resolution to the effect that they considered it impossible to participate in the work of the Chamber of Deputies while uncertainty prevailed about the fate of Matteotti, and that they all, therefore, would abstain from parliamentary activity until the situation should be clarified.[18]

Later that night, Dumini was arrested while trying to leave Rome by train. Questioned by Police Chief De Bono, who made it clear he was acting as a Fascist leader rather than as chief of police, Dumini was advised to deny everything, and he was promised that his loyalty would be rewarded. De Bono also went through Dumini's luggage and removed a bundle of papers and Matteotti's bloodstained trousers, perhaps taken by Dumini as proof of the deed or as a gory trophy.[19] Dumini asked to be defended by Farinacci, but the latter declined the appointment,[20] probably not realizing the importance which the trial would assume.

The arrest of Dumini and the opposition's decision, as well as the violent attacks which immediately began in the opposition press, were the signals for Mussolini to act. On the afternoon of June 13, he again rose to speak in the Chamber of Deputies.

"If anyone in this hall has the greatest right to be saddened and exasperated," he said, "it is I. Only my greatest enemy, one who had lain awake for long nights scheming a diabolical plot, could have conceived this crime." He went on to point out that his speech of June 7 had created a sort of *detente*. But he made it clear that if his opponents were to use this atrocious episode to try to bring down his government, he would resist such attempts with all the means at his disposal.[21]

Immediately afterward, the Chamber of Deputies, with only the pro-Fascist majority in attendance, approved the interim budget until December 31, 1924, and adjourned *sine die*.

Mussolini was now free from embarrassment within the Chamber of Deputies for at least several months; but he realized that,

18. De Felice, *Mussolini il Fascista*, I, 627.

19. Salvemini, *The Fascist Dictatorship*, p. 266.

20. Roberto Farinacci, *Andante mosso, 1924–25* (Milan: A. Mondadori, 1929) p. 60.

21. *Mussolini*, XX, 327–329.

in order to pacify public opinion, he would have to produce a certain number of scapegoats. The opposition press was well aware of the connection between the now captured Amerigo Dumini and such Fascist officials as Finzi, Rossi, Marinelli, and Filippelli, and it was losing no opportunity, in news stories as well as in editorials, to point out that any action of those Fascist leaders must have had the prompting or at least the consent of Mussolini himself. Stories were printed to the effect that Matteotti, on the day after his disappearance, had been scheduled to speak in the Chamber of Deputies on government finances and that he had planned to use that opportunity to deliver a scathing indictment of profiteering and corruption in the highest Fascist circles. He was reported to have been about to denounce and prove corrupt practices by Undersecretary Finzi in connection with an exploration concession to the Sinclair Petroleum Company.

Cesare Rossi's excited comment to the newsman after Matteotti's speech of May 30 was also given prominence in the opposition press, as was the fact that Dumini and his henchmen had been hangers-on of Marinelli and Rossi. In a rapid sequence of events, Mussolini forced the resignations of Rossi and Undersecretary Finzi on June 14, and of De Bono from his police post on the sixteenth. That same day, Filippelli was arrested while trying to escape to France, and the next day Volpi was captured near Milan. Rossi, who had been sought for questioning by the police since the day after his resignation, gave himself up in Rome on June 22.

Through these resignations and arrests, and by relinquishing the Interior portfolio to the Nationalist leader Luigi Federzoni on June 16, Mussolini hoped to show his detachment and determination to let justice prevail. He also had to contend, however, with the extremist faction of the Fascist party, led by Farinacci, who saw in the turmoil created by the Matteotti affair an opportunity to advocate what they called "the second wave" of the Fascist revolution. Parliamentary procedures to them were meaningless, and a situation in which the government appeared to be tottering seemed to them tailor-made for the setting up of a reign of terror against any and all opponents, in order to rule with absolute power. Hoping, perhaps, to control the extremists by satisfying the ambition of their leader, Mussolini made Farinacci a member of the party Directorate,[22] but the appointment was merely interpreted by the *ras* of Cremona as a vindication of his intransigent views. As a brutal answer to the Socialist press's requests that the government resign[23] and the militia be disbanded,[24] Farinacci at once encouraged thousands of militiamen to march through the streets of Rome singing war songs,[25] while Mussolini lamely claimed that they had "come only to welcome Ras Tafari, not to seize control."[26] Only a few days later, Farinacci gloatingly wrote: ([The sad Matteotti episode [has shown] most clearly that Mussolini cannot be left at the mercy of this or that faction, but must base his actions on our strength. The sad Matteotti episode, furthermore, has rid us of all our opponents who had surrounded the Duce, and whom we used to call "the Jewish courtiers."[27]

And the next day, having called a rally of the "old guard" of Fascism from the Po Valley in Bologna, Farinacci harangued more than 70,000 Blackshirts, attacking both the Fascist moderates and the opposition parties and warning the latter to surrender or face a fight to the finish.

This rally was the prelude to a six months' struggle during 1924 in which Mussolini tried to steer a middle course and keep the activities of his government within constitutional bounds, and Farinacci tried to goad him into repressive measures while insisting that "pacification" could only be obtained through force.

On June 24, Mussolini appeared before the Senate and, in a major speech, pointed out that within twenty-four hours of the report to the police of Matteotti's disappearance, the principal suspect had been arrested. He assured the Senate that all his po-

---

22. *Cremona Nuova* (Cremona), June 17, 1924.
23. *Avanti!* (Rome), June 15, 1924.
24. *Ibid.*, June 17, 1924.
25. *Cremona Nuova* (Cremona), June 18, 1924.
26. *The New York Times*, June 18, 1924.
27. *Cremona Nuova* (Cremona), June 22, 1924. Farinacci's anti-Semitism, which was to erupt with outspoken virulence after the promulgation of the Racial Laws in Italy in 1938, evidently had much earlier roots.

litical activities since the election had aimed directly at speeding up and perfecting the final entry of the Fascists into the constitutional fold and at making Fascism a nucleus of reunion and of national conciliation. He pointed out that his speech of June 7 in the Chamber of Deputies had undoubtedly established the terms of a possible coexistence necessary to the regular functioning of Parliament, while within the country the feeling had spread that a new period of peace and absolute tranquillity was about to begin. These results, Mussolini thought, had not been cancelled, but had been only interrupted by the tragic episode which had cost Matteotti his life. The object of the general policy of the government, Mussolini stated, remained unchanged: to reach at any cost, within the law, political normalcy and national pacification.[28]

While Mussolini was thus reassuring the Senate, Roberto Farinacci editorialized against the opposition, pointing out that the military cadres of Fascism were in full readiness, warning the opposition not to try to bring down Mussolini or to think hard of the certain consequences of any such attempt, and concluding: (We already know what we would do. We would simply . . . take our Duce with us to Bologna, and from there we would make him again march on Rome at the head of his columns. And our enemies should also consider that we have learned much from past experiences. During the second wave, we would see to it that those we once protected with excessive generosity could no longer laugh at us.[29]

And during the following days, Farinacci commented in an editorial on Mussolini's Senate speech; and while paying lip service to the Duce's statesmanlike attitude, he plainly stated his conviction that any attempt at pacification was in vain. Again he brought out his pet idea of instituting a harsh press censorship so that "the Fascist masses would not be provoked into burning entire issues of this or that [opposition] newspaper."[30]

The Milan police, in the meantime, had arrested Giuseppe

---

28. *Mussolini*, XXI, 4–11.
29. *Cremona Nuova* (Cremona), June 24, 1925.
30. *Ibid.*, June 24–25, 1924.

Viola, one of Matteotti's five attackers, on June 24; and on June 28, they captured Amleto Poveromo, another of the group. On the same day, in Rome, no less a figure than the Administrative Secretary of the Fascist party, Giovanni Marinelli, was arrested in connection with the kidnapping of Matteotti.

Meanwhile, on June 27, the opposition deputies had published a manifesto, accusing Mussolini and his Fascist henchmen of having broken the law and of being responsible for Matteotti's disappearance. The deputies officially announced to the Italian people that, as long as the regime of illegality prevailed, they would abstain from parliamentary activities. The *Aventine* secession, as the opposition styled itself, was again, after more than twenty centuries, on the Roman political scene.

Emboldened by the opposition's maneuver, which appeared to confirm Farinacci's own skepticism of the possibility of co-existence, the *ras* of Cremona kept pressing Mussolini to act, advocating "exceptional laws which should have been enacted immediately after our revolution."[31] He also published an appeal to Mussolini to stop seeking "normalization," warning the *Duce* that his conciliatory attitude was mistaken for weakness, and stating: "Just as in 1921 we denounced the 'peace pact' . . . we must today tell our adversaries: with men and parties of bad faith we cannot accept to coexist."[32]

Mussolini obviously realized that the situation was getting out of hand. On July 10, he prevailed on the Council of Ministers to enforce the press regulations which had been enacted a year earlier. Farinacci applauded this measure, but, still not satisfied, he demanded that anti-Fascists within Italy should be sentenced to house-arrest, and that those who had fled the country should be stripped of their Italian citizenship.[33] He also caused the Provincial Council of Cremona to pass a resolution stigmatizing the opposition and specifically declining to offer condolence to Matteotti's widow.[34]

The situation, however, in spite of Mussolini's efforts, did not

31. *Ibid.*, July 3, 1924.
32. *Ibid.*, July 4, 1924.
33. *Ibid.*, July 10, 1924. Both these measures were eventually enacted in 1926.
34. Farinacci, *Andante mosso*, p. 11.

show signs of improvement. During the month of July, the two principal associations of war veterans, the *Mutilati* and the *Combattenti*, which had previously been ardently pro-Fascist, held national congresses at which, without going openly over to the opposition, the leadership seriously criticized the government's policies and advocated a number of reforms.

The bureaucracy, also sensing tremors in the structure of the Fascist regime and trying to avoid being too deeply compromised in the event of its downfall, began to show less favoritism towards Fascist lawbreakers and bullies. In increasing numbers, latecomers resigned from membership in the Fascist party, and many deputies, who only a few months earlier had been eager to be included in the *listone*, began to waver and let it be understood that they might withhold their support from the government.[35] Farinacci, in turn, openly attacked the wavering rightist deputies, claiming that, should they defect, "they would make our movement more agile, and would allow us to pursue, with better results, a policy of absolute intransigence."[36]

Mussolini instead, being a great opportunist, always wanted to play both sides against the middle and keep all his options open. In this instance, he intended to seek the support of both the moderates and the extremists, and to this end he called, on July 22, a meeting of the Grand Council, which Farinacci attended.

In a speech which tried to promise something to every-one, Mussolini reaffirmed the government's determination to pursue a policy of national unity. At the same time, he defended the integrity of Fascism and disclaimed responsibility for Matteotti's murder.[37] During the same meeting, Mussolini and Farinacci decided that, since the opposition parties intended to use the trial of Matteotti's kidnappers to indict Fascism, Fascism would accept the challenge and would, in turn, try the opposition at the bar of public opinion. Accordingly, Farinacci wrote to the Rome *Procuratore Generale*, Luigi Crisafulli, that he would now accept the appointment as Amerigo Dumini's defender.[38]

Pursuing the same unifying tactics, Mussolini on August 7

35. De Felice, *Mussolini il Fascista*, I, 659–661.
36. *Cremona Nuova* (Cremona), July 18, 1924.
37. *Mussolini*, XXI, 21–29.
38. *Cremona Nuova* (Cremona), July 25, 1924.

convened the National Council of Fascism, which comprised a larger number of local leaders than the Grand Council and, in a major speech, managed to satisfy the demands of the moderates led by Giuseppe Bottai, who solicited the elaboration of social legislation, as well as those of the extremists, whom he assured that Fascism, if necessary, would fight to the finish and be invincible.[39]

Farinacci was ecstatic and lavish in his praise for Mussolini's speech and for the decisions reached by the National Council, and he took the opportunity, in his editorial comment, to reaffirm that the trial of Matteotti's kidnappers would not be allowed to degenerate into an indictment of Fascism.[40]

By the middle of August, it seemed that Mussolini had succeeded in reasserting his control over the Fascists as well as over their rightist collaborators; but on August 16, 1924, Matteotti's corpse was accidentally found by a hunter's dog, and the danse macabre was resumed more frenetically than ever. The opposition press indulged in the most fantastic speculation as well as in increasing attacks on Fascist policies and individuals, while the Fascist press responded with equal intemperance.

At the same time, a renewal of violent encounters between squadristi and members of opposition parties throughout Italy made many feel that a bloody showdown might be near. To calm public opinion, on September 6, Mussolini wired Farinacci, who was about to make a speech in Florence, asking him to use the utmost moderation and to "wave not just an olive branch but a whole olive forest."[41] Farinacci, in a rare show of discipline, devoted most of his address to eulogizing the Fascist "martyrs" and

---

39. *Mussolini*, XXI, 40–46. This speech provided a clear insight into Mussolini's political opportunism and cynical contempt for the masses. He was not speaking for publication, and looking at Farinacci and his followers, he stated: "We must anesthetize . . . the opposition, and in fact the entire Italian people. The state of mind of the Italian people is this: do whatever you want, but tell us afterwards. Do not bother us every day threatening to call out the firing squads. Some morning, when we wake up, tell us that you have done it, and we will be happy."

40. *Cremona Nuova* (Cremona), August 8, 1924.

41. Mussolini to Farinacci, September 6, 1924, ID–NA, T586, 030946.

to praising some of the liberal supporters of Fascism.[42] Less than a week later, however, there was a most serious incident in Rome with the fatal shooting of the Fascist Deputy Armando Casalini by a Socialist fanatic. The next day, Farinacci thundered in his newspaper against the *Aventine* deputies, whom he accused of having instigated the murder, and concluded his editorial: "If the broom is not enough, let us use the machine-gun."[43] In vain Mussolini's own newspaper pleaded: "Fascists, these are your orders: utmost discipline! No violence!"[44]

The street fights and attacks against the opposition newspapers and headquarters multiplied, while more and more numerous defections from the Fascist ranks developed. The business world made clear its disillusionment by having a delegation of the Federation of Industrialists present Mussolini with a number of demands for political and economic reforms.[45] Even small businessmen took a firmer stand than they previously had taken against the Fascists. As an example, the manager of the Verdi Theatre in Cremona refused to give *Cremona Nuova* more than two free passes and sarcastically asked "whether to review a play it was really necessary to send the newspaper's whole staff and their families?"[46] And the Liberal party, at its Congress at Leghorn at the beginning of October, gave clear indications that it might soon detach itself from the pro-Fascist majority.[47]

Farinacci attended the Liberal Congress as a journalist, and his vituperative articles[48] may have contributed to the Liberals'

42. *Cremona Nuova* (Cremona), September 7, 1924.
43. *Ibid.*, September 13, 1924.
44. *Il Popolo d'Italia* (Milan), September 13, 1924.
45. *La Stampa* (Turin), September 18, 1924.
46. Politeama Verdi to Farinacci, September 19, 1924, ICSA, Farinacci Fund, 1924 Correspondence, Folder 3, Env. V.
47. De Felice, *Mussolini il Fascista*, I, 679–680.
48. He accused the Liberals, for instance, of being "neither fish nor fowl . . . despicable [men] with little conscience," regretted that Fascist discipline had "prevented the intervention of a small squad of Blackshirts to 'disinfect' the [Liberal] meeting hall," and called the Liberals "mangy dogs licking after . . . Albertini" about whose resolutions "Fascism does not give a damn, as it pushes on its way against everything and everybody." (*Cremona Nuova* [Cremona], October 1–7, 1924.)

hardening attitude towards Fascism. More important, as an index of disenchantment with Fascism by a hitherto vital bloc of supporters, was the decision announced shortly afterwards by the leadership of the *Mutilati* and of the War Veterans Association not to participate in the ceremonies marking the second anniversary of the March on Rome. Farinacci, in a meeting of the Fascist party Directorate, advocated the expulsion from the party of some prominent leaders of those associations, but he was overruled. Resorting, as usual, to the columns of his newspaper, he began a series of sharp attacks against the veterans' organizations whom he accused of being fair-weather friends and of forgetting the benefits they had derived from the Fascist fight against Bolshevism.[49] So virulent were his criticisms, in fact, that Mussolini telegraphed him through the prefect of Cremona, pointing out that his attacks on the Veterans' Associations were harmful to the party and asking him to abstain from further polemics.[50] The same day, however, Farinacci printed his most violent denunciation of the Veterans' Associations, urging that the Fascist party break all relations with them and that the government place them under receivership.[51]

Another target of Farinacci's ire was Freemasonry, of which there existed in Italy two branches. One, which claimed to be purely Italian, was headed by Count Domizio Torrigiani and was generally called, after its headquarters in Rome, the Palazzo Giustiniani Masonry; the other, also identified by its Roman location, was the Piazza del Gesú Masonry, which followed the Scottish rite and had as its Grand Master an old rightist Liberal, Raoul Palermi. The Piazza del Gesú association was less extremely anticlerical than the other, but both masonries, because of their basically international character, were in obvious contrast with the nationalistic principles of Fascism, and in fact, as early as 1923, Mussolini had declared it incompatible for a Fascist to be also a Mason. Many of the *Aventine* deputies, furthermore, were Masons, and it was not surprising, therefore, that Freemasonry

49. *Ibid.*, October 12, 1923.
50. Mussolini to prefect of Cremona, October 23, 1924, ID–NA, T586, 034316.
51. *Cremona Nuova* (Cremona), October 23, 1924.

should be regarded by the Fascist extremists as an enemy to be fought with any means, and that Farinacci, even though in his youth he had been a Mason, would now often attack the institution in print and, on occasion, instigate the sacking of a lodge or the beating of some known Freemason.

Mussolini, meanwhile, again took other steps which seemed to prove his determination to uphold law and order. On October 10, Emilio De Bono was forced to resign from leadership of the militia,[52] and shortly afterwards the militia itself was incorporated into the armed forces, and its members swore allegiance to the king. During the second half of October, Mussolini made an extensive tour of Italy, making speeches intended to bolster his position. On October 31, addressing a Fascist rally in the Augusteo Theatre in Rome, he claimed that the opposition was finally defeated, but his assertion was promptly qualified as wishful thinking by Farinacci, who commented that the only places where the opposition was indeed powerless were a few provinces such as his own Cremona, where Fascist rule was established and maintained without any halfhearted measures.[53]

That the opposition to Fascism was far from defeated was clearly shown during the celebration of Armistice Day on November 4,[54] when violent clashes occurred between the Blackshirts and the war veterans in Rome, in Milan, and in several

52. Officially, De Bono wrote Mussolini, asking to be relieved, and received from him a warm note of thanks for his service. (*Mussolini*, XXI, 452.) In reality, however, the *Quadrumvir* protested bitterly and wrote Farinacci complaining that Mussolini wanted to "offer [De Bono's] head" to the opposition. (De Bono to Farinacci, October 10, 1924, ICSA, Farinacci Fund, 1924 Correspondence, Folder 3, Env. D.)

53. *Cremona Nuova* (Cremona), November 2, 1924. In spite of Farinacci's claim, it would appear that his control was not yet so complete, at least within the judiciary, because he had recently complained to Mussolini that the Fascist Minister of Justice, Aldo Oviglio, had refused his request to transfer away from Cremona two "anti-Fascist" judges. In typical Farinacci style, the *ras* of Cremona warned Mussolini that, at the first provocation, he would "ship the two judges to Oviglio by parcel post." (Farinacci to Mussolini, September 12, 1924, ID–NA, T586, 026226–026228.)

54. The armistice between Italy and Austria-Hungary was concluded on November 4, 1918, a full week before the one between the Allies and Germany which marked the end of World War I.

cities in southern Italy. Farinacci headlined his editorial "*Mea Culpa*" and commented that the incidents were in fact the Fascists' fault, because they had not physically eliminated their opponents much sooner.[55] There was scarcely a day now when Farinacci would not single out opposition newspapers or political leaders for attack in the most violent language. His favorite targets were Luigi Albertini, a senator as well as editor of the *Corriere della Sera*; Giovanni Amendola, editor of *Il Mondo* and, as a Liberal deputy, unofficial leader of the *Aventine* secession; and Filippo Turati, dean of Italian Socialist deputies.[56]

The *Aventine* deputies, meanwhile, continued to limit themselves to attacks in the press against Fascism, but they produced no concrete proposals for a parliamentary solution to the political impasse. When the Chamber of Deputies reopened on November 12, they reasserted their refusal to participate in its works and entrenched behind their "moral protest." All the while, however, they maneuvered behind the scenes, trying to detach a number of non-Fascist deputies from the majority as well as some of the more moderate Fascists, and hoping, by a series of revelations of Fascist wrong-doing, to provoke a crisis which might topple Mussolini's government.

The first of these revelations was the publication on November 26 of documents proving the participation of the *Quadrumvir* Italo Balbo in the beating of political opponents and in illegal interference with the police. As a result, Balbo, who had replaced Emilio De Bono as commander of the militia, was forced by Mussolini to resign.[57] Farinacci opposed the dismissal of Balbo as he had that of De Bono, six weeks earlier, because he considered these moves of Mussolini as concessions which only served to

55. *Cremona Nuova* (Cremona), November 7, 1924. The president of the *Arditi* Federation at this time wrote Farinacci asking him to intervene with Mussolini so that he would no longer "cheat the *Arditi* of what they had been promised." (L. Zaccherini to Farinacci, November 5, 1924. ICSA, Farinacci Fund, 1924 Correspondence, Folder 3, Env. V.)

56. Within a few years, Albertini would be forced to withdraw from journalism and from any form of public life; Amendola would die as a consequence of Fascist beatings; and Turati would escape to France to end his days in exile.

57. *Mussolini*, XXI, 455.

reinforce the opposition. Farinacci's dissent was widely known, and it was used by some opposition newspapers to spotlight the precarious situation of Fascism and the existence of a "vice-Duce" working to undermine Mussolini.[58] To these allegations, Farinacci replied with an editorial disclaiming any difference with Mussolini, to whom he pledged his unconditional obedience. Accusing in turn the opposition of trying to split the Fascist ranks and calling their efforts "perfidious daydreams," he concluded: *Our stubbornness in defending Fascism against those who slander it and want to divide and atomize it should not be mistaken for indiscipline: Fascism is our creature, and as such we love and defend it . . . As always, we reaffirm our unlimited faith in Mussolini, whom we cannot separate from Fascism, because they are both facets of a single soul and a single thought, belonging to the new Italy which will not prostitute itself to its enemies, even if now they masquerade as Italian patriots.*[59] These words clearly described the acute conclusion which Farinacci had reached: in order for Fascism to survive and become all-powerful, Mussolini and only Mussolini had to be its acknowledged leader with his name and person elevated far above any other. In a word, it was necessary to create a myth of Mussolini. It would then be possible, Farinacci hoped, for him and his followers to maneuver behind the scenes to bend Mussolini to their will in ruling Italy; but first Mussolini must, in spite of himself if necessary, be saved from the threatening ruin and placed on a secure pedestal out of reach of the enemies of Fascism. Farinacci pursued this theme for several days, extolling Mussolini as the creator of the new Italy and warning the opposition that any attempt to overthrow Mussolini would automatically result in their liquidation by the Fascist militia. One of his editorials, in fact, was entitled "Hands off Mussolini."[60]

The opposition, however, continued to attack Mussolini, charging him with at least "moral complicity" in Matteotti's murder[61]

58. *Il Corriere della Sera* (Milan), November 26–27, 1924.
59. *Cremona Nuova* (Cremona), November 28, 1924.
60. *Ibid.*, November 29, December 1, 1924.
61. *Il Popolo* (Rome), November 29, 1924.

and asking that he and his government resign.[62] These attacks, coming as they did only in the press and not in the Chamber of Deputies, from which more than one hundred Liberal, Popular, and Socialist members were abstaining,[63] had no constitutional significance. But the attitude of the Senate, which was now also in session, became increasingly critical and such as to cause Mussolini deep concern.

The Senate, it will be recalled, had voted its confidence in Mussolini on June 26. As an appointive chamber, composed of prominent personalities from the armed services and from industry and the professions, the Senate was a most conservative body and, as such, it had widely endorsed Fascism as Italy's savior from "Bolshevism." On December 3, however, Luigi Albertini, editor of the Liberal daily, *Corriere della Sera*, rose to deliver a sharp criticism of the Fascist government. He was followed by Senator Ettore Conti, a Milanese industrialist, who made it clear that the nation did not intend "to escape from one form of extremism in order to fall prey to another" and denied Mussolini's contention that Bolshevism was the only alternative to Fascism.[64] Mussolini defended his policies and, in the end, he again obtained a vote of confidence; but this time his majority had shrunk from 225 votes to 206, and the senators voting against him had increased in number from 21 to 54.[65] Farinacci pretended to ignore the significance of this rising disenchantment with Fascism on the part of the Senate and wrote an editorial claiming that Fascism was more vital than ever and that it would now "begin its counterattack and not stop until the state will have those laws and those reforms which are the birthright of our revolution."[66] The same day, however, as another step in the campaign to expose the crimes of Fascist leaders, Giuseppe Donati, publisher of the Popular newspaper *Il Popolo*, preferred formal charges against former Police Chief Emilio De Bono for complicity in the Mat-

62. *Il Mondo* (Rome), November 29, 1924.
63. The few Communist deputies had returned to the Chamber on November 12, 1924.
64. Acts of Parliament, Senate, 27th Legislature, pp. 344 ff.
65. De Felice, *Mussolini il Fascista*, I, 691.
66. *Cremona Nuova* (Cremona), December 6, 1924.

teotti murder. As a senator, De Bono could only be tried by the Senate, and a committee was formed to investigate the accusation. The committee, incidentally, pre-empted the entire files covering the Matteotti affair, so that, much to the satisfaction of Mussolini and Farinacci, prosecution of the jailed abductors was indefinitely postponed.

Responding to Farinacci's vituperation, the opposition press was equally vehement in attacking him and his views. It was hardly surprising, therefore, that on December 7, 1924, an attempt was made on Farinacci's life. As he was driving from Mantova to Cremona, two rifle shots were aimed at his car, and one bullet broke through the window, without, however, injuring any of the car's occupants. The would-be assassin was never identified,[67] and Farinacci received an avalanche of messages from the Fascist ranks congratulating him for his escape, while the opposition press played down the incident, even hinting that there had been no assassination attempt and that the car's window had been broken by a slingshot.[68] Farinacci redoubled his efforts to stiffen the Fascist attitude toward the opposition and the non-Fascist members of the Parliamentary majority, writing that the hour had come to launch an offensive to prevent the country from falling back into chaos.[69] An increasing number of former supporters and sympathizers, however, left the side of Fascism, and it was even reported that a number of senators and former prime ministers were asking the king to intervene and demand that Mussolini step down.[70] The *Aventine* deputies obviously felt that the time had come to use their strongest weapon. Consequently, on December 27, *Il Mondo* began publication of a memorandum which Cesare Rossi, Mussolini's former press secretary, had compiled back in June before giving himself up and which soon afterwards had reached the opposition leaders. In this document, the former press officer gave a detailed account of the events of June 1924, relating many instances of Mussolini's instigation to

67. Report of the Brescia District Attorney to the Minister of Justice, January 19, 1925, ID–NA, T586, 031110–031112.
68. *Il Popolo* (Rome), December 12, 1924.
69. *Cremona Nuova* (Cremona), December 19, 1924.
70. De Felice, *Mussolini il Fascista*, I, 691–692.

violence against political opponents and squarely placing the blame for the Matteotti murder directly on Marinelli and indirectly on Mussolini.[71]

The Fascist press tried to discredit Rossi's accusations. Farinacci wrote that the former press officer was clearly insane,[72] but the impression created by the Rossi memorandum was enormous everywhere. The opposition press pointed out that "the only political question is whether it is compatible with the dignity of a civilized country that there remain at the head of its government a man who is under the weight of such tremendous charges,"[73] and invited Mussolini to renounce his immunities and to put himself at the disposal of the judicial authorities.[74] The London Times's correspondent wrote: "It is said on good authority that even the pro-Fascist members of the Senate consider Signor Mussolini's position is untenable, and the opinion has been expressed in Senate circles that the magistracy should not allow forty-eight hours to elapse without taking steps to interrogate him."[75] So critical, in fact, was the situation, that the possibility of the government's resigning was discussed, even though inconclusively, during a meeting of the Council of Ministers on December 30, and the advisability of such a step was supported not only by the two Liberal Ministers but also by two Fascist ones.[76]

On December 31, the Fascist extremists made their move. Farinacci, in Cremona, while insisting that "Mussolini is Fascism, and Fascism means us," wrote: "Our loyalty is beyond doubt, but we must tell Mussolini that Fascism does not approve his moderate policies of the last two years."[77] That same day, translating Farinacci's prodding into action, a group of high militia officers confronted Mussolini in his office and presented him with an ultimatum: either he would abandon his wavering tactics, or

71. Rossi, Il Delitto Matteotti, pp. 163–188.
72. Cremona Nuova (Cremona), December 28, 1924.
73. La Stampa (Turin), December 28, 1924.
74. Il Corriere della Sera (Milan), December 30, 1924.
75. The Times (London), December 30, 1924.
76. Mussolini, XXI, 234.
77. Cremona Nuova (Cremona), December 31, 1924.

they would publicly disavow him. Mussolini, shaken, promised that on January 3, in the Chamber of Deputies, he would once and for all dispose of the opposition.[78] As Farinacci ascertained afterwards, some of the militia officers met later the same day with leaders of the Piazza Gesú Freemasonry, and there was talk of killing Mussolini if he did not keep his promise.[79]

At the same time, some opposition leaders were again vainly trying to induce the king to intervene, and rumors spread that the fall of Mussolini's government was imminent. As a result, in many parts of Italy there were popular expressions of jubilation, which in turn caused a violent reaction on the part of Fascist diehards; the disorders were numerous and bloody, particularly in Tuscany,[80] but also in the Cremonese countryside, where Farinacci bluntly ordered that "the manganelli (clubs) which had been put away in the attic must be dusted off and kept handy."[81] Commenting on the disorders in Florence, where more than ten thousand armed Fascists had taken the offices of several newspapers and opposition parties by storm and sacked them, Farinacci stressed again that he could not blame the Fascist rank and file for rebelling against the party Directorate and the government, "in order to defend Fascism and its Duce." He ended with an emotional appeal to Mussolini to put an end to compromises and to govern "fascistically," in accordance with "the true soul of Fascism, our intransigence, which alone has saved the party and which now allows us again to go on the offensive."[82]

In this charged atmosphere, Mussolini rose in the Chamber of Deputies on January 3, 1925, to deliver the speech which was to be the death sentence of Italian freedom for the next twenty years. He began by asking the deputies a loaded question: "Article 47 of the Constitution says: 'The Chamber of Deputies has the right to impeach the Ministers of the Crown, and bring them to the bar of the High Court of Justice.' I formally demand whether,

78. Tamaro, Venti anni, II, 60–62.
79. D. Negrini to Farinacci, February 5, 1926, ICSA, Farinacci Fund, 1926 Correspondence, Folder 1.
80. De Felice, Mussolini il Fascista, I, 715.
81. Cremona Nuova (Cremona), January 1, 1925.
82. Ibid., January 2, 1925.

in this chamber or outside of it, there is anyone wishing to avail himself of Article 47." Mussolini said that he knew he was accused of having created the Ceka, but that he denied it categorically. He declared that he, and he alone, assumed the full political, moral, and historical responsibility for all that had happened. Referring to the violent words attributed to him, he proclaimed: "If distorted phrases are enough to hang a man, bring on the rope and the scaffold. If Fascism is really a criminal association, I am the leader of this criminal association." He attacked the Aventine deputies, accusing them of sedition. "When two incompatible elements are at war," he continued, "the only solution is force. There has never been any other solution in history, and there never will be." He pointed out that the opposition had deluded itself in believing that Fascism was dead because he himself was repressing it and said that, if he were to unleash it, there would be plenty to see. "Italy," he concluded, "wants peace, tranquillity, calm in which to work. We shall give her this tranquillity and calm, with love, if possible, and with force if necessary. Be sure that in the forty-eight hours following this speech of mine the situation will be made clear on the entire front."[83]

The Duce was true to his word. Within twenty-four hours, it was indeed clear that the Fascist government had become the Fascist dictatorship. And Farinacci, who at the conclusion of Mussolini's speech had rushed down the steps of the Chamber to the front bench to be the first to shake his hand,[84] could claim vindication for his unwavering intransigence and gloat: "We were right in predicting that the Matteotti crime would bury all of Matteotti's friends."[85]

83. Mussolini, XXI, 235–238.
84. L. Federzoni in La Nuova Stampa (Turin), June 2, 1946.
85. Cremona Nuova (Cremona), January 4, 1925.

VIII

FARINACCI
AT THE HELM OF
THE PARTY

FARINACCI'S EDITORIAL of January 4 was titled "The Password is Counterattack," but it was not to the *squadristi* or to the Fascist militia that Mussolini entrusted the task of subduing the opposition. At 10:30 P.M. on January 3, 1925, the Minister of the Interior, Luigi Federzoni, dispatched a circular telegram to all prefects instructing them to inform the local Fascist leaders of the government's prohibition against any public demonstration or disorder in connection with Mussolini's speech.[1] Twenty-five minutes later, another telegram ordered the prefects to proceed to:

1. Close down all politically suspect clubs and meeting halls.
2. Disband all organizations which under any pretext might unite disorderly or anyhow subversive individuals.
3. Disband all chapters of Italia Libera[2] and prevent any further activity by them.
4. Effect closest surveillance of Communists and subversive individuals proven to engage or suspected of engaging in criminal activities, rounding up dangerous characters and remembering that any attempt at resistance must be repressed with any means necessary.
5. Collect illegally held arms, proceeding to frequent searches.
6. Maintain the most rigorous control over all public establishments.[3]

1. Quoted in A. Aquarone, *L'organizzazione dello stato totalitario* (Turin: G. Einaudi, 1965), p. 347.
2. *Italia Libera* was the organization which, after 1922, had united a large number of militant anti-Fascists.
3. Aquarone, *L'organizzazione*, p. 348.

The prefects and the police under their orders acted at once, so that three days later, on January 6, Federzoni could report to the Council of Ministers that 95 suspicious clubs and 150 public establishments had been closed, 25 subversive organizations and 120 chapters of *Italia Libera* had been disbanded, 111 "dangerous" individuals had been arrested, and 655 house searches had been effected.[4]

Faced with this openly dictatorial onslaught, the *Aventine* deputies retreated even more disdainfully into their attitude of abstentionism and moral superiority. On January 8, they met and issued a manifesto, pointing out the unconstitutionality of the Fascist government's actions and deprecating its repression and violation of all fundamental liberties.[5] They reiterated their determination to abstain from further participation in the work of Parliament, in the obvious but futile hope that Fascism would topple under the weight of moral reprobation. The parliamentary majority, on its part, carried on its rubber-stamp mission, ratifying, on January 14, over 2,000 decrees issued by Mussolini during the preceding months.

Farinacci, however, even though applauding Mussolini's speech and the lightning speed with which its threats had begun to be translated into action, was far from willing to remain on the sidelines while Mussolini and Federzoni carried out their repressive program. More obstreperous than ever, Farinacci began at once a press campaign against a number of high functionaries in several ministries, especially those of Justice, Public Instruction, Finances, and Public Works, accusing them of being Masons and insisting that they be replaced with Fascists of proven loyalty and that, in fact, the entire bureaucracy be "fascistized."[6]

Also, partly as a result of Farinacci's pressure, exerted mainly through his editorials, the resignations from the Cabinet of the two Liberal Ministers, Gino Sarrocchi and Alessandro Casati, were followed by that of his old enemy, Aldo Oviglio, who was replaced as Minister of Justice by a more intransigent Fascist,

4. *Ibid.*, pp. 48–50.
5. Quoted in Salvatorelli e Mira, *Storia d'Italia*, p. 354.
6. *Cremona Nuova* (Cremona), January 10, 11, 13, 15, 21, 1925.

Alfredo Rocco.[7] And Farinacci again took up the cudgels against the Veterans' Association[8] and strongly criticized the proposed reform of the armed forces, causing Mussolini to wire him to stop embarrassing the government.[9]

Mussolini, at this point, was indeed faced by a serious dilemma. It was clearly essential, for the success of his drive towards even a forced "normalization," to prevent a resurgence of excesses by *squadristi* and the realization of Farinacci's famous "second wave." It was equally essential to strengthen and streamline the Fascist ranks, and this task could best be accomplished by a fanatically intransigent Fascist. In order to give a sop to the extremists, weed away dissident and revisionist Fascists, and put Farinacci in a post where he might be more easily controllable, Mussolini announced to the Grand Council meeting of February 12, 1925, his decision to put the Fascist party under the rule of a secretary general and to appoint Farinacci to that post. Significantly, the *Duce* pointed out that Fascism had "won a battle, but not yet the war," but he stressed that he demanded and expected from everyone the utmost "discipline without personal exhibitionism."[10]

From the very outset, the warning was lost on Farinacci, who five days later, addressing the Provincial Congress of the *Fasci* at Cremona, boasted that his appointment as Secretary General of the party was the result of the party's gratitude for his "energetic attitude after the Matteotti crime" and stated: *I am convinced that only through force can Fascism give the nation peace and prosperity and dispose of internal enemies. But in order to gain victory Fascism must remain fully efficient and leave to us—who intend to take full responsibility before history—the task of ruling alone while interpreting faithfully the Duce's thoughts.*[11]

That Farinacci interpreted his appointment as Secretary General as a personal victory for his intransigence was made even clearer

7. *Ibid.*, January 6, 1925.

8. *Ibid.*, January 23, 1925.

9. Mussolini to prefect of Cremona, February 6, 1925, ID–NA, T586, 034313.

10. *Il Popolo d'Italia* (Milan), February 13, 1925.

11. Roberto Farinacci, *Un periodo aureo del Partito Nazionale Fascista* (Foligno: Campitelli Editore, 1927), pp. 7–20.

in his speech of February 22, 1925, to a Fascist rally on the Island of Elba, when he pointed out that the Fascist government had wasted two years because of excessive indulgence and recalled the many times when he had advocated a stronger stand. On this occasion, he pronounced for the first time what was to become his favorite slogan. "We want," he shouted, "to insert the Fascist Revolution into the state. What does this mean? It means to legalize Fascist illegality "[12]

Having thus made his position clear to friends and foes, the next day Farinacci arrived in Rome to take up his duties as Secretary General of the Fascist party, and he issued a proclamation recalling Mussolini's order to "win the war" and spelling out the various problems to which he wanted Fascism to provide prompt solutions: muzzling of the press, control of banks, "fascistization" of the bureaucracy, establishment of Fascist syndicalism, and abolition of secret societies, meaning Freemasonry.[13] These goals, of course, were in addition to others which Farinacci had already repeatedly stated, such as the elimination of the parliamentary opposition, the subjugation of the Veterans' Associations, and the "purification" of party membership rolls. Nor, to be sure, did he forget the Matteotti affair. Less than a month after his appointment, for instance, commenting on the acquittal of several *squadristi* on trial for a number of killings of Socialists in the Bolognese countryside, Farinacci came out editorially, as well as officially as Secretary of the party, with high praise for the Fascist judges and the prediction that the trial of Matteotti's killers would have a similar outcome.[14] And a few days later, addressing a Fascist rally in Rome celebrating the anniversary of the founding of the *Fasci di Combattimento*, Farinacci spoke of himself as the head of the party and openly attacked the judiciary still investigating Matteotti's murder, saying that "in trying one

---

12. *Ibid.*, pp. 23–33.
13. ID–NA, T586, 034285. It was, in a way, providential for Mussolini that the reins of the party at this moment be held by a strong leader able to face internal and external opposition, because on February 15, the Fascist Duce was struck by an acute attack of duodenal ulcers from which he did not recover for several weeks.
14. *Cremona Nuova* (Cremona), March 6, 1925.

or two Fascists one can never try the Revolution, because all of us then are culprits. One cannot bring our revolution into a courtroom. For us there is only one judge: history."[15]

These were for Farinacci days of feverish activity, forced as he was to divide his time between Rome and Cremona. On weekdays, he could generally be found in his office at the Palazzo Littorio on Piazza Colonna, meeting with Fascist leaders from the outlying provinces, phoning or writing notes to Mussolini on this or that policy matter, or dictating the daily editorial to be telephoned to Cremona for the next day's issue of *Cremona Nuova*. He had taken up residence in a suite in the Hotel Bristol, on the nearby Via del Tritone, where he occasionally entertained some woman who had struck his fancy. On Fridays, Farinacci would generally board the overnight train to Cremona, where early on Saturday morning he would be met at the station by the triumvirate he had left to watch over his bailiwick during his absence: Cesare Balestreri, a prosperous landowner and secretary of the Cremona *Fascio;* Vincenzo Sanipoli, a militia warrant officer, well known for his bloody exploits during the heyday of *squadrismo*, as well as for his blind devotion to Farinacci; and the faithful secretary and mistress, Maria Antonioli. The group would proceed to Farinacci's home, where, after a perfunctory greeting to the good Anita and a romp with the two children, Farinacci would be briefed in minute detail concerning events and developments in the province of Cremona. The rest of the weekend would then be spent in meetings with local officials and businessmen and visits to this or that village or town where some problem seemed to require Farinacci's personal intervention. There would also be conferences with his law partner, Professor Alessandro Groppali, or with the journalists who were in charge of *Cremona Nuova*, Giorgio Masi and Paolo Pantaleo. At meal times, in true seigneurial style, Farinacci would often hold open table at one of his old haunts, the Cafe Nautilus or the Albergo Roma. On Sunday night, he would again leave for Rome, there to start work anew on what he claimed to be the mission en-

15. Farinacci, *Un periodo aureo*, pp. 53–62. Farinacci's definition of himself as head of the party did not go unnoticed and was widely criticized by other Fascist newspapers. (ID–NA, T586, 030533–030534.)

trusted to him by Mussolini: to make the Italian state into a Fascist state.

It is abundantly clear from a wealth of documentary evidence that Mussolini had not intended to invest Farinacci with any such task. In fact, as will be seen, Farinacci's aggressive tactics and undisciplined behavior were frequent causes of friction between the two men and eventually resulted in Farinacci's downfall and virtual banishment. During the thirteen months of his tenure as Secretary General of the Fascist party, however, Farinacci was indeed instrumental, directly or indirectly, in steering the course of the government as well as of the party, so that when he left office the Fascist dictatorship was well established. That he was not to participate in its leadership on a national scale was the result of a number of factors; but during this period, Farinacci spoke and acted as if, having virtually deified Mussolini, *"il Gran Segretario"* ("the Great Secretary,") as Farinacci was soon nicknamed, were the real arbiter of the Italian situation.

The first success of the new policy of force was, strangely enough, achieved by using that old Socialist weapon, the strike.

Ever since Fascism's advent to power, Fascist labor organizations had been formed in many fields, paralleling the older Socialist ones and vying with them for preponderance. On January 23, 1925, the Grand Council of Fascism had issued a bulletin, proclaiming as the task of the national Fascist syndicates "the defense of labor, without denying the proper role of capital." Then, in late February, Fascist-inspired strikes in northern Italy brought to a virtual standstill the building trades and the iron and steel industry, until, with the personal intervention of Farinacci, an agreement was reached with the employers in mid-March, and work was resumed. Speaking at Cremona on April 21, on the anniversary of the founding of Rome—the day had been chosen to replace May 1 as Labor Day—Farinacci bluntly stated that "Fascist syndicalism must be controlled and must be at the direct orders of the party."[16] And, commenting on the decision

16. Farinacci, *Un periodo aureo*, pp. 93–99. In the same speech, in a typical Farinacci outburst, the *ras* of Cremona noted that the opposition accused him of trampling liberty, and shouted: "Let us say frankly that we don't give a damn about liberty!"

taken on April 24 by the Grand Council to have provincial party leaders named jointly by the *Fasci* and by the Fascist syndicates and to forbid strikes unless authorized by the party, Farinacci pointed out that he had long since instituted these procedures at Cremona and rejoiced that they would now be applied on a national scale.[17] The leaders of the Socialist unions, continuously assailed by Farinacci and harassed by Luigi Federzoni's police, were unable to control the rank and file of the workers, who increasingly drifted into Fascist organizations. On October 2, 1925, the Federation of Industry and the Fascist labor "corporations" were officially recognized as the only authorized representatives of employers and workers. A few months later, on April 3, 1926, a comprehensive law formalized that relationship in minute detail, abolishing all freedom of collective bargaining and explicitly subordinating all trades, professions, commerce, and industry, to the directives of the government, aiming at the final establishment of the "corporative" state.[18]

Another early victory for Farinacci's viewpoint was registered on March 2, 1925, when a special decree removed from office the leadership of the National Association of War Veterans and placed the organization under the rule of a Fascist three-man commission.[19]

Turning to the reorganization of the Fascist party, whose membership had declined from 782,979 in 1923 to 642,246 by the end of 1924,[20] Farinacci began a double process of weeding out those whom he considered lukewarm or undesirable elements and attracting new recruits, especially from the younger segments of the population. He did not hesitate to disband any *Fascio* whose leaders he considered for any reason unfit or to expel from the party any member who incurred his displeasure; as many as eighteen deputies, including Aldo Oviglio the former Minister of Justice, as well as a substantial number of militia officers, saw their party membership revoked by Farinacci. As a result, while

17. *Cremona Nuova* (Cremona), April 26, 1925.
18. Salvatorelli e Mira, *Storia d'Italia*, pp. 370–371.
19. *Il Corriere della Sera* (Milan), March 3, 1925; *Cremona Nuova* (Cremona), March 3, 1925.
20. De Felice, *Mussolini il Fascista*, II, 57.

the Fascist youth organizations had attained a membership of 118,365[21] by June, adult members were further reduced by the end of 1925 to slightly under 600,000, after Farinacci on November 25 had prevailed on the party Directorate to approve his decision to close temporarily the membership rolls.[22] Farinacci's reorganizing activities, however, and especially his efforts to attract the young, were undoubtedly beneficial to the party, whose membership rose to 937,997 in 1926 and to 1,023,998 in 1927.[23]

While applying the acid test of doctrinaire conformism to Fascist party members, Farinacci missed no opportunity to push his attacks against the opposition outside the party. In editorials and speeches, time and again, he advocated the harshest measures against the *Aventine* deputies and their followers, specifying as he did, for instance, on April 12, at Robecco d'Oglio, near Cremona, that "all those suspected of being subversives must be confined under strict surveillance," that Luigi Albertini, Giovanni Amendola, Filippo Turati, and others must be "banished," that all leaders of the *Aventine* secession must be immediately arrested and charged with "criminal conspiracy against the State," and, finally, that the death penalty should be instituted against the enemies of Fascism.[24]

This speech made of course a great impression on the reading public and caused the opposition press to appeal to the government to disavow Farinacci's threats.[25] Mussolini wrote Farinacci a personal and rather tame note, warning him that "certain parts of . . . recent speeches . . . could give the world the impression that the Fascist government is in serious danger, and it might therefore institute a reign of terror . . . while instead the Fascist regime 'is strong as never before."[26] But the irrepressible "Great Secretary" kept right on, writing that the opposition should welcome such laws as a protection for them, since they should prefer "the rule of harsh laws rather than the explosion

21. Farinacci, *Un periodo aureo*, p. 156.
22. *Cremona Nuova* (Cremona), November 26, 1925.
23. De Felice, *Mussolini il Fascista*, II, 57.
24. Farinacci, *Un periodo aureo*, pp. 76–83.
25. *Il Giornale d'Italia* (Rome), April 14, 1925.
26. Mussolini to Farinacci, April 14, 1925. ID–NA, T586, 026560–026562.

of the just wrath of the party." "Mussolini," Farinacci concluded, "is arbiter of the situation, but he cannot remain deaf to the voice of Fascism "[27] That Farinacci's pressure was achieving some results was shown by the introduction in the Chamber of Deputies on May 27 of several laws aimed at curbing "activities against the State."[28] The legislative process would still delay the enactment and application of the "leggi Fascistissime," the "most Fascist" laws; but within less than a year, both through legislation and through police tactics, the Fascist dictatorship would indeed dispose of the opposition. Not quickly enough, however, to satisfy Farinacci, who kept clamoring for the elimination of the "enemies of Fascism" and took every opportunity to reassert his intransigence. On June 10, 1925, for instance, having learned that the Socialist leader Filippo Turati had called a meeting of the Aventine deputies in the lobby of Parliament to commemorate Matteotti, Farinacci summoned the Fascist deputies[29] and threatened to intervene forcibly "to commemorate the Fascist dead."[30] The meeting was then forbidden by the Fascist president of the Chamber of Deputies, and Farinacci triumphantly harangued a Fascist crowd assembled before party headquarters, boasting that he had succeeded in "de-Matteottizing" the nation.[31]

It was also undoubtedly as a result of Farinacci's daily vilification that the main leader of the Aventine deputies, Giovanni Amendola, who had already been assaulted by Fascists on the streets of Rome in December 1923, was waylaid on July 20 by a band of squadristi on a highway near Florence and given such a beating that he was crippled and died eight months later.

Several opposition leaders had meanwhile managed to emigrate, and against them Farinacci unleashed a particularly vicious campaign, urging that they be considered criminals and traitors. Accordingly, on January 31, 1926, the Senate approved a measure which gave the government the right, without process of law, to strip away citizenship and confiscate the property of any Italian

27. Cremona Nuova (Cremona), April 16, 1925.
28. Ibid., May 29, 1925.
29. Farinacci, Un periodo aureo, p. 138.
30. Tamaro, Venti anni, II, 115–116.
31. Farinacci, Un periodo aureo, p. 140–141.

who, while abroad, engaged in any activity against the Fascist government.[32]

As to Farinacci's fight against Freemasonry, it was punctuated by a series of rather embarrassing disclosures concerning his own past membership in the Piazza del Gesú Masonry, which culminated in the opposition press printing photographs of Farinacci's application and oath of loyalty to the Quinto Curzio Lodge of Cremona, dating as far back as July 1915.[33] There were also statements by various known Masons as to Farinacci's continued activity in the brotherhood.[34] Farinacci at first denied ever having belonged, but later admitted having joined the lodge before the war "for the sole purpose of destroying it from within."[35] The polemic continued more and more acrimoniously, with the opposition press pointing out that the Lodge Farinacci claimed to have joined to destroy in 1915 had not ceased activities until 1923,[36] and with Farinacci labelling Masons as "enemies of the Motherland" and vowing that the Fascist state would "trample on the corpses of all the parties and associations which stood in its way, including Freemasonry."[37]

Luckily for Farinacci, an opportunity to end the matter was soon afterward offered by an abortive attempt on Mussolini's life made on November 4 by a Socialist deputy, Tito Zaniboni. The police, made aware through an informer of Zaniboni's intentions, arrested him a few hours before he was to shoot Mussolini from a hotel room opposite the Foreign Ministry. Since Zaniboni was a Freemason, all Masonic lodges in Italy were occupied by the police and, on November 26, 1925, a law was passed regulating and generally abolishing sects and fraternal associations.[38]

Farinacci took the pretext of the plot to assail more vehemently

32. Salvatorelli e Mira, Storia d'Italia, p. 366. Among the first victims of this law, aimed at self-exiled anti-Fascists, was one of the greatest Italian historians, Gaetano Salvemini.

33. La Voce Repubblicana (Rome), September 10, 1925.

34. ID–NA, T586, 033944–033955–6/030832–030833.

35. Cremona Nuova (Cremona), September 11, 1925.

36. La Tribuna (Rome), September 17, 1925.

37. Cremona Nuova (Cremona), September 17, 1925.

38. Salvatorelli e Mira, Storia d'Italia, pp. 363–364. The Unitarian Socialist Party, of which Zaniboni was a member, was also ordered dissolved.

than ever the opposition press, specifically demanding that *Il Popolo*, *Il Mondo*, and *Il Corriere della Sera*, which he accused of being "financed by Masonic and foreign gold" and of having instigated the assassination attempt, be forced to pass into Fascist ownership or be closed down.[39] Farinacci's greatest victory in this fight was the conversion of the *Corriere della Sera* to Fascism. The great liberal daily was owned jointly by the Albertini brothers, Luigi and Alberto, respectively editor and publisher, and by two wealthy textile industrialists, the brothers Crespi. The latter, anxious to be on what they felt was the winning side, and knowing that the Albertinis were not independently wealthy, insisted on dissolving the partnership. Since the Albertinis were unable to buy out the Crespis, in November 1925 they were forced to sell to them their shares, and they were immediately replaced on the newspaper by pro-Fascist journalists.[40] Other newspapers, such as *La Tribuna* and *Il Messaggero* at Rome and *Il Mattino* at Naples, were similarly forced to join the Fascist ranks or to cease publication, as *Il Popolo* did at the end of November. Finally, on December 31, 1925, a law was passed establishing regulation of the press more stringently than ever before.[41]

With regard to Roberto Farinacci's attitude and behavior towards the world of business, banking, and finance, his motives were a combination of self-interest and of ingrained distrust towards the large institutions with international connections. From time to time, he exerted his influence on behalf of some large company, as shown by his intervention on behalf of *Societá Italiana Edison di Elettricita* to obtain for it a contract for the electrification of Italian state railways,[42] but Farinacci was by nature a provincial, a member and champion of the small bourgeoisie, be it agricultural or urban, and it was to this class that he looked for support and for the rewards he felt due for his ac-

39. *Cremona Nuova* (Cremona), November 12, 1925.
40. Ivon De Begnac, *Palazzo Venezia, Storia di un regime* (Rome: Editrice La Rocca, 1950), p. 270.
41. Salvatorelli e Mira, *Storia d'Italia*, p. 367.
42. Giacinto Motta, Managing Director of *Societa Edison*, to Farinacci, January 19, 1924, ICSA, Farinacci Fund, 1924 Correspondence, Folder 3, Env. M.

tivities on its behalf. These rewards manifested themselves in various ways. Through his intervention, for instance, a Cremona manufacturer of artificial silk obtained in 1924 import permits for machinery at reduced custom duties and showed his gratitude with a payment of 50,000 *lire*.[43] Another company, this one located at Vercelli, obtained a similar special treatment and compensated Farinacci with 15,000 *lire*.[44] During the same period, a dispute over business methods arose among the owners of a sugar refinery at Cremona, and Farinacci intervened, siding with one of them, Giovanni Bastoni. Farinacci ended up with a share in the firm.[45] In July 1925, Farinacci was instrumental in obtaining for a group of his friends the concession of the Mineral Waters Spa at Salsomaggiore and received 35,000 *lire* for his efforts.[46]

As to banks, Farinacci had a natural predilection for relatively small ones, and he held posts in a number of them. In 1924, for instance, he was appointed president of the National Credit Institute of Farm Co-operatives; and in 1925, he became a director of the United Lombardy Savings Banks. Farinacci was also an intimate friend of Count Luigi Lusignani, a Parma nobleman who founded the *Banca Agricola di Parma* in 1925 and was arrested in 1926 and accused of having looted its treasury. No evidence of embezzlement could ever be found, but it was widely rumored at the time that Farinacci had had a hand in the looting, and that in fact he had arranged for Lusignani's alleged suicide in prison.[47]

Documentary evidence exists, however, of Farinacci's part in forcing the main shareholders of the *Banco di Roma* to cede their controlling interest in the bank to the Fascist government. Mussolini's brother, Arnaldo, and the former founder of the *Arditi* Association, Ferruccio Vecchi, were also instrumental in the take-over, but it appears that Farinacci was the prime mover

43. ID–NA, T586, 030891. A *lira* was, at this time, worth about 5¢, U.S.
44. *Ibid.*, 030892.
45. G. Bastoni to Farinacci, March–October 1924, ICSA, Farinacci Fund, 1924 Correspondence, Folder 3, Env. B.
46. ID–NA, T586, 030892.
47. Farinacci's law partner, Professor Alessandro Groppali, was actually arrested and indicted for fraud in connection with the bank's failure, and it was Farinacci's refusal to intervene in Groppali's behalf that led to the lasting enmity between the two men. Groppali was later acquitted and transferred to a university chair in Sardinia.

Roberto Farinacci during the heyday of *squadrismo*.

July 1919: The police move to disperse a leftist protest rally on the **Piazza Venezia** in Rome.

1921: A truckload of *squadristi* about to leave for a "punitive expedition."

October 28, 1922: Troops deploy on a Roman *piazza*.

October 28, 1922: A Fascist column approaching Rome.

1924: Farinacci on the stump.

March 1925: Farinacci, in homburg and spats on the right, soon after his appointment as Secretary General of the Fascist Party. Next to him, facing the camera, is Militia General Attilio Teruzzi. The man on the left is not identified.

March 1926: Farinacci, center, with mustache, with a group of admirers as he appears to serve as attorney for Matteotti's killers at the Chieti trial.

April 1936: Farinacci in the hospital after his grenade-throwing accident. With him, on the right, is Attilio Teruzzi.

Farinacci during the "lean years."

Farinacci after his return to Italy from Ethiopia.

Farinacci, at far right, with other veterans of the *Disperata* air squadron. Fourth from left is Galeazzo Ciano, Mussolini's son-in-law and commander of the squadron.

1934: Mussolini, center, with back to camera, visits the Palestine Pavilion at the Bari Trade Fair.

1937: Uniform spattered by rain, Mussolini decorates Farinacci after the latter's return from a mission to Spain.

The church of Sant'Angelo in Pescheri, in the Roman ghetto. Until 1870, Jews were required to hear sermons once a year in this church.

A corner of the Jewish quarter in Rome. From here, almost 1,000 Jews were deported during the SS raid of October 16, 1943.

May 1939: At center, German Foreign Minister Joachim von Ribbentrop being received on his visit to Milan. His official hosts are immediately behind him: Galeazzo Ciano and Farinacci.

May 1939: German Foreign Minister Joachim von Ribbentrop, center, raising his hand in the Nazi salute, during a tour of Lombardy. Farinacci, his official host, is third from left in the circle surrounding Ribbentrop.

April 13, 1939: Following the occupation of Albania, the Fascist Grand Council resolves to offer the Albanian crown to Victor Emmanuel, King of Italy and Emperor of Ethiopia. Standing, addressing the council, is Achille Starace, Secretary General of the Fascist Party. Farinacci is seated third from right.

October 28, 1940: Hitler and Mussolini in Florence.

(*Il Meridiano* [Naples])

1942: Hitler receives Farinacci, second from left, in Berlin.

April 28, 1945: Farinacci, at center, with priest, after being sentenced to death in Vimercate.

(*Il Meridiano* [Naples])

(*Il Meridiano* [Naples])

April 28, 1945: The firing squad readies weapons.

April 28, 1945: Farinacci against the wall.

(*Il Meridiano* [Naples])

in bringing this major bank into the Fascist fold.[48] Not so successful was Farinacci in the fight against the *Banca Commerciale* of Milan. This bank's chairman, Giuseppe Toeplitz, being Jewish as well as unwilling to subsidize *Cremona Nuova*, was one of Farinacci's *bêtes noires*. Early in 1925, the *ras* of Cremona had spoken in the Chamber of Deputies accusing Toeplitz of financial maneuvers detrimental to the Italian national interest and demanding the banker's arrest. Toeplitz had, in turn, wired Farinacci, accusing him of "either deep ignorance of the facts or premeditated viciousness."[49] After becoming Secretary General of the Fascist party, Farinacci continued to attack Toeplitz personally, as well as attacking the *Banca Commerciale*, which he accused of being a tool of Anglo-American capitalism. He also tried in vain to promote the cause of an obscure American private bank, Sillit & Son, which was trying to negotiate dollar loans to the Italian government in competition with the Morgan Bank, represented in Italy by *Banca Commerciale*.[50]

No summary of Farinacci's activities in the economic field during his rule over the Fascist party would be complete without mention of his transformation of *Cremona Nuova* into *Il Regime Fascista*, which raised it from a provincial to a national level, and of his acquisition of new funds and machinery for his publishing ventures. Ostensibly, ownership of Farinacci's newspaper was vested in a corporation, managed by another of Farinacci's faithful followers, Vittorio Varenna. Varenna was indefatigable in obtaining subsidies and subscriptions for the newspaper, and it appears that he was not above using Farinacci's influence to push through currency speculations, part of whose profits would go to the newspaper.[51] Using the funds thus accumulated during 1925, Farinacci arranged for the transfer to larger quarters of the editorial offices and printing plant of *Cremona Nuova*, whose name

48. Ferruccio Vecchi to Farinacci, April 8–11, 1925, ICSA, Farinacci Fund, 1925 Correspondence, Folder 5, Env. V.

49. Toeplitz to Farinacci, January 16, 1925, *ibid.*, Folder 4, Env. T.

50. Farinacci to Mussolini, August 19, 1925, ID–NA, T586, 034244–034245. Morgan naturally prevailed, extending to Italy a line of credit of one hundred million dollars early in 1926.

51. Gualtiero Anelli to Farinacci, June 14, 1925, ICSA, Farinacci Fund, 1925 Correspondence, Folder 4, Env. A.

he changed on January 1, 1926, to *Il Regime Fascista*. He also obtained the valuable support of one of Italy's largest book publishers, Arnoldo Mondadori, who was in fact instrumental in modernizing Farinacci's printing plant by supplying him with two linotypes and larger presses. Currying favor with Farinacci, Mondadori repeatedly assured the Fascist Secretary General that he would be "satisfied soon with a perfect newspaper" and asked that he "have confidence" in Mondadori and Varenna.[52]

Examining, finally, Farinacci's activities to accomplish the "fascistization" of Italian bureaucracy, it is evident that from the outset his press campaign against specific high functionaries in a number of ministries was successful, because many of them, especially in the Ministry of Justice, were in fact demoted, transferred, or forced to retire, and Farinacci did not fail to publicize his victories.[53] As usual, however, he kept on pressing for more drastic and general measures, arousing the resentment of the various ministers—particularly Luigi Federzoni, Minister of the Interior—and incurring the annoyance of Mussolini. The *Duce*, on one occasion, asked Farinacci to stop seeing prefects because "otherwise it would seem that there be two Ministers of the Interior, which is not true and no good."[54] In any event, Farinacci's ultimate goal in this field was achieved, because on December 24, 1925, a new law made all public employees subject to immediate dismissal whenever their views or actions might not be in accordance with the political directives of the government—in other words, not abjectly pro-Fascist.[55]

By the end of 1925, there remained, in Farinacci's view, the task of using the trial of Matteotti's killers to "put on trial the opposition" and at the same time win vindication for Fascist extremism. Against the instructions of Mussolini, and against all principles of reason and decency, Farinacci now turned to this task with single-minded intransigence.

52. Arnoldo Mondadori to Farinacci, January 4, 5, 10, 1926, ICSA, Farinacci Fund, 1926 Correspondence, Env. 9 (miscellaneous telegrams).

53. *Cremona Nuova* (Cremona), May 13, 1925.

54. Mussolini to Farinacci, November 16, 1925, ID–NA, T586, 026532–026534.

55. Salvatorelli e Mira, *Storia d'Italia*, p. 362.

IX

THE TRIAL
OF MATTEOTTI'S
KILLERS

As HAS been noted, in August 1924 Mussolini had agreed with Farinacci that the *ras* of Cremona should undertake the defense of Amerigo Dumini, arrested as one of the killers of Giacomo Matteotti. According to plan, Farinacci would use Dumini's trial as a forum to defend Fascism and attack the opposition. Since then, however, the situation had changed drastically. Driven by the urge to survive and egged on by Farinacci and his followers, Mussolini had successfully surmounted a most critical period and had laid a solid foundation for his totalitarian rule. The opposition, instead, had progressively grown weaker, through unwillingness or inability to take concrete action against the Fascist takeover of the Italian state. The aristocracy, the military leadership, and the ruling circles of industry and finance, animated sometimes by fear but more often by self-interest, were increasingly declaring their support of the Fascist government; and the mass of the population, understandably more preoccupied with pursuit of the daily bread than with political principles, showed every intention of acquiescing in the transformation of the government into a dictatorship.

By the summer of 1925, therefore, Mussolini had decided that the Matteotti Affair should be treated as just another episode of violence, shorn of political connotations, and in any event not to be regarded as a *cause célèbre* on which Fascist supremacy hinged. Farinacci, instead, continued to insist that the crisis sparked by Matteotti's killing had saved Fascism by forcing it to be intransigent, and he missed no opportunity to reawaken the echoes of the affair. Some of Farinacci's outbursts in this connection

117

have already been mentioned; but as time passed, it seemed more and more as if he were openly defying Mussolini by his treatment of the Matteotti crime.

In June 1925, for instance, the High Court of Justice absolved Emilio De Bono from complicity in the Matteotti Affair, although it stated that there was a lack of evidence as to the charge of aiding and abetting the killers, and it did not fully clear him of any involvement. The president of the Court, General Vittorio Zuppelli, was therefore attacked so strongly by Farinacci's newspaper[1] that Mussolini, incensed, wired the prefect of Cremona, ordering that any future issue of *Cremona Nuova* containing articles which might embarrass the government should be confiscated.[2] Farinacci immediately wrote Mussolini protesting the apparent attempt to subordinate the Secretary of the party to a mere prefect and submitting his resignation,[3] whereupon Mussolini wired the prefect countermanding the order and stating that he had "given instructions directly to the Hon. Farinacci as to the behavior of his newspaper."[4]

During the summer of 1925, Farinacci travelled extensively through southern Italy and Sicily, endeavoring to rally to the support of Fascism the generally apathetic masses of those backward regions. But he was as intemperate as ever in his speeches, forcing Mussolini to wire the prefect of Messina, instructing him to transmit the Farinacci this message: "I have ordered the [Italian Press Agency] Stefani to delete from your speech sentences which, having been repeated a thousand times, have lost much of their value. I deny that Fascism owes its success to the Matteotti crime."[5] Farinacci, however, irrepressible as usual, continued to harp in his public speeches on the relationship between the opposition's alleged exploitation of the Matteotti Affair and Fascism's triumphant counteroffensive—as he

1. *Cremona Nuova* (Cremona), July 2, 1925.
2. Mussolini to Prefect Rossi, July 4, 1925, ID–NA, T586, 030626.
3. Farinacci to Mussolini, July 4, 1925, *ibid.*, 030623–030624.
4. Mussolini to Prefect Rossi, July 5, 1925, *ibid.*, 030625.
5. Mussolini to prefect of Messina, July 18, 1925, *ibid.*, 030532. In fact, in the published version of Farinacci's speech at Messina on that day, there is no mention of Matteotti. (Farinacci, *Un periodo aureo*, pp. 195–200.)

did, for instance, in his speech at Bari on September 27.[6] He was equally aggressive and unreasoningly partisan in his relationship with the attorneys representing Amerigo Dumini's codefendants, and in fact had a violent altercation with one of them who objected to Farinacci's boast that the trial would "follow his own orders."[7]

Meanwhile, on July 31, 1925, King Victor Emmanuel proclaimed an amnesty reprieving all those serving sentences for political crimes, except for those convicted of murder and manslaughter, and reducing the sentences even for these crimes. It has been aptly stated that "while appearing to be useless to the murderers of Matteotti, the amnesty was, in reality, the key to the door of their prison."[8]

On December 1, the investigating magistrates announced their conclusion that the five *squadristi* had planned to kidnap Matteotti, but not to kill him. Rossi and Marinelli were found to have merely ordered the abduction, a political crime covered by the recent amnesty, and they were therefore released, with Rossi going into exile in France, and Marinelli being immediately named Inspector General of the Fascist party by Farinacci.

Matteotti's widow realized the hopelessness of trying to obtain justice; and to avoid endangering her two lawyers, the Socialist deputies Emanuele Modigliani and Enrico Gonzales, she then withdrew as civil plaintiff from prosecution of her husband's abductors.

In a further effort to take the trial of the five *squadristi* out of the spotlight, Mussolini arranged to have the trial moved to Chieti, a remote town near the Adriatic, northeast of Rome, where it was scheduled to open on March 16, 1926.

Farinacci, however, never one to miss an opportunity for fanfare, summoned the secretary of the Chieti *Fascio* to Rome and ordered him to organize a vast Fascist rally to give Farinacci a tumultuous reception on his arrival at Chieti for the opening of the trial. It was also arranged that the Fascist women of Chieti

6. Farinacci, *Un periodo aureo*, pp. 274–277.
7. G. Vaselli to Farinacci, September 25, 1925, ICSA, Farinacci Fund, 1925 Correspondence, Folder 5, Env. V.
8. Salvemini, *The Fascist Dictatorship*, p. 287.

would present Farinacci with a silk barrister's gown. The prefect of Chieti got wind of this plan, and immediately informed Mussolini,[9] who reacted with a sizzling telegram ordering Farinacci to use utmost discretion and to prevent any Fascist meetings or celebrations.[10] Farinacci merely replied acknowledging the message and promising to discuss the matter.[11]

He did, apparently, talk on this subject with Mussolini shortly afterward, promising to abide by Mussolini's wishes; but as events were to prove, Farinacci's promises were not kept. In his newspaper, meanwhile, he continued to sound off on the forthcoming trial.[12]

A few days before the trial, Mussolini set down his views on the trial in a handwritten memorandum which specified:

1. The trial must absolutely end before March 28.
2. We must avoid during the court sessions any and all elements of drama, which might arouse public opinion, domestically and abroad. Therefore no noisy incidents or political excursions.
3. The trial must under no circumstances take on the character of a political inquest involving in any way the party or the Regime. Let the opposition try to do that.
4. The accused must also be prevented from trying to change the character of the trial—therefore, no wearing of black shirts.
5. The trial must take place amidst the indifference of the nation, and we must avoid that Italy become again "Matteottized" two years after its recovery.[13]

Just how completely Farinacci flouted Mussolini's instructions was shown first of all by the circumstances of his arrival at Chieti on March 15. A crowd of several thousand Blackshirts, assembled from the surrounding countryside, met him at the station and,

9. Prefect of Chieti to Mussolini's Chief of Cabinet. February 26, 1926, ID–NA, T586, 030806.

10. Mussolini to Prefect Pacces, February 28, 1926, ID–NA, T586, 030813.

11. Prefect Pacces to Mussolini, March 1, 1926, ID–NA, T586, 030814.

12. *Il Regime Fascista* (Cremona), March 11, 1925.

13. Quoted in G. Rossini, *Il delitto Matteotti tra il Viminale e l'Aventino*, (Bologna: Il Mulino, 1966), p. 892.

chanting Fascist slogans, accompanied him to the headquarters of the Provincial Council.[14] There, the leader of the Fascist Women's Group, Baroness Sanitá, presented him with a barrister's gown. Farinacci then harangued the crowd, reviewing the Fascist crisis of 1924, claiming the merit of having defended and saved Fascism and repeating that the impending proceedings would indeed place the opposition on trial.[15]

During the following days, as the trial unfolded, Farinacci was the only one of the five attorneys defending the accused *squadristi* who repeatedly interjected outbursts of partisan politics in the proceedings, and he also saw to it that the trial received full coverage in the domestic and foreign press, going so far as taunting the correspondent of *L'Humanité*, the French Communist daily, by daring him in public to report the trial truthfully.[16]

Mussolini was incensed at Farinacci's tactics, and caused his own newspaper to print an editorial sharply refuting any political connotations of the trial.[17] At the same time, he wrote Farinacci: *(I see that not one of your promises has been kept, because the trial, despite the denials of the accused, has become a political one. I judge all this with extreme severity, and great uneasiness is spreading within the party. The language of Chieti's Fascist newspaper is simply vile and grotesque! I warn you that I will not tolerate any rallies or celebrations at the end of the trial, if it will end with a universal whitewashing.*[18] [Emphasis in the autographic text.]

With unconcealed arrogance, Farinacci replied the next day: *(This morning your messenger brought me one of your usual "epistolar tantrums." I have fulfilled the engagements made at Rome, and you amaze me by saying I did not keep my promises. You wanted the trial over by the 26th, [sic] and it will end sooner. That the regime and the party should be kept out, and I*

14. Salvatorelli e Mira, Storia d'Italia, p. 374.
15. Farinacci, Un periodo aureo, pp. 372–374.
16. Ibid., pp. 393–394.
17. Il Popolo d'Italia (Milan), March 21, 1925.
18. Mussolini to Farinacci, March 21, 1925, ID–NA, T586, 026549–026550.

have said so several times. *The trial has become political? But this was known long ago; otherwise I would not be at Chieti. But it is political only because it attacks the opposition, unless the "uneasy ones" within the party are annoyed because:*

a. *The trial will end as we anticipated.*
b. *The evidence emerging at the trial is not that touted for a year by the opposition press.*
c. *Matteotti, when alive, was a great pig.*

To these "uneasy ones" we could suggest that they join the Children of Mary.[19] [*Emphasis in the autographic text.*]

Three days later, the "Great Secretary" rose in the Chieti courtroom to deliver his summation in defense of Amerigo Dumini. After paying tribute to the judge for his fairness, to the Public Prosecutor for agreeing to drop the charge of premeditation, and to the jurors for being "worthy Italians" able to "give a verdict such as the nation expects," he waded right into a reconstruction of the struggle between Fascism and the opposition during the second half of 1924.

He attacked indiscriminately the *Aventine* deputies, the investigating magistrates, Matteotti's family and their lawyers, accusing them all of having speculated on Matteotti's death to try to destroy Fascism.

"Our enemies," Farinacci orated, "who had long been conspiring against the state, were only too happy to seize upon a corpse . . . to create a united front against Fascism." He continued: *We saw Populars and Freemasons, Republicans, Socialists and phony Liberals, climb arm in arm the Aventine to ask for the resignation of the government, the dissolution of the Chamber of Deputies, the disbanding of the militia. And they put our revolution on trial, a trial in which our defeated enemies tried in cowardly fashion for revenge against our victorious valor by using the most vile slander. And if, during this trial, I have cast aspersions on the investigating magistrates, I was justified. . . . The investigating*

19. Farinacci to Mussolini, March 22, 1925, ID–NA, T586, 034255–034261. The "Children of Mary" are the Catholic groups of small children organized by each parish, and in Italy the expression is often used to indicate a meek and ineffectual group.

magistrates, by accepting memoirs, anonymous letters, and depositions based on the rancor of the regime's enemies, thought they would catch some big fish; but they found nothing in their net, not even minnows. Gentlemen of the jury, the opposition wanted to ask your verdict to be the condemnation of our revolution. But the revolution is victorious, the situation is reversed, and those who should have been our inquisitors, the attorneys for the civil plaintiff [Matteotti's widow], have shamefully withdrawn.[20]

Stooping, then, to unprecedented depths of brutal cynicism, Farinacci launched an attack on the career of the martyred deputy. "He was never a sincere Socialist," shouted Farinacci. ⁅He organized strikes on other people's farms, but he kept his own workers in slavery and forced them to the most inhuman labors. . . . He worked against his own country in the service of foreigners . . . and published a pamphlet full of shameless lies telling foreigners that the first year of Fascist rule was a year of terror and destruction. . . . Was not such a man, gentlemen of the jury, a permanent provocation to all those who love the Motherland?[21]

Farinacci then went on with a hodgepodge of ill-grounded legal references, eulogies of Fascist "martyrs," further vilifications of Matteotti and other anti-Fascists, and harebrained theories concerning Matteotti's "accidental" death. He stressed that he had spoken as Secretary of the party, "sounding the death knell for the opposition," and, unable to resist an opportunity for self-glorification, he concluded: ⁅The mail, these days, has brought to my desk mountains of anonymous, threatening letters. I am not perturbed. Just as I let myself be arrested when it was a crime to speak of Motherland, just as I shed my blood when we had to fight in the streets to defend the moral values of the nation, the feelings of the Motherland, the religion of the family, so today I am ready to face any sacrifice. And if I should be struck down, let it not be said that a deputy was killed, but that a man was killed because he defended his idea and his flag.[22]

Farinacci's demagoguery and histrionics, gratifying as they may

20. Roberto Farinacci, In difesa di Dumini (Rome: Libreria dell'800, 1944), pp. 50–52.
21. Ibid., p. 53.
22. Ibid., p. 65.

have been to him, were of course unnecessary, because, as Mussolini and almost everybody else expected, the verdict was a foregone conclusion. The jury, stage-managed by a Fascist public prosecutor, a Fascist judge, with the Secretary General of the Fascist party as chief defense attorney, acquitted Viola and Malacria, and found Dumini, Volpi, and Poveromo guilty of complicity in involuntary homicide. The minimum penalty of five years and eleven months was reduced by four years, thanks to the recent amnesty, and, being credited with the time served while awaiting trial, the three killers were freed less than two months later.[23]

In the meantime, however, Mussolini had decided to tolerate no longer Farinacci's defiance and insubordination, and the rule of the "Great Secretary," after little more than a year, had abruptly come to an end.

23. Salvemini, *The Fascist Dictatorship*, p. 293.

X

THE
DOWNFALL OF
A CYCLOPS

It seems abundantly clear that Farinacci's behavior at the Chieti trial was the final determining factor in Mussolini's decision to remove the ras of Cremona from national leadership of the Fascist party. This decision, however, had been maturing for a long time, under the influence both of specific incidents and of a basic divergence of ideas, goals, and methods between the two men.

Farinacci's conception of the Fascist party was a more truly revolutionary one, envisaging for the party a dominant role in forcibly shaping the nation into a monolithic Fascist state governed by an intransigent elite for the alleged benefit of the laboring masses. Mussolini instead, consummate opportunist that he was, saw his greatest chances of success in the gradual application of authoritarian techniques to the existing institutions, in concert with the old privileged classes, and with the Fascist party relegated to an ancillary role as just one agency of the government.

Given this sharp dichotomy at the very top of Fascism, it is also essential, in order to understand why Mussolini was bound to prevail, to consider two other elements of the struggle. The ras of Cremona drew his main support from the small bourgeoisie and from a relatively small number of fanatic activists, the squadristi. The first group, in Italy as anywhere else, was weak and divided by conflicting interests and unwilling to consider joining forces with the proletariat to achieve a strong revolutionary bloc. The squadristi, for their part, capable only of isolated and spasmodic outbursts of destructive violence, were intrinsically unfit to take part in any long-range organizational program. Mussolini, on the other hand, had now the backing not only of the monarchy, the aristocracy, and the armed services, but also of the wealthiest bourgeoisie and the leaders of commerce and industry, an influential class which considered Mussolini, as did the Pope three years later, "a man sent by Divine Providence." Consequently, the other element in favor of Mussolini was the increasingly all-pervasive effects of the "myth" of Mussolini as an omniscient, omnipotent, benevolent semigod to whom would soon be applied the slogan *"Mussolini ha sempre ragione"* (Mussolini is always right). Farinacci himself had been instrumental in fostering the rise of this myth, hoping to control and maneuver Mussolini for his own ends, but Farinacci's plan backfired. As Mussolini became stronger in the exercise of power based on the growing consensus—or, at least, acquiescence—of the Italian people, he realized that the nation had not accepted and would not truly accept Fascism, but that it would and did accept him as its protector and leader. To fulfill this role, of course, it was also necessary for Mussolini to eliminate or somehow neutralize Farinacci and his more unruly followers, who, by their revolutionary activism and terroristic tactics, stood in the way of the "normalization" at which Mussolini aimed in order to justify and strengthen his personal dictatorship. The task of removing Farinacci was made relatively easy for Mussolini by Farinacci himself, who, during the period of his Secretaryship, committed a number of blunders and provoked incidents of such gravity as to make his dismissal virtually inevitable.

The relationship between the Fascist government and the Vatican, for instance, was seriously compromised by Farinacci's sanctioning of Fascist violence against Catholic organizations, and by his polemics with the Catholic press.

The Holy See, both before and after the Matteotti episode, had been maintaining a cautiously watchful attitude, endeavoring to restrain the Popular party from concretely collaborating with the Socialists, and above all carefully avoiding a confrontation with the Fascist government, which it considered a preferable alternative to a "bolshevik" regime. Mussolini was well aware of the Vatican's policy. As early as 1923, he had held a secret meeting with the Vatican's Secretary of State, Cardinal Pietro Gasparri, at which there had been mention of the desirability of reconciling the Papacy and the Kingdom of Italy in the near future. Soon after

Farinacci's assumption of leadership of the Fascist party, however, a rash of muggings and beatings by Fascist youths was unleashed against individual members and against local headquarters of the Catholic youth organizations.

Luigi Federzoni, as Minister of the Interior and a faithful executor of Mussolini's directives, had personally intervened with Farinacci, asking him to co-operate "in quickly restoring calm and discipline in the Fascist ranks,"[1] but new and especially brutal incidents had nevertheless taken place in Rovigo and Padua. The Vatican continued for a while in its attitude of reserve, but when Federzoni made a speech at Brescia exhorting all Fascists to refrain from violence and promising that normalization would be quickly achieved, the semiofficial Vatican newspaper published an editorial pointedly questioning the reliability of the promises of the Minister of the Interior, since, while the government deplored violence, Farinacci openly advocated it.[2]

Farinacci promptly replied to L'Osservatore Romano, taking the Vatican newspaper to task for presuming to speak of Fascist violence while ignoring that allegedly used by Catholics against Fascists and boasting that "in certain circumstances violence is a christian virtue, because it serves . . . that christian civilization which would have been overthrown in Italy if Fascism's holy violence had not reacted against the barbarian hordes in the service of Moscow."[3]

A few days later, Farinacci again harped on the same theme, accusing the Osservatore Romano of "impudence."[4] Finally, speaking on August 23 to a Fascist rally at Desio, a small town near Milan noted as the birthplace of Pius XI, Farinacci addressed a "Fascist salute" to the Pontiff and boasted of the benefits the Church had reaped from the Fascist victory. Then he issued a sharp warning and a virtual ultimatum. "Fascism," he said, "cannot be partially accepted: it must be either fully accepted or completely rejected. . . . Let [Catholics] know that just as Fascism has de-

1. Federzoni to Farinacci, May 28, 1925, ICSA, Farinacci Fund, 1925 Correspondence, Folder 2, Env. F.
2. L'Osservatore Romano (Rome), July 28, 1925.
3. Cremona Nuova (Cremona), August 7, 1925.
4. Ibid., August 13, 1925.

fended religion, so it will fight to the finish, with no holds barred, against those who might use religion as a political weapon."[5] Through Father Pietro Tacchi-Venturi, the same Jesuit priest who would remain for two decades the unofficial intermediary between the Holy See and Mussolini, the Vatican made it clear to Federzoni and to Mussolini that no formal accord between the Vatican and the government was possible as long as the episodes of violence instigated and sanctioned by Farinacci continued. It was only with difficulty, in fact, that Father Tacchi-Venturi managed to delete a sentence deploring Fascist violence from a speech the Pope made on December 14.[6] But the net result of Farinacci's actions was a delay in the beginning of negotiations and the eventual conclusion of the Concordat.

Another blunder by Farinacci, this time concerning the monarchy, occurred in June 1925, when he publicly criticized King Victor Emmanuel for having received Giovanni Amendola, Alcide De Gasperi, and other *Aventine* leaders, and "warned" the king not to have any contacts with the opposition.[7]

Farinacci's most fatal mistake, however—and perhaps it was one which his nature and character would not permit him to avoid—was the unofficial but well-publicized support he gave to the renewed organization of *squadre d'azione* and to a recrudescence of *squadristi* activities which culminated in October in the "Florence massacre." Mussolini was well aware of Farinacci's tactics in this field, and at the National Fascist Party Congress held in Rome on June 21, 1925, after Farinacci had boasted of his intransigence and of the splendid virtues of thousands of *squadristi*, "a ruling class matured through life's battles,"[8] Mussolini had pointedly exhorted the assembled Fascist leaders to "banish brutal and unintelligent violence."[9] Urged on by Farinacci, however, who often quipped that "in order to serve Mussolini, one

5. Farinacci, *Un periodo aureo*, pp. 219–223.
6. Father Tacchi-Venturi to Mussolini, December 13, 1925. Quoted in De Felice, *Mussolini il Fascista*, II, 113.
7. *Cremona Nuova* (Cremona), June 13, 1925.
8. Farinacci, *Un periodo aureo*, p. 155.
9. *Mussolini*, XXI, 358.

must disobey him,"[10] the *squadristi* had continued to engage in rowdyism and violence against political opponents and, not infrequently, against personal enemies. The province of Florence, which had already been the scene of bloody turmoil in December 1924, had perhaps the largest concentration of Fascist extremists of all Italy, and it was there that the conflict between Farinacci's activists and the government's efforts towards normalization finally came to a head.

On October 3, 1925, a gang of *squadristi*, shouting that Masonry had to be destroyed at all costs, broke into the home of a known Freemason, who, in self-defense, shot and killed one of the Fascist ringleaders, Giovanni Luporini. The incident sparked an outbreak of *squadrista* violence of unprecedented proportions, which lasted through the night of October 3 and the day and night of the fourth. Fascist gangs roamed the city in a veritable manhunt, killing seven anti-Fascists and severely beating hundreds of others before the police were able to restore a semblance of order by arresting fifty-eight of the *squadristi*.[11]

News of what was immediately called the "Florence massacre" was received throughout Italy with dismay and apprehension by the mass of the population and with ghoulish glee by other *squadristi* who planned similar exploits in their own areas. Mussolini, who was about to leave for the Locarno Conference, was furious, accusing the extremists of trying "to ruin [him] by creating a whole series of Matteotti crimes."[12] Realizing that he could not abruptly dismiss Farinacci without risking a general uprising by the extremists in the Fascist party, Mussolini saw that he had to take decisive steps to prevent a return of anarchy. He acted swiftly to put an end to organized Fascist violence. Early on October 5, he dispatched Farinacci to Florence, with strict injunctions to put an end to the turmoil and to report that same night to the Grand Council which was called into emergency session. At the Council's meeting, Mussolini sharply criticized Fari-

---

10. Farinacci to Mussolini, June 19, 1926, ID–NA, T586, 031335–31337.
11. A detailed account of the "Florence Massacre" can be found in Salvemini, *The Fascist Dictatorship*, pp. 145–162.
12. Tamaro, *Venti anni*, II, 11.

nacci and his unruly followers and forced the approval of a resolution ordering that all *squadre d'azione* be immediately dissolved, that all former *squadristi* be enrolled in the ranks of the militia, and that any Fascist refusing to obey these orders be expelled by the party.[13]

The resolution was not publicized, and, as a sop to Farinacci's *amour propre*, it was left to him to announce its contents as his own idea to the Fascist National Council which he called to a meeting in Rome on October 19. He did in fact issue the Grand Council's orders by inserting them in a decalogue which he labelled as "my will, which is the will of the party." The decalogue went as far as demanding that the "morality" of all Fascists be investigated. The tone of Farinacci's speech, however, was still defiant. "If we have dissolved the *squadre d'azione*," he concluded, "it is because we wanted to create a single well-organized *squadra d'azione*, the party, always ready to answer any provocation and defend itself with any means!"[14] Mussolini, well aware that Farinacci could not and would not truly change his attitude, had in the meantime given strict orders to the Minister of the Interior to proceed without mercy against any new outbreak of *squadrista* activity. The changed atmosphere was immediately noticeable. On October 12, some *squadristi* were arrested for having tried to break into the headquarters of both Freemasonries. Consequently, the secretary of the Rome *Fascio*, Italo Foschi, a creature of Farinacci, was dismissed on Mussolini's direct orders.

Another rebuff to Farinacci in connection with the "Florence massacre" resulted from the appointment of three separate boards of inquiry to look into the activities of the Florentine Fascists: one by the government; one by the militia; and the third,

13. While the official communique of the Grand Council meeting did not even mention the events of Florence, Mussolini's attack on Farinacci is revealed by a telegram sent eighteen months later to the prefect of Cremona, ordering the confiscation of an issue of *Il Regime Fascista* because of Farinacci's editorial praise for the Florentine *squadristi* on trial. In this telegram, Mussolini told the prefect to remind Farinacci of the "mark of shame" given him "before the full Grand Council" because of the "Florence massacre and devastation." (Mussolini to prefect of Cremona, May 23, 1927, ID–NA, T586, 030657.)

14. Farinacci, *Un periodo aureo*, pp. 293–299.

on behalf of the party, under the chairmanship of one of the leaders least well disposed towards Farinacci, Italo Balbo. In vain Farinacci intrigued with his Florentine friends to try to whitewash the recent events and maintain in positions of leadership intransigent Fascists such as the secretary of the Florence *Fascio*, Tullio Tamburini.[15] The Florence *Fascio*, following Balbo's inquest, was dissolved, and a two-man commission of moderate Fascists was charged with its reorganization. Mussolini, furthermore, began to exercise a much closer supervision over Farinacci's activities, placing stringent restraints on his functions. On October 13, for instance, having learned that Farinacci was planning to hold a secret meeting with Fascist leaders of the War Wounded Association, he wired Farinacci, expressing disapproval of such an initiative which, by fomenting unrest within that association, "would be a colossal mistake to be absolutely avoided" and ordered him to cancel the meeting.[16] The same day, another sizzling wire from Mussolini informed Farinacci of the government's order to disband immediately the Turin *squadristi*. "Many of these [*squadristi*] are of dubious faith, as the recent criminal chronicles amply show . . ." Mussolini stated. "It is high time to make the necessary separation: the Fascists with the Fascists, the criminals with the criminals, the profiteers with the profiteers, and above all we must practice moral—I repeat, moral—intransigence."[17]

Farinacci's reply to these telegrams was ambiguous,[18] and he did not in fact proceed with vigor to repress his activist followers, even though, under Mussolini's strict orders, he paid lip service in his editorials to the need for discipline and for avoiding reprisals after the abortive attempt on Mussolini's life on November 4 by Socialist deputy Tito Zaniboni.[19] That Farinacci was not in good faith following the directives of the government and of the Grand Council was shown by the fact that, during this same

15. T. Tamburini to Farinacci, October 17, and 25, 1925, ICSA, Farinacci Fund, 1925 Correspondence, Folder 4, Env. T.
16. Mussolini to prefect of Cremona, October 13, 1925, ID–NA, T586, 030834.
17. Mussolini to prefect of Cremona, October 13, 1925, *ibid.*, 030837.
18. Prefect of Cremona to Mussolini, October 14, 1925, *ibid.*, 030830.
19. *Cremona Nuova* (Cremona), November 6, 8, 12, 1925.

period, Mussolini again had to take him to task in a long letter defining *squadrista* activity as "grotesque . . . and a derision of [Farinacci's] decalogue," and asking him to take real and serious action.[20]

Mussolini was by now convinced that Farinacci had outgrown his usefulness; and while he took no concrete action during December, in order not to compromise legislative action on the *"leggi Fascistissime,"*[21] he began, immediately after the turn of the year, to move towards removal of the "Great Secretary."

On January 3, 1926, the Grand Council decided to reopen Fascist membership rolls, thus countermanding Farinacci's action in closing them two months earlier. During the same meeting, the Grand Council again prohibited the organization of any "special units within the party," in an obvious reproach to Farinacci for not having effectively carried out the disbanding of the *squadre d'azione.*[22]

A few days later, in a letter ordering Farinacci to cancel an "unnecessary" Fascist convention at Milan, Mussolini bluntly told him: "You must not give the impression that the Fascist legislation is the work of the party, as if the government had stood by idly, while instead the government anticipated the party and took the full initiative."[23] This was followed by verbal orders not to go on an inspection tour of the Fascio at Turin, which caused Farinacci to protest bitterly. *(Today in Italy and in the whole world there is no man more hated than I. Why? Let Federzoni answer! What saddens me is that little by little you view with suspicion my most Fascist and above all Mussolinian activity, and paralyze it with prohibitions which humiliate me be-*

20. Mussolini to Farinacci, November 16, 1925, ID–NA, T586, 026532–026534.

21. Besides the ones already mentioned, a law passed on December 24, abolishing parts of the Constitution revised the entire administrative structure of the Italian state, making the prime minister no longer a *primus inter pares* but, rather, the Head of the Government, in whom was vested all executive authority, and without whose previous approval no new law could be proposed.

22. *Il Popolo d'Italia* (Milan), January 5, 1926.

23. Mussolini to Farinacci, January 12, 1926, ID–NA, T586, 026547–026548.

fore some faithless ones. *Yet I do not despair. Time will tell, and . . . he laughs best who laughs last.*[24] [*Emphasis in the autographic text.*]

Mussolini did not relent. In fact, that same week, Farinacci's unruly behavior in the Chamber of Deputies provided Mussolini with another opportunity to chastise him sharply.

On January 8, 1926, the Popular deputies had decided to "descend from the *Aventine*," and on the sixteenth, they again took their seats during the session held to commemorate the recent death of Queen Mother Margherita. At the end of the meeting, Mussolini arose to demand that the Chamber of Deputies, rather than adjourn for three days in sign of mourning, meet again the next day "to settle a moral question which brooks no delay." Farinacci, realizing that Mussolini intended to use this opportunity to administer the *coup de grace* to the parliamentary opposition and eager to keep the executioner's role for himself, spoke in opposition to Mussolini's request, claiming that any dialogue with the Populars would be demeaning for Mussolini and therefore inconceivable. When Mussolini insisted, the proposal was naturally accepted; but as the Popular deputies were leaving the Chamber, they were assaulted by Farinacci and other Fascist extremists, who punched and manhandled them, warning them to stay away from the Chamber.

A few hours later, Farinacci received a curt note in which Mussolini accused him of having acted "in a non-Fascist style" and having displayed "a show of indiscipline." Mussolini stressed that the Populars' attempt to re-enter the Chamber of Deputies was a matter on which he had the paramount authority. He brusquely ordered Farinacci to remain completely silent in the next day's debate.[25] The *ras* of Cremona replied the same evening, protesting his loyalty and claiming he had only acted "to defend [Mussolini's] myth" and because he had "long accounts to settle" with the opposition; but he promised to remain silent the following day.[26] What he did, trying to save face, was to publish an edi-

24. Farinacci to Mussolini, January 14, 1926, *ibid.*, 030780–030790.
25. Mussolini to Farinacci, January 16, 1926, *ibid.*, 030812.
26. Farinacci to Mussolini, January 16, 1926, *ibid.*, 030801–030805.

torial insisting that the calling of a special session was superfluous and repeating that Mussolini should not lower himself to speak to the Popular deputies.[27]

However, he need not have worried, for no *Aventine* deputies were in the Chamber when Mussolini rose to speak on January 17. The *Duce* stated unequivocally that any deputy wishing to come back into the Chamber and be "tolerated" there must first publicly accept the victory of the Fascist revolution, confess the failure of the *Aventine* secession, and solemnly disown all anti-Fascist exiles. "Unless these conditions are accepted and fulfilled," Mussolini concluded, crashing his fist on the table, "as long as I am in this seat, and I intend to stay in it for a long time, they will not be allowed back in, tomorrow or ever!"[28]

After this latest rebuke, even Farinacci could see that his days as Secretary General were numbered, and, speaking to a meeting of the Cremona *Fascio* on January 18, he said: *(I accepted the post of Secretary General of the party, declaring to the Duce, to the Grand Council, and to the National Council, that I would remain in that office until the liquidation of the Aventine and the conclusion of the Matteotti trial. I will do just that. Afterwards I will return to my province, which has given me the greatest satisfaction, having given back to the Duce the party strong as never before and victorious as our martyrs dreamed of it.*[29]

Farinacci's announcement, which took Mussolini by surprise,[30] was in all likelihood a tactical maneuver to forestall an immediate dismissal and to permit Farinacci to finish the appointed task by taking part in the Chieti trial while still wielding the prestige of the party secretaryship. In this, the move was successful, although Farinacci's activities during the next two months continued to be closely watched and severely restricted. Early in March, for instance, Mussolini had occasion to write Farinacci, "Professor Dinale tells me that, when he discussed with you the situation of

27. *Il Regime Fascista* (Cremona), January 17, 1926.
28. Salvatorelli e Mira, *Storia d'Italia*, pp. 373–374. A few days later, three Popular deputies did the required penance; none of the other opposition deputies ever came back to Parliament.
29. Farinacci, *Un periodo aureo*, p. 363.
30. De Begnac, *Palazzo Venezia*, p. 302.

Treviso, you answered him that you would anyway do the opposite of whatever the president [Mussolini] might say, 'because I am the head of the party.' These stupid words, if they are true, repeated and amplified in the provinces, are very harmful to the party."[31]

In any event, as has been seen, Farinacci's handling of the Chieti trial left no doubt in Mussolini's mind as to the need to take him out of the limelight. As soon as the trial was over, Farinacci returned to Rome, only to be informed by Mussolini that the Grand Council would meet on March 30 and that a new Secretary General of the party would then be appointed. As a face-saving move, on the morning of the thirtieth, Farinacci was allowed to submit his resignation, which was accepted that same night by the Grand Council. At the meeting, Mussolini appointed as the new Secretary General of the party Augusto Turati, a much more docile subordinate who would in fact hold the post for almost five years. Entirely for the eyes of the world, the Duce caused the Grand Council to vote a resolution thanking Farinacci for his work on behalf of the party.[32] Mussolini's true feelings, however, were clearly expressed by an editorial in which his newspaper, while praising Farinacci for having reorganized the party, mentioned disapprovingly "his [treatment of the] press question, his polemizing with the Church, and his pitting the provincial Fascist cadres against the government hierarchy."[33] Farinacci in turn replied with an acrimonious article accusing Mussolini's newspaper of "ingratitude,"[34] and he began printing column after column of "messages of solidarity" sent to him by *squadristi* throughout Italy.[35] The *ras* of Cremona, as his activities of the next few months would show, was obviously not resigned to disappearing from the national scene.

31. Mussolini to Farinacci, March 3, 1926, ID–NA, T586, 025559.
32. De Felice, *Mussolini il Fascista*, II, 174–175.
33. *Il Popolo d'Italia* (Milan), April 3, 1926.
34. *Il Regime Fascista* (Cremona), April 3, 1926.
35. *Ibid.*, April 4, 8, 10, 11, 1926.

XI

A DECADE
ON THE
FRINGES

THE IMMEDIATE aftermath of Farinacci's dismissal from the Fascist party's top command was, not unexpectedly, marked by a convulsive reaction on the part of Fascist extremists in several provinces.

The tone and inspiration for this reaction were provided by Farinacci himself, who, on returning to Cremona to take up the post of secretary of the local Provincial Fascist Federation, harangued a vast multitude meeting him at the railroad station. There he promised that he would not "defect the continuing battle" and that he would "remain a watchful sentry to insure . . . the survival of the revolutionary spirit and intransigence."[1]

A few days later, Farinacci travelled to Venice, where he was given an enthusiastic reception, and again, while reasserting his loyalty to Mussolini, he told his cheering audience that he would see to it that the party would "maintain its purity, with no room for opportunists."[2]

Moving on to Trieste, a notorious hotbed of extremism, Farinacci was again wildly acclaimed by a mob of intransigent Fascists. Speaking from a balcony on the main square, he repeated his invectives against lukewarm Fascists, whom he swore to purge from the party. That same evening, posters acclaiming Farinacci and intransigent Fascism and ridiculing the party's directives ordering discipline appeared on buildings throughout the city, and

1. *Il Regime Fascista* (Cremona), April 13, 1926.
2. *Il Giornale del Veneto* (Venice), April 17, 1926.

fistfights broke out between extremists and moderates.[3] Similar outbreaks occurred in the towns of Udine and Rovigo. The attitude of the authorities with regard to breaches of the peace, however, had changed, and what Farinacci might have hoped to be the beginning of a triumphal comeback quickly ended in a fiasco. The police acted swiftly, breaking up the riots and arresting eight of the extremist ringleaders. The prefect ordered Farinacci to leave Trieste, and the former Secretary General meekly returned to Cremona.

The incidents, while carefully kept out of the Italian press, were reported by some foreign newspapers,[4] prompting Mussolini's accusations that Farinacci's activities were grist to the mill of the anti-Fascist press in exile. Mussolini was further incensed when Farinacci began publishing sharp attacks against the moderates' leader, Giuseppe Bottai, whom Mussolini had installed as editor of *Il Mattino* at Naples. Bluntly telling Farinacci that he considered the slurs on Bottai as directed at himself, Mussolini reminded the former Secretary General of a number of improper appointments made during his tenure, and concluded: "In a very, very friendly manner, I ask you once more to keep quiet before it is too late."[5]

As usual, Farinacci replied with protestations of "affectionate devotion to the *Duce*,"[6] but he continued to polemize with Bottai and with another Fascist journalist, Curzio Malaparte, editor of the weekly *La Conquista dello Stato*, who now, obviously with Mussolini's blessing, unleashed an all-out attack against Farinacci, accusing him of demagoguery and indiscipline and of having fostered his personal ascendancy in the provincial organizations of the party.[7] Farinacci replied somewhat lamely, stating

3. Federzoni to Mussolini, April 24, 1926, ID–NA, T586, 031063–031064.

4. *Vossische Zeitung* (Lugano), April 25, 1926; *Quotidien* (Paris), April 28, 1926.

5. Mussolini to prefect of Cremona, May 22, 1926, ID–NA, T586, 030553–030554.

6. Prefect of Cremona to Mussolini, May 24, 1926, *ibid.*, 030552.

7. At Catania, in Sicily, for instance, the local Fascist newspaper was named "Farinacci." (ICSA, Farinacci Fund, 1926 Correspondence, Folder 2, Env. F.

that "at the proper time [he would] demonstrate with irrefutable proofs" the truth of his assertions,[8] and the polemic for the time being ended.

What did not end, however, was the unrest in Cremona and the surrounding countryside, where the month of June saw repeated clashes between supporters of Farinacci and other Fascists who tried to take advantage of his fall from national prominence to put an end to his local rule. Farinacci, however, was too strongly entrenched, and his followers were more numerous and skilled in *squadrista* violence, so that the encounters ended with their victory. After a particularly bloody skirmish, in fact, the extremists plastered the city's streets with large printed posters boasting of the beatings inflicted on "a few hoodlums who wanted to purge and govern [the] city," and concluding: (*Fascists of Cremona,*

Our enemies, the enemies of the one who cannot be praised enough for having saved Fascism after the Matteotti crime, have dared to bring the fight into our province and our city. Let us therefore raise the cry that rallied us in times of anguish and sorrow and shout loudly: Hands off our Duce! We are receiving wires and letters of support from all over Italy, but even if we were alone we shall know how to defend, arms in hand, the one who led us to the supreme victory. Long live Farinacci, only true Duce of Fascism![9]

While the literary style of the poster was clearly Farinacci's, the *ras* of Cremona was shrewd enough not to take active part in the street fights and, as soon as he realized that no concerted action on his behalf was forthcoming from extremists in other provinces, he repeatedly wired Mussolini blaming the outbreaks on "unworthy elements expelled from Fascism for moral indignity" and asking that the government and the party take steps to re-establish order.[10]

---

8. *Il Regime Fascista* (Cremona), May 27, 1926. Farinacci's technique of promising the proof of his allegations at some future time bears a strong resemblance to the tactics used thirty years later by U.S. Senator Joseph McCarthy.

9. ID–NA, T586, 031326.

10. Farinacci to Mussolini, June 26 and 28, 1926, *ibid.*, 026233–026234.

Several Fascists on both sides were in fact arrested, but Farinacci managed not to be officially implicated. His fast footwork, however, did not save him from a blast by Mussolini, who wired rejecting "the conventional order of the day assuring loyalty, which is contradicted by street posters, and by well-known private utterances."[11]

Even if Farinacci had ever hoped to spark an insurrectional movement within Fascism and to take Mussolini's place—and there is no concrete evidence that he ever consciously entertained such a plan—he was by now convinced that Mussolini's position was too strong, and that the scattered extremist pockets could never hope to succeed against the organized forces of the state. It is legitimate to ask, in fact, why Mussolini did not deal with Farinacci with the same brutal severity used against other Fascist dissidents, expelling him from the party or even restricting his personal freedom. The answer to this question, of course, can only be based on surmises, but there are sufficient elements to provide a logical and probably correct explanation. First of all, Mussolini had in the recent past endorsed a number of Farinacci's initiatives in party policy, and to eliminate him completely from the political scene would have implied the disavowal of those policies. Second, Mussolini's drive towards normalization would undoubtedly have suffered from the repercussions of Farinacci's expulsion, both vis-a-vis public opinion and within the ranks of the party. Finally, it is possible that Farinacci, as he often hinted, did in fact possess documents which could incriminate or tarnish the image of Mussolini and his closest collaborators.

In any event, early in July 1926, the *ras* of Cremona wrote Mussolini a thirteen-page letter obviously designed to forestall punitive action and to insure Farinacci's political survival. Accusing Mussolini of trying to "assassinate [him] morally and politically," Farinacci reviewed in detail his own exploits on behalf of Fascism and of the *Duce* since 1919. He then listed the many hostile actions to which he had been subjected by the present party leadership since the end of his own secretaryship, and even earlier by

11. Mussolini to prefect of Cremona, *ibid.*, 031324. The telegram is undated, but a specific reference to a sentence in the poster quoted above assures its being contemporaneous.

Federzoni, who "had ordered two individuals well known to you to search my room at the Bristol Hotel in Rome trying to steal some documents which I hold, which nobody will ever find, and which some day may be of help to me."[12] Mussolini wrote a brief reply, denying Farinacci's accusations, blaming him in turn for having brought about his own downfall through indiscipline and loose talk, and concluding: (Once more, and it is the last time, I repeat: obey Turati, cutting out your pose of being an anti-Pope who waits or pretends to wait for his hour to come; make your peace with Federzoni . . . reconcile yourself with Balbo . . .and above all stay away from Freemasonry. The atmosphere will clear, the future will be open to you, and the enemies will not have the satisfaction of seeing you banished from political life.[13]

This letter, however, was stopped at the last minute, and Mussolini instead asked his brother Arnaldo, who was not only the editor of Il Popolo d'Italia and the chief fundraiser for the party, but also his closest confidant, to write to Farinacci and to set him straight. Arnaldo's letter, while sufficiently diplomatic, warned Farinacci that "Fascism could not base its future policy on the situation which existed in 1924" and that no one should "remain stuck on personal situations made obsolete by the events of today and by the tasks of tomorrow."[14] Farinacci's reply was rather subdued and generally friendly,[15] and Arnaldo, in forwarding a copy of it to his brother, wrote him: "I do not deem it politic on our part to insist too much on isolating him [Farinacci]. Maybe a good talking to will bring him back on the path of wisdom and make him fit into our times according to his possibilities."[16]

Thus the summer of 1926 marked the beginning of an uneasy truce between Farinacci and Mussolini. It was in effect an armed truce, punctuated by spasmodic outbursts of verbal defiance or reproach on the part of Farinacci and by periodic blasts, also verbal, from Mussolini and the party leaders who obviously did not dare mount an all-out public attack against the intransigent

12. Farinacci to Mussolini, July 8, 1926, ibid., 031189–031201.
13. Mussolini to Farinacci, July 10, 1926, ibid., 031185–031187.
14. Arnaldo Mussolini to Farinacci, July 12, 1926, ibid., 030745–030747.
15. Farinacci to Arnaldo Mussolini, July 16, 1926, ibid., 030750.
16. Arnaldo Mussolini to Benito Mussolini, July 20, 1926, ibid., 030749.

chieftain. The net result, however, was to allow Farinacci to continue, as he would until the end of the Fascist regime, to pose as the Cato of Fascism and to goad Mussolini, by reaction, into transforming Italy more and more into a police state.

In August 1926, for instance, Farinacci editorialized on the troubled Greek situation, stating: "Only one thing Fascism should learn from Greece, namely, that each government liquidates its opponents."[17] Mussolini wired him that "Italian Fascism . . . [had] nothing, but nothing, but absolutely nothing to learn from Greece" and that "the French Terror did nothing but hasten the Restoration."[18] Barely two months later, however, immediately following an attempt on his life at Bologna on October 31,[19] Mussolini went much further even than Farinacci, who advocated deporting all anti-Fascists to Italian Somaliland.[20] Mussolini caused the immediate enactment of a series of laws which removed any remaining vestige of democracy from Italian governing institutions.[21]

17. *Il Regime Fascista* (Cremona), August 28, 1926.

18. Mussolini to prefect of Cremona, August 29, 1926, ID–NA, T586, 030641.

19. A pistol shot which missed its mark was fired against Mussolini allegedly by an anarchist youth, Anteo Zamboni, who was lynched on the spot by the Fascist mob. If the frustrated plot by Socialist deputy Tito Zaniboni of the previous November is counted, this was the fourth attempt on Mussolini's life, since his nose had been scratched by a bullet fired by an Irish spinster, Violet Gibson, early in April, and a bomb had been thrown against his car in September by an anti-Fascist anarchist, Gino Lucetti, wounding eight bystanders but leaving Mussolini unscathed.

20. *Il Regime Fascista* (Cremona), November 2, 1926.

21. In summary, the new laws provided:

1. The institution of the death penalty against anyone guilty of attempts on the life of members of the royal house or the head of the government, or of crimes against national security.

2. The dissolution of all political parties or organizations "acting in opposition to the [Fascist] regime" (in other words, all parties except the Fascist party).

3. Revocation of publishing permits of all newspapers and magazines "acting in opposition to the [Fascist] regime" (again eliminating, in fact, all but the Fascist press).

4. Severe jail penalties for anyone trying to reconstitute the dissolved parties and organizations.

5. The creation of a special court (the infamous *Tribunale Speciale per*

Trying, perhaps, to regain the initiative as the prime exponent of intransigence, Farinacci immediately announced that at the next session of the Chamber of Deputies he would move that the *Aventine* deputies be formally expelled and their seats declared vacant.[22] When Parliament met on November 9, however, on Mussolini's orders it was the new Secretary General of the Fascist party, Augusto Turati, who sponsored a motion for the expulsion not only of the *Aventine* deputies but also of the nineteen Communist deputies who had remained active in the Chamber.[23] In any case, Farinacci was emboldened by the new turn of events and began spreading rumors concerning his impending comeback, allegedly as Minister of Communications. He also opened negotiations for the purchase of a large Milan daily, *Il Secolo*, arranging for loans of several million *lire* with provincial banks in Lombardy and Piedmont. Mussolini was promptly advised of these maneuvers by his brother Arnaldo and, since nothing came of them, he must have taken steps to keep Farinacci in limbo.[24]

It was a comfortable limbo, however. The new building which during Farinacci's secretaryship had been erected to house the enlarged offices and plant of his newspaper also included an apartment in which he lived with his family. The practice of criminal law, which Farinacci pursued in any Italian city where clients felt his name as defense attorney might help in swaying a judge or jury, brought him a comfortable income. There was no scarcity of buxom country maidens or sophisticated ladies eager for an adventure with such a notorious swashbuckler. And with the local

---

la *Difesa dello Stato*), composed of militia and army officers to have jurisdiction over anyone accused of political crimes.
6. The establishment of the *"confino di polizia"* (a measure whereby individuals suspected of political feelings adverse to Fascism would be compelled to move and reside in isolated villages under constant police surveillance).
(De Felice, *Mussolini il Fascista*, II, 210–212.)
22. *Il Regime Fascista* (Cremona), November 7, 1926.
23. The motion was naturally passed, 232 to 10.
24. Arnaldo Mussolini to Benito Mussolini, November 27, 1926, ID–NA, T586, 030751.

Fascist organizations completely under his control, Farinacci's rule over the city and the Province of Cremona was despotic and absolute.[25]

Outside of Cremona, however, his activities and contacts were closely watched and reported to Mussolini, who obviously placed no reliance on Farinacci's continuous protestations of affection and loyalty. The files, in fact, are full of letters in which the *ras* of Cremona, while pledging his undying devotion to Mussolini personally, complained bitterly of the persecution to which he and his friends and even casual acquaintances were subjected by the party leaders and by various members of the government, citing names and specific instances of actual or imagined incidents. These letters, some of which rambled for ten or twenty pages, remained generally unanswered, as Mussolini usually left the task of handling Farinacci to his brother Arnaldo or to the Secretary of the party. It is in fact from some of Arnaldo Mussolini's reports to the *Duce* that a clear insight can be gained into Farinacci's character, mentality, and attitude.

After a long meeting with Farinacci early in 1927, for instance, Arnaldo wrote Benito: *(He [Farinacci] still thinks that outside the government there must be a vanguard ready for battle, showing open and hidden enemies that Fascism . . . can never lay down its arms. . . . I asked him for what reasons and for what goals Fascism should maintain this warlike mentality, and he cited the syndical regulations, the enemies of the regime, and the intransigent hostility of the Church. He fears that the class struggle, banished by Fascism, might reappear through corporativism. Finally, he would advocate a certain amount of discussion within the party, the better to define the goals and lines of action for the future. He shows himself unable to consider or understand*

25. Any sporadic attempts at resistance were still ruthlessly repressed with *squadrista* methods, as shown by Farinacci's reply to the party's undersecretary, Achille Starace, who inquired as to whether a gang of Fascists had beaten two men on Cremona's main square. "My Fascists," wrote Farinacci, "are only to be blamed for not having given them a beating sooner." (A. Starace to Farinacci, November 23, 1926; Farinacci to Starace, November 30, 1926, ICSA, Farinacci Fund, 1926 Correspondence, Folder 4, Env. S.)

the great problems of the economy, of finance, of military efficiency. *He only thinks of the domestic situation and of the best ways to run the party efficiently.*[26]

A few months later, having met Farinacci in Rome, Arnaldo wrote: "these talks with him may start out well, but in the end one is always left with a bitter taste in one's mouth from the realization of his lack of political tact and his exaggerated pretensions."[27]

And again, in October, informing his brother of a lengthy interview in which he had reproached Farinacci for not following the directives of the party's Secretary General, Arnaldo Mussolini wrote that Farinacci considered Turati "inadequate to lead the party" and would not, because of "personal dignity," call on him at party headquarters.[28]

The enmity between Farinacci and his successor had begun during his tenure of the General Secretaryship, and it continued unabated as long as Augusto Turati held the post. Writing to Farinacci after a meeting of the party Directorate called specially to "examine [his] attitude toward the National Directorate and [his] polemic criticisms of its orders," Turati stated in no uncertain terms: *During the period of your Secretaryship, you rightly demanded that your orders be obeyed without discussion. You cannot now pretend that the new Directorate forego this necessary discipline. . . . It is deplorable that you go around claiming to interpret the feelings of the Fascist masses in contrast to what is the thought of the Party's Directorate.*[29]

Farinacci, of course, paid no attention to the warnings which concluded Turati's letter; he continued to take positions which were at variance with the government's policies. When the Italian press, for instance, almost unanimously condemned the execution

26. Arnaldo Mussolini to Benito Mussolini, February 14, 1927, ID–NA, T586, 030752–030753.

27. Arnaldo Mussolini to Benito Mussolini, August 5, 1927, ibid., 030754.

28. Arnaldo Mussolini to Benito Mussolini, October 19, 1927, ibid., 030755–030758.

29. A. Turati to Farinacci, September 7, 1927, ibid., 031348–031351.

in America of Sacco and Vanzetti in August 1927, Farinacci came out editorially praising the results of the trial and assailing his journalistic brethren for their "weakness."[30]

Turning to the economic crisis created by Mussolini's insistence on revaluation of the lira, Farinacci took up the cause of the Po Valley landowners, who were being forced to sell their crops for less than they cost to produce. Farinacci had the Fascist Federation of Cremona issue an order of the day blaming the Fascist syndicates for the unsettled agricultural situation. He sent Mussolini a copy, prompting the Duce to answer curtly that the party's Secretary General had since the previous month issued directives on the matter, and Farinacci should simply follow them.[31]

The ras of Cremona, undaunted, continued to editorialize on Italy's economic problems, stressing the plight of the farmers,[32] so that Mussolini sent him a long wire pointing out that "the Fascist government [had] done for Italian agriculture in one month more than had been done for it in a whole century,"[33] to which Farinacci replied with a ten-page letter full of unsupported statistics, trying to prove that farmers were being ruined and accusing the syndicates' officials of double-dealing.[34]

It was at this time, as a result of rifts among the Fascist leadership of Cremona caused by Farinacci's stand on the agricultural situation, that two of his former lieutenants, Cesare Balestreri and Giulio Orefici, tried to break Farinacci's hold on the province by appealing for the intervention of the party's Secretary General. Farinacci in turn wrote Mussolini, quoting Turati as having told his opponents: "Don't worry, if I find the least thing to blame on Farinacci I'll fix him for good. Then we'll clean up the prefecture, the Questura, and the courts. If I find nothing now, in a couple of months we'll start again." "As you can see,"

30. Il Regime Fascista (Cremona), August 26, 1927.

31. Farinacci to Mussolini, June 20, 1927, ID–NA, T586, 031074–031078; Mussolini to prefect of Cremona, June 21, 1927, ibid., 031079.

32. Il Regime Fascista (Cremona), July 9, 1927, August 30, 1927.

33. Mussolini to prefect of Cremona, August 31, 1927, ID–NA, T586, 031084–031086.

34. Farinacci to Mussolini, September 24, 1921, ibid., 030621–030622.

Farinacci wrote, "Orefici and Balestreri are tools of Turati against me. . . . Only you must judge everybody."[35]

Whether or not Turati's investigations produced any evidence damaging to Farinacci, either Mussolini's fear of repercussions, or Farinacci's hold on the *Duce*, or both, worked in his favor, because no official action was taken against him and he continued to rule over the province of Cremona. Unofficially, however, the party leadership intensified its underground campaign against Farinacci and his followers, especially in Milan, where there were even public demonstrations by Fascist groups carrying placards attacking Farinacci.[36] Milan, as the cradle of Fascism and the unofficial bailiwick of Arnaldo Mussolini, was always most responsive to directives from the party leadership, and it is not unlikely that the inspiration for the open attacks on Farinacci had in fact come from Rome. Never one to let a challenge go unanswered, Farinacci now decided to take up the cudgels against the Milanese hierarchy and thus became embroiled in an affair which was to bring him no end of trouble, while at the same time providing another instance of Mussolini acting under Farinacci's prodding.

Early in April of 1928, the city of Milan obtained a substantial loan from the private bank of Dillon, Read of New York. The mayor of Milan, Ernesto Belloni, conducted the negotiations personally and, as it later appeared, concluded the deal with Dillon Read even though another bank had offered better terms. There were, soon thereafter, rumors of bribery, as well as hints that Arnaldo Mussolini had also had a hand in the transaction. On September 5, obviously under pressure, Belloni resigned as mayor, and soon thereafter Farinacci began a campaign of innuendo, writing, for instance, that there were "many parasites hidden in the crevices of the *Duomo* of Milan."[37] To Mussolini's request for explanations, Farinacci answered disclaiming any "personal character" to his remarks, in which, he said, he merely meant to "compare Fascism to an artistic masterpiece." "But," he went on, "I would not exclude that at Milan there are some parasites and men who, paupers like me in October 1922, are now in splendid

35. Farinacci to Mussolini, December 7, 1927, *ibid.*, 030621–030622.
36. Farinacci to Turati, February 6, 1928, *ibid.*, 031695–031698.
37. *Il Regime Fascista* (Cremona), September 23, 1928.

economic conditions."[38] Mussolini's reaction was caustic, as he wired: (Your reply is just as vague as your previous allegations. As to poverty, I don't refute that you were a pauper in 1922, but I deny most strongly that you are still a pauper in 1928, sixth year of the [Fascist] regime. True paupers don't ride in limousines or reside in luxury hotels. . . . When one makes accusations he must have the courage to bring the parasites to the bar of justice, otherwise this generic puritanism logically becomes the best accomplice of the criminal masonic anti-Fascism which tries to sling mud on the regime and on the leaders of the regime.[39] Farinacci's answer was again vague, devoted mostly to justifying his own relative affluence; but he set out to gather proofs against Belloni and finally, in July of 1929, he sent Mussolini a number of documents[40] and published a detailed list of accusations against Belloni, in connection both with the Dillon, Read loan and with a number of other contracts concluded by Belloni on behalf of the city of Milan during his administration.[41]

Mussolini, no longer able to ignore the matter, appointed a three-man commission to investigate the charges. When he received the report that the Dillon Read matter seemed to be aboveboard, but that serious irregularities had in fact occurred during Belloni's administration, he punished the former mayor with a temporary suspension from the party, and Farinacci with a "note of censure."[42]

Farinacci protested bitterly with another of his lengthy unanswered letters to Mussolini, pointing out that any censure should have been directed to the party leadership and to the prefect for not having acted against Belloni sooner, and not against himself, who had only acted in this matter to defend "the sanctity and the purity of our cause," but Mussolini was unmoved.[43]

38. Farinacci to Mussolini, September 24, 1928, ID–NA, T586, 026296.

39. Mussolini to Farinacci, September 25, 1928, ibid., 031181–031182.

40. Reference to this action is made in a later letter. Farinacci to Mussolini, September 27, 1928, ibid., –031163–031166.

41. Il Regime Fascista (Cremona), July 12, 13, 1929.

42. Il Popolo d'Italia (Milan), August 3, 1929.

43. Farinacci to Mussolini, August 8, 1929, ID–NA, T586, 026305–026314.

It was indeed lucky for Farinacci that he had been re-elected to the Chamber of Deputies in the so-called plebiscite of March 1929, as otherwise in all likelihood he would not have been included in the single slate of candidates presented to Italian voters in what was to be the last election under the Fascist regime. He was, however, further rebuffed when Mussolini revised the composition of the Grand Council, cutting its size from fifty to fewer than twenty members,[44] among whom the *ras* of Cremona was not included. This was perhaps the lowest point of Farinacci's political disgrace, and he went as far as writing Turati a fairly subdued letter, declaring himself ready to "regularize [his] position" towards the party's Secretary General,[45] but he received a sharp reply reminding him of the times when he, "banging [his] fist on [his] briefcase full of papers, would claim to possess documents seriously incriminating men of the government and men of the party" and accusing him of disloyalty and obstructionism.[46] Turati, furthermore, urged Belloni to take revenge on Farinacci, so that in January of 1930 the former mayor of Milan started a suit for defamation and slander against Farinacci's newspaper, *Il Regime Fascista*. The *ras* of Cremona, with his back to the wall, resorted once more to veiled blackmail. Already, a month earlier, he had wired a German newspaper, denying any truth to reports printed therein concerning his alleged possession of "documents of such gravity as to destroy the *Duce*'s brother, Arnaldo Mussolini."[47]

He now wrote Arnaldo, informing him of Turati's collusion with Belloni, and asking that Arnaldo seek his brother's intervention.[48] Soon thereafter, a meeting was held in Rome between Farinacci, Turati, Arnaldo Mussolini, and a few other top party leaders. The minutes of the discussion, which lasted several hours, clearly show anxiety on the part of the ruling group to settle

44. *Il Regime Fascista* (Cremona), October 2, 1929.
45. Farinacci to Turati, October 30, 1929, ID–NA, T586, 031167–031168.
46. Turati to Farinacci, October 31, 1929, *ibid.*, 031160–031162.
47. Farinacci to editor of *Dresdener Volkszeitung*, undated but referring to article of December 2, 1929, *ibid.*, 030768.
48. Farinacci to Arnaldo Mussolini, February 20, 1930, *ibid.*, 030870.

the matter to Farinacci's satisfaction.[49] A few months later, the trial was held in Cremona, and when the verdict was finally issued on October 10, Farinacci's newspaper was cleared of all charges, whereupon Mussolini expelled Belloni from the party and revoked the censure inflicted on Farinacci fifteen months earlier.[50]

Although he thus grudgingly admitted that Farinacci had been right, Mussolini did not in effect modify his attitude towards Farinacci. An examination of the voluminous files of Mussolini's private Secretariat shows that every move or utterance of the *ras* of Cremona was reported to the *Duce*, either by police informers or by transcriptions of telephone wiretaps. While still refusing, as he would until the end of 1933, to meet Farinacci, or to answer directly the voluminous letters which the former Secretary General continued to address to him, Mussolini scanned regularly the columns of *Il Regime Fascista* and, whenever he found an editorial not to his liking, he ordered that the issue be confiscated. In the last four months of 1931, this happened no less than three times in connection with Farinacci's comments on the reorganization of the armed forces[51] and on the Italian situation,[52] and even with specific reference to a single sentence saying that, unlike Farinacci, in October 1922 many Fascist leaders had "run to Rome to grab portfolios and honors."[53] Orders were even given to the prefect of Cremona to take the initiative and "confiscate *Il Regime Fascista* whenever it might contain open or veiled attacks against the *Banca Commerciale* or [its] Chairman Toeplitz."[54]

Farinacci, in turn, kept off the national political stage by Mussolini, expanded his legal practice and became also associate editor of *Vita Italiana*, a political monthly, founded in 1913 by

49. Minutes of meeting at Palazzo Littorio, March 5, 1930, *ibid.*, 031202–031252.
50. *Il Regime Fascista* (Cremona), October 11, 1930.
51. *Ibid.*, September 18, 1931.
52. *Ibid.*, October 3, 1931.
53. *Ibid.*, October 24, 1931.
54. Minister of Interior to prefect of Cremona, September 5, 1931, ID–NA, T586, 030678.

another journalist, Giovanni Preziosi. Preziosi was just as sectarian and intransigent as Farinacci, besides being a notorious anti-Semite. It was in fact an article by Farinacci on *Vita Italiana* in which he referred with veiled contempt to the lukewarm spirit of the current party leadership which prompted Giovanni Giuriati, who had shortly before succeeded Turati as Secretary General of the Fascist party, to take Farinacci to task for "publishing statements which discredit the party and can be exploited by the enemies of Fascism."[55] Farinacci replied in his usual defiant tone, rehashing his exploits on behalf of the party and complaining of the persecution to which he was subjected for his intransigent Fascist faith. He pointed out the many times when his warnings had gone unheeded, only to be proved correct later. He wrote:

([Many times I have denounced to the leadership that the party is seriously menaced by the worst kind of anti-Fascism, represented by prostitutes, pimps and ex-convicts . . . who work to discredit those who are politically and morally strong . . . but I have never received a word of reassurance. . . . It is natural that my articles sometimes reflect my anguish in seeing the regime so ill-served.[56]

It is obvious from this exchange and from many other letters and documents spread through Mussolini's and Farinacci's correspondence files, and from the study of contemporary and subsequent events, that there were in fact good grounds for Farinacci's apprehension as to the future of Fascism, and that the *ras* of Cremona had a clearer insight into the Italian political situation than did Mussolini. The Duce was by now succumbing to the adulation of his cohorts and choosing to believe what he was told by his subordinates without verifying whether they might, as they increasingly did, only report good news and suppress unpleasant reports.[57] It is also evident that Farinacci, in spite of

55. G. Giuriati to Farinacci, October 23, 1931, *ibid.*, 031177.

56. Farinacci to Giuriati, October 30, 1931, *ibid.*, 031169–031176.

57. Mussolini's egocentrism is nowhere better exemplified than in a handwritten memorandum he gave Turati in February 1927, explaining the reasons why all positions of leadership must be appointive, and saying that he would himself decide on all appointments. He wrote:

1. *The revolution has one chief, who has prepared it from 1914 to 1922,*

many and frequent rebuffs, did not waver from his determination to fight against what he and his followers dubbed the "*imborghesimento*" of the party: the transformation of revolutionary Fascism into a bourgeois establishment.

Farinacci expressed his views most clearly in another of his periodic outpourings to Mussolini, a 27-page letter following the confiscation of several issues of *Il Regime Fascista*. The origins of this latest confrontation lay in one of the many financial scandals which were rocking the Italian economy, deep in the throes of the depression gripping the world in the early thirties. A certain Giovanni Manzoni, close friend of the Milanese Fascist leadership and particularly of Arnaldo Mussolini, had a few years earlier founded a savings bank which had branched out throughout Lombardy. The institution had attracted vast numbers of depositors by paying a high dividend rate and by exploiting its managers' connections with the Fascist hierarchs; but early in 1932, it had declared bankruptcy, wiping out the savings of thousands of families. Farinacci had immediately thundered not only against Manzoni, who had been arrested, but against the man's friends who, by their "support and moral influence," had helped Manzoni in defrauding the public.[58] The inference was clear, and Mussolini, still deeply affected by his brother Arnaldo's sudden death a few weeks before, reacted with extreme severity, wiring the prefect of Cremona that he should have taken the initiative of confiscating *Il Regime Fascista* because of its article "which cast a shadow on the entire regime, a scandalistic, dema-

---

has willed it in 1922, and has led it until today: *everything depends on him.*

2. It would be sublimely grotesque to have abolished electioneering in the nation and preserve it in the party.

3. [We will thus] safeguard the party's directives, not letting them be compromised by electoral procedures which usually do not bring the best men to the fore.

4. [This decision derives from] our concept of the state, [a concept which is] authoritarian and therefore antiliberal and antidemocratic. A ship is guided by one pilot, not by the entire crew.

(Quoted in De Felice, *Mussolini il Fascista*, II, 178.)

58. *Il Regime Fascista* (Cremona), January 9, 1932.

gogic, deplorable article which greatly harmed Fascism." And he dismissed the poor prefect on the spot.[59]

A few days later, another issue of *Il Regime Fascista*, reporting further details of the Manzoni Bank's crash, was confiscated,[60] and Mussolini decreed that Farinacci could not, while a member of the Chamber of Deputies, also be Secretary of the Provincial Fascist Federation of Cremona.

Farinacci then addressed himself "no longer to the friend, to the brother . . . but to the Chief of the Grand Council," in the formal, third-person *voi*, rather than the usual and familiar *tu*, asking that his position be reviewed to decide once and for all whether he deserved to remain in the ranks of the Fascist party and, if so, that he again be accorded the *Duce's* trust and confidence. He reviewed at length once more both his activities in the service of Fascism and the insults and humiliations suffered at the hands of the party's rulers, stressing his anguish at seeing "our party being worn down . . . its energies destroyed by the miserable manhunts . . . by the bureaucratic stifling of initiatives," and his desire to bring to Mussolini's attention what was being hidden from him, a desire which Farinacci could only fulfill in the columns of his newspaper in view of the ostracism to which he was subjected. Denying any intention to foster dissension within the Fascist ranks for personal ambition, and defining himself as "a most intransigent Fascist, stronger when things are most difficult and dangerous, who does not curry popular favor, who provokes and scourges those who have joined the party without faith and without backbone, and who tells unpleasant things to many people without metaphors," Farinacci went on to tell Mussolini in no uncertain terms his concern over the future of Fascism in the event of the *Duce's* death. He declared himself convinced that the regime would remain solid as long as God kept Mussolini alive, but he pointed out that Mussolini was, after all, made of flesh and blood and reproached him for taking unnecessary risks such as flying or riding motorcycles.

59. Mussolini to prefect of Cremona, January 11, 1932, ID–NA, T586, 030692.

60. Prefect of Cremona to Ministry of Interior, January 14, 1932, *ibid.*, 030690.

"Do you think," he went on, ([that the Italian people would then find a solution coherent with their recent past? I don't believe so. There is no ideal strong enough to overcome within the leaders of the regime cannibalism, envy, diffidence, and you would be succeeded by a fratricidal struggle, in which the non-Fascist part of the population and . . . of the army . . . would tear down splintered Fascism.*

Farinacci pointed out, with undeniable sincerity, that it was the realization that the death of Mussolini would mean the end of Fascism which encouraged the hopes of the anti-Fascists and engendered fear and perplexity in many otherwise good Fascists, including even several members of the Grand Council, "who, however, prefer to be yes-men and reserve their doubts and protests for private conversations, far from [Mussolini's] presence." He also repeated that, in attacking profiteers and opportunists, he felt he was only doing so for the benefit of Fascism and that punishment of such unworthy Fascists should be merciless. "Russia," he added, "is a good teacher in this; she teaches by shooting without mercy anyone who offends the honor or weakens the solidity of [the] regime. . . . But those who know that you dislike scandal take advantage of it to act with impunity."[61]

To such a scathing indictment of the men surrounding him, Mussolini did not answer directly, but he asked Achille Starace, a nonentity who was now Secretary General of the Fascist party, to ask Farinacci to explain certain of his allegations. Starace did so, and Farinacci must have backtracked somewhat because, according to the report of the meeting, he promised in future not to write about any scandals which might occur, and he admitted that the party had undergone a useful reconstruction after 1926, even though with methods not to his liking.[62]

Mussolini, at this point, was evidently divided between his hate and contempt for Farinacci and his fear of the scandal which would inevitably result if any drastic measures were publicly taken against the irrepressible ras of Cremona. What he did was launch a thorough investigation into the background of Farinacci,

61. Farinacci, to Mussolini, January 20, 1932, ibid., 030130–030156.
62. A. Starace to Mussolini, February 10, 1932, ibid., 031128–031129

going as far as reviewing the records of his military service[63] and obtaining, through his police informers, detailed lists of financial supporters and subscribers to Farinacci's newspapers.[64] He also obtained a copy of the voluminous report of the investigation on Farinacci's dissertation and other alleged improprieties which had been made by Senator Alberici for the Minister of the Interior in 1930.

Mussolini obviously found nothing of sufficient gravity to justify expelling Farinacci from the party, and he must have been surprised by the number of high-placed individuals and large corporations who appeared among Farinacci's financial backers.[65] In any event, he officially did nothing against Farinacci, who continued as in the past to write and speak without restraint and to complain periodically but vainly to Mussolini of various imagined or real grievances against the party leadership. He complained, too, of government policies which he considered harmful to the true spirit of Fascism, such as, for instance, Mussolini's secret order to all Fascist organizations not to commemorate any longer the anniversary of the January 3, 1925, speech,[66] in which the Duce had openly proclaimed his dictatorial aim.

Farinacci's enemies among the Fascist hierarchy, however, were many, and it was probably at their prompting, rather than that of Mussolini, who disliked scandal and newspaper polemics, that in the summer of 1933 a Roman Fascist daily, L'Impero, began a series of articles accusing Farinacci of cowardice and of having enriched himself during the period of his Secretaryship.

63. Ministry of War to Mussolini's private secretary, February 13, 1932, ibid., 030942–030946.

64. Ibid., 030699–030702.

65. Whether because of true sympathy for his views or, more likely, succumbing to the insistence of Farinacci's administrator, Vittorio Varenna, and to fear of being attacked by Il Regime Fascista, virtually all major Italian manufacturers and many leaders of banking and finance contributed important sums to Farinacci's newspaper. A favorite method of Farinacci's helpers was to badger businessmen and officials of public agencies, especially the railroads, into buying a bloc of yearly subscriptions which they in turn would foist off on their own workers and employees. (See, e.g., transcriptions of telephone wiretaps, November 23, 1932, ID–NA, T586, 030710–030712.)

66. Farinacci to Mussolini, January 8, 1933, ibid., 026359.

The *ras* of Cremona, for all his many and grievous faults, was not really lacking in personal courage, and he replied by publishing detailed accounts of the many duels he had fought during the early years of Fascism. He was also able to deny the accusations of having used his high office for personal gain, because, as it happened, it had really been only after his resignation that he had gone all out to solicit and obtain financial support for his publishing ventures. The matter culminated in Farinacci's addressing an open letter to the present Secretary General of the Fascist Party, Achille Starace, asking him to intervene and reprimand *L'Impero*.[67] He wrote another letter to the Rome *Procuratore Generale*, charging *L'Impero* with defamation and slander.[68]

Mussolini, through the party's Secretary, prohibited any further publication of "open letters"[69] and continued to follow Farinacci's activities through police reports. The *ras* of Cremona, however, had obviously decided that the time had come for him to force his way back into Mussolini's good graces because, after some more generic and fruitless appeals,[70] he finally wrote the *Duce* a relatively brief letter which ended: ❲*To clarify everything, to acquaint you with some of my ideas, to tell you some things in confidence, and to inform you of certain decisions of mine, it is imperative that you grant me an audience so that I may speak with absolute frankness. I trust you will appreciate the desirability* [*of granting the audience*].[71] [Emphasis added by Mussolini in ink on the typewritten original.]

Farinacci's apparently innocent words could of course also be interpreted as a threat of blackmail. Assuming that the former Secretary General did in fact possess documents damaging to Mussolini and Fascism, had he now, exasperated by the continuing ostracism, decided to publish them unless he was readmitted to the inner councils of Fascism? Was this the meaning of Farinacci's reference to his "decisions"? Farinacci was certainly not

67. *Il Regime Fascista* (Cremona), June 15, 1933.

68. *Ibid.*, June 20, 1933.

69. *Il Messaggero* (Rome), June 23, 1933.

70. Farinacci to Mussolini, June 25, 1933 and July 28, 1933, *ibid.*, 031253–031260 and 030569.

71. Farinacci to Mussolini, October 21, 1933, *ibid.*, 030570–030572.

above blackmail, and Mussolini in turn was not one to succumb to sentimental appeals based on earlier comradeship. The only evidence supporting the blackmail theory is circumstantial, but the fact remains that Mussolini this time relented, and on November 21 a meeting between the two men finally took place in Rome.

Nothing in the records indicates what happened at this meeting, but again the evidence of subsequent events shows that an agreement for peaceful coexistence and renewed collaboration must have been reached, because during the following months Farinacci had no difficulty in gaining access to the *Duce*,[72] and his attitude became much more reserved and considerate. He now submitted articles to Mussolini for approval before publication and sent him letters received from third parties asking for instructions on what to answer.[73]

The news of his return to favor must also have been spread, because important industrialists such as the owners of the Gaslini Oil Refineries and those of the Dell'Acqua Cotton Mills now used him as intermediary in petitioning Mussolini for favors.[74] It was evident that, after a quarrel lasting almost ten years, the two men had finally arrived at a *modus vivendi*, and Farinacci's good behavior was rewarded soon thereafter. Taking the pretext of an imminent celebration to commemorate the first meeting of the Grand Council, the *ras* of Cremona wrote Mussolini a plaintive note, claiming to seek no other reward than "to serve the cause and you in a different way . . . as a watchdog ready to spring if some day you should really need me," but declaring himself to be "melancholy for sentimental reasons" and asking as his only wish to be "readmitted to the great revolutionary body."[75]

Mussolini, already planning his African adventure, saw the obvious advantage of having Farinacci's full support at a time when

---

72. Farinacci to Mussolini's private secretary, January 1, 1934, *ibid.*, 034175; Farinacci to Mussolini, February 23, 1934, *ibid.*, 034172; memo of Mussolini's private secretary, March 21, 1934, *ibid.*, 034171.

73. Farinacci to Mussolini, January 30, 1934, *ibid.*, 030934.

74. Farinacci to Mussolini's private secretary, April 13, 1934 and December, 19, 1934, *ibid.*, 028756 and 034211.

75. Farinacci to Mussolini, January 11, 1935, *ibid.*, 030930–030931.

Italy would have to present a united front to the outside world and was more than receptive to the request. On January 15, while Farinacci, in full Fascist regalia and with a militia honor guard, was giving away the bride at the wedding of his daughter Adriana to a Cremonese pharmacist, Palmiro Mola, the *Duce's* largesse made him not only a member of the Grand Council of Fascism, but also a *Ministro di Stato*, the highest government post below cabinet rank.

Appropriately, with the approach of Italy's first war of aggression, Roberto Farinacci was again riding high.

XII

THE CLARION
SOUNDS
AGAIN

ON THE desirability of a military take-over in Ethiopia, Mussolini and Farinacci, for once, saw eye to eye. Reasons for thinking of such a take-over were many and convoluted. Ethiopia was, after all, the only land in Africa not occupied or protected by a major power; it bordered on both Eritrea and Somaliland; and the British had already, or so Mussolini thought, given a green light to Italian expansion into Ethiopia.[1]

The conquest of Ethiopia could also be rationalized as justification for the failure at the Versailles Peace Conference to assign colonies to Italy; it could be considered as a means of providing living space for those workers and peasants who since the enactment of the quota provisions of the 1924 Immigration Act in July 1929 could no longer seek their fortune in the United States. It was, furthermore, a suitable objective for Mussolini's oft proclaimed dreams of bringing Italy back to the imperial grandeur of ancient Rome. Finally, a nice little colonial war would furnish a unifying goal for the Italian people, an outlet for many unemployed workers, and a suitable sounding board for the most bellicose Fascist slogans: "Live dangerously!," "Better to live one day like a lion than a hundred years like a sheep!," "Believe, obey, fight!"

Planning for the conquest of Ethiopia had in fact begun since 1933, when the elderly *Quadrumvir* Emilio De Bono had been

1. As early as 1925, Mussolini had met with British Foreign Secretary Austen Chamberlain and had reached with him an agreement for a new apportionment of interests in Ethiopia and for mutual support in the pursuit of such interests.

sent to reconnoiter in East Africa. A *casus belli* was conveniently provided on December 5, 1934, at Wal Wal, 60 miles within Ethiopia, when, challenged to withdraw by Ethiopian troops who were escorting an Anglo-Ethiopian boundary commission, the Italian garrison of the fortified post refused and attacked with tanks and planes, killing several scores of the Ethiopians. The Ethiopian Emperor Haile Selassie appealed to the League of Nations, where for the next ten months French and British representatives would successfully connive to sidetrack the issue and prevent any positive action. Meanwhile, the Fascist government, amid great fanfare, began to mobilize men and supplies and transfer them through the Suez Canal to the staging area of its colonies on the Red Sea.

Farinacci took part in the preparations, advising Mussolini with regard to the deployment of special battalions of younger and more enthusiastic militiamen[2] and addressing mass rallies such as the one at Camogli, near Genoa, where on May 19 he exhorted the assembled Fascists to "be ready to answer the call of history and make Italy great" and brought them to such a pitch of enthusiasm that they carried him from the square on their shoulders.[3]

At the same time, Farinacci, having finally emerged from the shadows of political disgrace, was not neglecting his personal affairs. In anticipation of a growing demand for war material, he succeeded in making arrangements for the establishment at Cremona of a new plant for the manufacture of machine guns,[4] in which, according to later police reports, he secretly held a financial interest.[5]

He also, according to a detailed account sent to Rome by the Milan police, blackmailed a former financial contributor who had become disillusioned and, with threats of having the man sen-

2. Farinacci to Mussolini, February 8, 1935, ID–NA, T586, 034279–034280.
3. Police Report of May 20, 1935, with stenographic text of speech, *ibid.*, 034042–034047.
4. Farinacci to Mussolini's private secretary, February 21, 1935, *ibid.*, 034212.
5. Police Report of September 27, 1941, *ibid.*, 033998.

tenced to the *confino di polizia*, Farinacci extorted from him 1,400,000 *lire*.[6] And, more in keeping with his regained status in the Fascist hierarchy, he took on as his "permanent" mistress the well-known opera singer Gianna Pederzini, leaving to the dowdy Maria Antonioli the role of private secretary and chief lieutenant in the ruling of his Cremonese fief. Farinacci's liaison with the young and beautiful diva was in fact quite open, and he was often seen with her in luxurious resorts such as the Lido and St. Moritz.[7]

As the hour for the Fascist invasion of Ethiopia drew nearer, Farinacci decided that it would be fitting for him to take active part in the fighting. After obtaining from Mussolini the use of a military airplane for a training course,[8] he won his wings and volunteered for service as a pilot in East Africa, with a letter to the *Duce* in which he asked to be allowed "to lead the old comrades in continuing to write glorious pages in [the history of] the Revolution."[9] Mussolini replied five days later, appointing Farinacci a first lieutenant in the Air Force, "a youthful rank which is a stepping-stone to the higher ones."[10]

The *ras* of Cremona, meanwhile, continued his propaganda campaign in preparation for the imminent outbreak of hostilities. A typical example of his methods is contained in a brief note he sent Mussolini at the end of September 1935. "By shaking him up without respite," he wrote, "and by making life impossible for him, I finally got my bishop to talk the way I wanted. Enclosed please find a sample."[11] The pastoral letter issued a few days earlier by the Bishop of Cremona was indeed abjectly pro-Fascist, exhorting the faithful "to be ready to make any and all sacrifices which the Motherland's drive to greatness might require" and praying that "all citizens obey the authorities, and the army be equal to the arduous task of moving forward the country's glorious flag."[12]

6. Police Report of November 8, 1935, *ibid.*, 034036–034037.
7. Police Report of August 20, 1935, *ibid.*, 034041.
8. Farinacci to Mussolini, September 4, 1935, *ibid.*, 033970.
9. Farinacci to Mussolini, September 4, 1935, *ibid.*, 033972–033973.
10. Mussolini to Farinacci, September 19, 1935, *ibid.*, 033971.
11. Farinacci to Mussolini September 30, 1935, *ibid.*, 033855.
12. *La Vita Cattolica* (Cremona), September 27, 1935.

The invasion of Ethiopia began on October 3, but it was not until four months later that Farinacci, having repeatedly requested to be assigned to active duty,[13] left Italy to join an elite bomber squadron commanded by Mussolini's son-in-law, Galeazzo Ciano, among whose members were Mussolini's two older sons, Vittorio and Bruno, and party Secretary General Achille Starace. The *ras* of Cremona had only time to engage in bombing and strafing the defenseless tribesmen for a few weeks, however, because early in April, while he and some friends were fishing with hand grenades in a small lake near Dessié, he waited too long before throwing a grenade and the explosion completely severed his right hand.[14] After spending several weeks in a field hospital, during which time the war ended with the occupation of Addis Ababa, Farinacci received a hero's welcome when he landed at Venice.[15] Then he spent several months being treated and fitted with a metal hand at the famous Rizzoli Orthopedic Institute at Bologna. He had meanwhile written Mussolini asking to be excused from any political tasks for the duration of his convalescence;[16] but, aside from the mutilation, for which he quickly compensated by learning to write and drive with the left hand, his health was obviously excellent, because he found time not only to resume his journalistic and forensic activities, but also to engage in a full social life at the Lido with the ever-present Pederzini woman and other members of his *clique*, including financier Vittorio Varenna and the general manager of the Fascist controlled *Banca Nazionale del Lavoro*, Aldo Osio.[17]

By the early fall of 1936, in any event, Farinacci was back in his self-assumed role of critic, choosing as his first target the victor

13. Farinacci to Mussolini, January 8, 1936, ID–NA, T586, 033861–033862.

14. The official version of the accident reported Farinacci as having been engaged in a grenade-throwing training exercise, but the truth soon leaked out and was widely known even if discreetly unmentioned. (Police Report of July 6, 1936, *ibid.*, 034030.)

15. Police Report of May 24, 1936, *ibid.*, 034031.

16. Farinacci to Mussolini, June 6, 1936, *ibid.*, 033863.

17. Police Reports of July 15, August 7, August 24, 1936, *ibid.*, 034027–034029.

of the Ethiopian campaign, Marshal Pietro Badoglio, whom he accused of military ineptitude and of lukewarm devotion to Fascism.[18] He also chose to write disparagingly of the Fascist movement started in Great Britain by Oswald Mosley as not being sufficiently versed in the *squadrista* tactics which were for Farinacci the only true way to achieve victory.[19]

Meanwhile, the outbreak of civil war in Spain had presented Mussolini with an excellent testing ground for new weapons and tactics, as well as an outlet for many unemployed veterans of the Ethiopian campaign. Early in 1937, after the conquest of Malaga by a strong contingent of Italian "volunteers," the Fascist dictator, possibly to obtain a first-hand appraisal of the chances of extablishing a Fascist regime in Spain, dispatched Farinacci on a personal mission to the insurgents' leader, Francisco Franco, introducing his envoy as "one of the pioneers of Fascism . . . a true fighter . . . [who] comes to review the situation of Nationalist Spain . . . and to acquaint you with my ideas for the future."[20] Farinacci arrived at Franco's headquarters in Salamanca on March 3, and held several meetings with the General's brother, Nicolas, after which he forwarded to Mussolini a lengthy but confused report on the political and military situation.[21] He also set out in detail for the Franco brothers a program of political organization which was merely a carbon copy of the Italian Fascist regime, spelling out that the future "Spanish National Party [would have to be] inserted in each and every agency of the state, and any other political party [would have to be] banished" and that "there can only be one press, the national press." "To achieve all this," Farinacci wrote, "the right men are needed, but there is no better crucible than war to bring to the surface the new lead-

18. Farinacci to Mussolini, September 11, 1936, *ibid.*, 033965–033968. As will be seen, Farinacci's enmity for the man who in July 1943 would replace Mussolini as head of the government kept growing with the passing years and resulted in December 1940 in the end of Badoglio's tenure as Chief of the General Staff.

19. *Il Regime Fascista* (Cremona), October 6, 1936.

20. Mussolini to Franco, March 1, 1937, ID–NA, T586, 033899.

21. Farinacci to Mussolini, March 5, 1937, *ibid.*, 026380–026384.

ers . . . [of] a new power structure which must be totalitarian and authoritarian."[22]

As luck would have it, Farinacci's mission coincided with the bloody defeat suffered by the Italian expeditionary corps at Guadalajara, and the *ras* of Cremona had an opportunity to observe at first hand failures of Italian equipment and strategy which he would later use to support his claims as a military expert. At the beginning of April 1937, Farinacci submitted his report in person to Mussolini and followed it up with a sharp criticism of the Italian Ambassador to Spain, Roberto Cantalupo.[23] A few months later, he submitted a realistic analysis of the Spanish military situation and of the Italian interests and involvement in Spain. Pointing out alleged strategic mistakes by Franco, rifts in the nationalists' political unity, and the Spaniards' "general dislike of Italians," Farinacci concluded: *We must find a way out, because Fascist prestige is deeply compromised. . . . What, after all, do we want in Spain? That at the time of the struggle for the Mediterranean which sooner or later will break out, they [the Spanish nationalists] at least be neutral. We must go all out in this direction . . . as it is very difficult to pretend that they be our allies. . . .*

I do not think it would pay us to get together for real with the English. . . . We must obstinately support Franco, giving him what he does not have, otherwise cut our losses as best we can getting back what we spent. I am for the first alternative, but then we must stop the half-measures, we must give all the means necessary to win rather than scanty and miserly aid (which in the end costs more), getting, in return, serious and adequate political guarantees for the future.[24] [*Emphasis in the original.*]

22. Farinacci to Nicolas Franco, March 10, 1937, ICSA, Farinacci Fund, 1937 Correspondence. Attached to the copy of this letter is a handwritten list of names of Spanish generals and politicians suggested as candidates for the various top posts in Franco's future government.

23. Farinacci to Mussolini, April 11, 1937, ID–NA, T586, 033867–033869.

24. Farinacci to Mussolini, ICSA, Farinacci Fund, 1937 Correspondence. The letter is undated, but reference in the text to military events permits placing its writing in July/August 1937.

Farinacci's political insight was, in this instance, acute and correct, and Mussolini did in fact follow his advice. Different treatment was reserved instead for a series of four articles which Farinacci published in June under the title "Tactical Lessons of the Spanish War." The articles, ghost-written by *Il Regime Fascista*'s military analyst, Emilio Canevari,[25] ridiculed the concept of offensive operations by fast motorized units and took particular aim at the light tanks being built for the Italian army. The tanks were described as "mere tin cans," and the writer advocated instead the creation of larger infantry divisions and the building of heavy tanks.[26]

Such an open attack on the pet theories and innovations of the Italian General Staff could not remain unanswered, and it fell to the Undersecretary of War, General Giuseppe Pariani, to write Farinacci a sharp rejoinder which, among other things, rejected *Il Regime Fascista*'s articles as "smacking of defeatism."[27] To this accusation, Farinacci retorted that to refuse to learn the lessons imparted by the Spanish Civil War "would be to fool ourselves, and thus to do ourselves great damage" and that "being immersed in thoretical studies and army maneuvers one may sometimes forget that in a war there is also a real enemy, who is not always cowardly or incapable or unarmed so as to run away at the first shot."[28]

Farinacci then forwarded to Mussolini the exchange of correspondence, together with letters from several retired generals and Fascist senior officers, supporting the views expressed by him in *Il Regime Fascista*[29] but, as later events on African and European battlefields were to show, Mussolini chose to believe what his generals told him rather than the warnings of Farinacci, Cane-

---

25. Canevari, formerly a colonel in the army, had been cashiered in Ethiopia because of shady financial dealings, and he had soon thereafter joined the staff of Farinacci's newspaper. He enjoyed a fair reputation as a military historian, and, after the Fascist debacle, he worked with Marshal Rodolfo Graziani in reorganizing the armed forces of the Saló Republic.

26. *Il Regime Fascista* (Cremona), June 3, 1937.

27. Gen. Pariani to Farinacci, June 22, 1937, ID–NA, T586, 026447–026448.

28. Farinacci to Pariani, July 7, 1937, ibid., 033890–033892.

29. Farinacci to Mussolini, July 7, 1937, ibid., 033880–033894.

vari, and their adherents. Being ignored, however, had never deterred Farinacci. Ten days later, apparently, he submitted to Mussolini a lengthy report on the preparedness of the Italian navy.[30] It is quite clear from the available documents that sycophancy was not among Farinacci's many grievous faults as a man or as a political leader. Throughout his association with Mussolini, Farinacci was perhaps the only Fascist hierarch who invariably "told it like it was." No blame can attach to him for Mussolini's preference for hearing and believing what he probably wanted to hear and believe from the start. A good example of this was the long, detailed report Farinacci submitted to the *Duce* after an inspection tour of Italian East Africa. No aspect of Italian military, political, and economic activities in the newly conquered empire was overlooked, and criticism of the many glaring sins of omission and commission was merciless.[31] The report, however, was not even acknowledged, and when Farinacci again went to Addis Ababa in the fall of 1939 in connection with some legal matters, he found the situation had deteriorated further. Again he forwarded to Mussolini a scathing indictment of the colonial administration and of the many commercial enterprises which had been formed for the exploitation of Ethiopia. Farinacci went into great detail, accusing regional governors of spending millions on lavish headquarters palaces while the Italian immigrant workers lived in squalor and describing newly built highways already becoming impassable because of defective materials and workmanship. "We can hope to gain much from the Empire," Farinacci concluded, "but we must lose no time and not waste uselessly more billions. . . . I felt it to be my duty to tell my Chief the truth, unpleasant as it may be . . . [because] those who keep telling you that things are going well are guilty of the blackest treason against your gigantic and sleepless efforts."[32]

If Farinacci was undoubtedly truthful in his open criticism of official mismanagement, there seems to be little or no justification for his moralistic attitude against profiteering, for it was just

30. Memo to file of Mussolini's private secretary, July 17, 1937, *ibid.*, 034218. The actual report is not in the archives.

31. Farinacci to Mussolini April 24, 1938, *ibid.*, 033990–033994.

32. Farinacci to Mussolini, December 21, 1939, *ibid.*, 026384–026393.

during this period, in 1939, that a new and larger building was erected in the center of Cremona to house the offices and presses of Farinacci's newspaper. The upper floors contained nine luxury apartments, of which Farinacci occupied one, his daughter and her family another, and the rest were profitably rented. The following year, furthermore, Farinacci bought several plots of land in Rome, and on one of them built a villa which became his residence in the capital.[33]

Life was indeed good to Farinacci now; and even if Mussolini paid little or no heed to his warnings and advice, the *ras* of Cremona was well rewarded for his recent displays of respect and discipline, being appointed president of the Legislative Committee on the Judiciary in the Chamber of Fasci and Corporations which early in 1939 replaced the elective Chamber of Deputies. A few months later, he was made a lieutenant general in the Fascist militia.

In 1939, he was also allowed to publish a three-volume *History of the Fascist Revolution*, which showed him as sole author even though it had been almost completely ghost-written by his chief editorial assistant, Paolo Pantaleo.[34] The book was promptly ruled required reading in all Italian secondary schools, besides being translated and printed in Germany.

Aside from Farinacci's relative reconciliation with the establishment, Mussolini's benevolence may have been due to the fact that, almost from the beginning of the Rome-Berlin Axis in October 1936, a close relationship was established between Farinacci and some members of the Nazi leadership, notably Goebbels and Himmler. Mussolini, especially in the early stages of his *entente* with Hitler, may have looked upon Farinacci as a potentially useful tool in dealing with the Germans. The basis for

33. According to an investigation made in May 1941 by the fiscal authorities, it seems probable that in these purchases Farinacci was guilty of fraud by declaring fictitiously low valuations to escape taxes. (ID–NA, T586, 034049–034057.) The *ras* of Cremona wrote indignantly to Mussolini, protesting his innocence, and once more no further action was taken in the matter. (Farinacci to Mussolini, June 8, 1941, *ibid.*, 026431–026434.)

34. Angelo Tasca, *Nascita e avvento del Fascismo: L'Italia dal 1918 al 1922*, 2nd edition (Florence: La Nuova Italia, 1963), p. 65.

an understanding of Farinacci's fascination with the Nazi regime, in turn, may be sought in the fact that Hitler and his followers had succeeded in pursuing and establishing in Germany the kind of revolution which Farinacci had always envisaged as the true goal of Fascism, and which in Italy, to his great chagrin, Mussolini and his closer collaborators had allowed to degenerate into a bourgeois dictatorship. As early as 1932, in fact, Farinacci had interviewed the Nazi writer Alfred Rosenberg during the latter's trip to Italy. He also had editorially admired the National Socialist political program, even though he had expressed the opinion that, in view of its latest poor showing at the polls, National Socialism was "on the way to oblivion."[35] As it became clear that Hitler and his cohorts were instead solidly in control of Germany and embarked on an aggressively expansionist course, the *ras* of Cremona commented favorably on the various phases and milestones in the rise of the Third Reich. After his political comeback, then, Farinacci took a decidedly pro-German stance, and he was appointed to lead the Italian delegation to the Nazi Party Congress at Nuremberg in September 1937. It was there that he first met Adolf Hitler and the major Nazi leaders, who were obviously impressed by Farinacci's intransigent Fascist faith and by his admiration for the Nazi version of Fascism. The following May, therefore, Farinacci received the Grand Cross of the Order of the German Eagle, and until the fall of Fascism he was considered the most pro-German of the Fascist leaders. He was, in Goebbels's words, "not only an energetic man, but also a pronounced friend of Germany" upon whom the Nazi leaders could "depend blindly."[36]

It was not surprising, therefore, that Farinacci, who had applauded the conclusion of the Pact of Steel in May 1939, as well as Hitler's invasion of Poland on September 1, was bitterly disappointed by Mussolini's decision to keep Italy out of the conflict. Consquently he expressed his views in a letter to Mussolini couched in terms reminiscent of his former virulence. Pointing out that the Italian press was generally assuming an anti-German

35. *Il Regime Fascista* (Cremona), December 13, 1932.
36. *The Goebbels Diaries, 1942–1943*, edited and translated by Louis P. Lochner (Garden City, N.Y.: Doubleday and Company, Inc., 1948), p. 403.

tone, Farinacci noted that ❪many officials feel authorized to consider our agreement with Germany a dead issue . . . a feeling which receives support from indiscretions about the many open secrets, such as the disagreement between Galeazzo Ciano and von Ribbentrop at Salzburg,[37] the commitment not to go to war before 1942, the instructions given by the [Propaganda] Ministry to the journalists . . . not to play up German successes. Naturally, all the fellow travelers and philodemocratic cretins who were opposed to the Axis policy, that policy which helped us to conquer the Empire, win in Spain, and occupy Albania, are beginning to say that if ever we intervene we will do so on the side of France against Germany.[38]

Going on to state his conviction that Germany's victory would be fast and decisive, Farinacci reminded Mussolini that "in five years, eating potatoes and black bread, the Germans created an army which is nothing short of a steamroller," and asked the Duce urgently to allow the press to take a more friendly attitude towards Germany, to find a way, at least unofficially, "to let it be known that . . . the Italians do not intend to follow the path of treason and violate their commitments" and to"punish severely those who talk against the Axis policy." The ras of Cremona then accused the Italian General Staff of ineptitude bordering on treason for having allowed the armed forces to find themselves grievously unprepared, listing many examples of shortages and neglect. He concluded with an appeal to Mussolini to give clear directives so that the situation could be rectified.[39] A month later, having been given by Mussolini a copy of an optimistic report prepared by War Undersecretary Pariani on the status of the

37. At a meeting in Salzburg in August 1939, von Ribbentrop informed Ciano of Hitler's decision to make war on Poland soon, causing a violent reaction on the part of the Italian Foreign Minister who, in signing the Pact of Steel the previous May, had stressed its peaceful and defensive aims, while Mussolini himself had sent Hitler a personal message on May 30 making it clear that Italy could not be ready for war for several years. (See Mario Toscano, *The Diplomatic Origins of the Pact of Steel*, revised edition [Baltimore, Md.: The Johns Hopkins Press, 1967] pp. 376–380, 400–401.)

38. Farinacci to Mussolini, September 13, 1939, ID–NA, T586, 031590–031602.

39. *Ibid.*

Italian army, Farinacci forwarded to the Duce a critique, probably ghost-written by Colonel Canevari, which sharply dissected the report and spotlighted many alleged inaccuracies and faulty judgments.[40]

It was in this mood of belligerent dissatisfaction and criticism that Farinacci attended the meeting of the Grand Council of December 7, 1939. The highest consultative body of Fascism, which in fact would not meet again until the final crisis on July 24, 1943, had been called in session to ratify, in the name of the party, the decision taken on the previous September 1 by the Council of Ministers of withholding military support from the German ally. According to the recollection of a participant, Giacomo Acerbo, Farinacci insistently but vainly proposed that Italy enter the war on the side of Germany. When none of the other members supported him, the *ras* of Cremona pointed out that Hitler might repeat the accusation of treason launched against Italy by Emperor Franz Joseph of Austria in 1915, but he was sharply rebuked by Mussolini himself.[41]

After this reprimand, Farinacci reverted to a great extent to his earlier role as censor of Fascism, starting with a nationwide radio speech on January 3, 1940, in which he exhumed all the intransigent Fascist tenets of the *squadrista* period, evoked the uncompromising tactics which had permitted Fascism to survive the Matteotti crisis in 1924, and called on all Fascists to display similar fortitude in the coming struggles.[42] A month later, he called Mussolini's attention to a meeting at Rhodes of the three surviving Quadrumvirs, Emilio De Bono, Cesare Maria De Vecchi, and Italo Balbo, hinting at the possibility of a conspiracy between them and pointing out that Lybia, of which Balbo was governor, "would be, in case of war, the most crucial spot in the Empire."[43] Typically, Farinacci saw treason and traitors everywhere, whether it be among the generals who had allowed Italian military pre-

40. Farinacci to Mussolini, October 14, 1939, *ibid.*, 031603–031625.

41. Quoted in Gianfranco Bianchi, 25 *Luglio, crollo di un regime* (Rome: U. Mursia & Co., 1963), p. 111.

42. *Il Regime Fascista* (Cremona), January 4, 1940.

43. Farinacci to Mussolini, February 5, 1940, ID–NA, T586, 033930–033932.

paredness to fall behind schedule, or among the Vatican prelates, some of whom, after Italy's attack on prostrated France in June 1940, he accused of espionage and of anti-Italian activities.[44]

By the spring of 1940, in any event, Mussolini had decided to bring Italy into the conflict on the side of Germany. Disregarding the warnings of his military advisers about Italy's lack of armaments and supplies, as well as warnings of political figures such as Grandi and Ciano about the Italian population's opposition to war and to Germany, Mussolini had clearly expressed this determination in a memorandum submitted to King Victor Emmanuel on March 31. According to Mussolini, the monarch had characterized the memorandum as "geometrically logical."[45] On May 29, speaking to Marshals Pietro Badoglio and Rodolfo Graziani, Mussolini stated that he had originally intended to wait to declare war against France and Great Britain until the spring of 1941, that after the fall of Norway and Denmark he had advanced the date to September 1940, but that in view of the situation created by the surrender of Belgium and the German conquest of Holland and France, he now considered any day after June 5 suitable for the start of hostilities.[46] There seems little reason, therefore, to doubt the truth of the cynical remark attributed to Mussolini at this time, namely, that he needed a few thousand dead Italian soldiers to obtain a seat at the Peace Conference. In vain were appeals directed to the Italian dictator by the Pope, by Winston Churchill, by U.S. President Franklin Roosevelt. Having obtained the king's consent to plunge the country into war, Mussolini decided not to consult the Grand Council, knowing that Quadrumvirs Balbo, De Bono, and De Vecchi were against going to war on the side of Germany and fearing that other members might join them in their opposition.

On June 10, in what was to be his last appearance on the Palazzo Venezia balcony, Benito Mussolini harangued a hastily assembled and definitely unenthusiastic crowd and announced

44. Farinacci to Mussolini's private secretary, June 18, 1940, ibid., 033938–033940.

45. Emilio Canevari, La guerra italiana—retroscena della disfatta (Rome: Tosi Editore, 1949), II, 33.

46. Ibid., p. 34.

to the world that Italy had "taken the field against the western reactionary and plutocratic democracies," because "a people of 45 million souls [could] not be really free unless it [had] free access to the oceans."[47]

Despite the obvious reference to Gibraltar and Suez, the first assault took place on the French Alpine frontier, which Italian troops crossed on June 17, 1940, the very day when France's newly formed Petain government sued for an armistice. During the following week, hampered by severe snowstorms, the Italian armies made little progress; and on June 25, an armistice between France and Italy was signed in Rome. Nothing had really been gained by this campaign, and consequently Mussolini sought other theatres of operations, unleashing attacks against Egypt on September 16 and against Greece on October 28.

Farinacci, at the outset, had naturally applauded Mussolini's decisions, in which he saw a vindication of his own earlier warmongering posture.

When, however, a few months later, the Italian divisions in Greece met with unexpected and serious reversals, Farinacci lost no time in making odious comparisons between the ineptitude of the Italian commanders and the efficiency of the German General Staff, bewailing the resulting injury to national pride, going into great detail as to Marshal Badoglio's anti-Fascist and defeatist views, and calling on Mussolini to dismiss the marshal from the top command.[48] Farinacci followed up with a pointed article in which he repeated the accusations against Badoglio, heaping on him the blame for the Greek debacle.[49] Badoglio, incensed, handed Mussolini his resignation, expecting that it would be rejected, and demanded from Farinacci a retraction which the ras of Cremona vehemently refused to grant. This time, Farinacci's pressure was successful; on December 4, Mussolini accepted Badoglio's resignation and replaced him as Chief of the General Staff with General Ugo Cavallero, who was not only an ardent Fascist but also a long-time friend and confidant of Farinacci.

47. Tamaro, Venti anni di storia, III, 413–414.
48. Farinacci to Mussolini, November 9, 1940, ID–NA, T586, 026411–026417.
49. Il Regime Fascista (Cremona), November 23, 1940.

As the Italian armies suffered further reverses in Greece and in North Africa, Farinacci's warmongering made him increasingly unpopular among the Italian population, as he himself acknowledged to Grandi. "As you know," he wrote, "you and I are right now the chosen scapegoats of public opinion. I am said to be working and scheming to put Italy under German rule, while you would try to organize a government . . . acceptable to those . . . who would gladly see the disappearance of Mussolini."[50] It was probably to bolster his popularity among the militia ranks and to keep himself in the limelight that, at the beginning of 1941, Farinacci asked to be recalled to active duty despite his mutilation.[51] The Duce granted his request by naming him Inspector General of the militia contingents in Albania.

Arriving in the theater of operations on January 21, 1941, Farinacci lost no time in touring the various headquarters. By January 27, he had forwarded to Mussolini a report in which he spotlighted the logistic and strategic errors of the Italian high command and recommended drastic changes.[52] During the following months, Farinacci continued to visit troops at the front, endeavoring to bolster their morale and to foster co-operation with the Germans, who had meanwhile intervened to save the military situation in the Balkans.

Shortly after his return to Italy at the end of April 1941, Farinacci reported in person to Mussolini. He found the Duce furious because of the overbearing attitude taken by Marshal Erwin Rommel in North Africa and by the German commanders in the Balkans. "In Albania too," Galeazzo Ciano noted in his diary under the date of May 3, 1941, "the feeling of resentment toward our Allies is marked. The Duce realizes this and gives Farinacci the responsibility of drafting a letter to Hitler to call attention to what has happened. He has chosen Farinacci because he has no official position and because there are no possible doubts as to his pro-German feelings."[53] The May 5 entry, how-

50. Farinacci to Grandi, January 2, 1941, ID–NA, T586, 033928–033929.

51. Farinacci to Mussolini, January 10, 1941, ibid., 031659.

52. Farinacci to Mussolini, January 27, 1941, ibid., 026435–026438.

53. The Ciano Diaries, edited by Hugh Gibson (Garden City, N.Y.: Doubleday & Co., Inc., 1946), p. 346.

ever, begins: "Farinacci's letter to Hitler is not sent. The Duce is satisfied with the Fuehrer's explanation, and, on the other hand, does not like the introduction of Farinacci's letter, which vaunted his own exploits in Albania."[54] Unabashed, Farinacci continued to criticize the organization of the Italian armed forces, at the same time extolling German bravery and efficiency. One of his articles, praising the clean-up efforts of General Ugo Cavallero, was so openly critical of the War Ministry[55] that Mussolini ordered the newspaper's issue confiscated "because it contained inaccurate and damaging statements on such a delicate subject as the organization of the army."[56]

By this time, Mussolini obviously regretted having brought Farinacci back into the limelight; but in view of the friendship between the *ras* of Cremona and the Nazi hierarchy, it was impossible to put him again completely in the background. His activities, of course, continued to be watched, and the police reports of this period are particularly full of derogatory remarks about Farinacci, a clear indication that the *ras* was again in disfavor with Mussolini. Special efforts were also made to play down his influence in Germany. When he went there in 1941 to visit Hanover and Berlin, the Italian Ambassador Dino Alfieri, clearly on instructions from Mussolini, prevailed on the Hanover authorities not to bestow on Farinacci honorary citizenship as originally planned. Furthermore, having made direct arrangements with Goebbels during a meeting with him in Venice, Farinacci expected to visit Hitler's headquarters and make an appearance before the Italian troops on the Russian front. But again, much to his displeasure, the Ambassador's intervention prevented the realization of both plans. "Farinacci's visit to Berlin has gone well," wrote Alfieri to Mussolini in the last of his daily reports about Farinacci, "in spite of the strong enmity between the two ministries (Foreign Affairs and Propaganda). Farinacci, who is very smart, has quickly grasped the situation, and he left with

54. *Ibid.*, p. 347.
55. *Il Regime Fascista* (Cremona), July 31, 1941.
56. Mussolini to prefect of Cremona, August 1, 1941, ID–NA, T586, 031663.

Weiszker [sic]—whom he had been invited to visit—a violin for Ribbentrop (who is said to be a great music lover)."[57]

Other proofs of Mussolini's displeasure with Farinacci can be found in the Duce's refusal to approve the award to Farinacci of a medal for bravery during his stint in Albania, in spite of Farinacci's insistent solicitations[58] and General Cavallero's glowing citation,[59] and in the fact that no more missions were entrusted to him.

As usual, however, Farinacci was undeterred by snubs or rebuffs, and he continued from time to time to importune Mussolini with denunciations of treason on the part of Italian generals in all theatres of operations and with reports (well grounded, in this case) of inadequate supply and equipment of the Italian troops on the Russian front.[60]

As 1942 progressed and it became increasingly clear that any hopes of victory for the Axis forces were fast receding, Farinacci's extravagant eulogies of the Germans and his intransigent attacks against the Catholic Church made him more than ever an object of hate and contempt for the Italian population. When, for instance, he published an editorial assailing war profiteers,[61] the widespread public reaction reported by the police was that the ras of Cremona should practice what he preached.[62] Farinacci, on the other hand, was either unaware of his growing unpopularity, or he felt that resort to violent tactics would always see him and his followers through. He continued to flaunt his intransigence while depriving himself and his mistress, Gianna Pederzini, of no comforts in his new villa on the Via Nomentana in Rome, for which he obtained a permanent police guard.[63]

57. Dino Alfieri to Mussolini, September 5, 8, 10, 1941, ibid., 031666–031668.

58. Farinacci to Mussolini, December 14, 1941 and January 20, 1942, ibid., 033983–033984 and 033978.

59. Ibid., 033979–033981.

60. Memos to file of Mussolini's private secretary, November 9 and 14, 1941, ibid., 034082–034083.

61. Il Regime Fascista (Cremona), July 29, 1942.

62. Police Report of July 30, 1942, ID–NA, T586, 033991.

63. Questore of Rome to Police Station of Monte Sacro Precinct, May 12, 1942, ibid., 034065.

By the fall of 1942, morale was at a low ebb, both in Germany and in Italy. "The most pessimistic report which has lately come to us from Germany," confided Ciano to his diary on September 25, "is from young Consul Farinacci. What would his father think?"[64] A month later, however, the *ras* of Cremona himself expressed his dissatisfaction and concern, as Ciano wrote on October 23: "I see Farinacci and Bottai. They are both exasperated by the internal situation, which is aggravated by the absolute inadequacy of the Party."[65] Shortly after the American landings in North Africa on November 8, 1942, which in Mussolini's own view marked the beginning of the end for the Axis powers,[66] Farinacci sent Mussolini one of his bulky epistles, complaining bitterly of the failure of the party leadership to punish with utmost severity the manifestations of defeatism and disenchantment with Fascism which were becoming more and more common among party cadres as well as with the population in general.[67] He followed this up the next day with a sharp attack against the Ministry of Finance, which had been unable to prevent a run on the banks, immediately after the North African landings, and which allegedly mismanaged the Italian economy.[68] In the columns of his newspaper, Farinacci also redoubled his efforts to bolster the population's morale, efforts which back-fired, however, when he found no better way to exhort the Italian people to bear up under Allied bombing than to urge them to take example from German civilians.[69] At the same time, he began to hold increasingly frequent meetings with Fascist chieftains, government

64. *The Ciano Diaries*, p. 523. Farinacci's son, Franco, who was at this time Italian Consul in Hamburg, was notoriously not on good terms with his father. In the fall of 1943, in fact, he managed to reach southern Italy and fought in the Italian Corps of Liberation after Italy's declaration of co-belligerence with the Allies in 1944.

65. *Ibid.*, p. 533.

66. Benito Mussolini, *The Fall of Mussolini*, edited by Max Ascoli, translated by Frances Frenaye (New York: Farrar, Straus and Company, 1948), p. 5.

67. Farinacci to Mussolini, November 19, 1942, IN–DA, T586 031551–031556.

68. Farinacci to Mussolini, November 20, 1942, *ibid.*, 026674–026667.

69. *Il Regime Fascista* (Cremona), November 27, 1942.

officials, and high army officers, whom he invited almost daily to lunch or to dine at his new Rome villa, in an obvious effort to strengthen and widen the ranks of his adherents. "His Excellency Farinacci," wrote a police informer reporting on a luncheon attended by the secretaries of the Fascist Federations of Milan and Bergamo, "continues in his work aimed at increasing the number of his followers, in order to put into effect his plan to replace the Duce at the right moment."[70] There is no documentary evidence that such was indeed Farinacci's intention, but his actions immediately before and after the fall of Mussolini justify the assumption that the thought may have crossed his mind, especially as he also sought to strengthen his German contacts.

In February of 1943, Farinacci visited Danzig and other cities in northern Germany. On his return, he wrote Hitler, thanking him for having been allowed "to express to the people of the great Reich the solidarity of Italian Fascism, which more than ever feels bound by the Pact of Steel which we wanted and defended, and which today we honor before the whole world with our blood and common sacrifice." "Wherever I had occasion to speak," Farinacci continued, "I assured the German comrades that Italy, faithful to the orders of Mussolini, will follow her ally to the end, and, if necessary, down to the ultimate consequence." The rest of this long letter was a diatribe against the Vatican and the Catholic clergy in general, whom he accused of being opposed to Fascism and Nazism. It ended with the suggestion that Hitler take steps to counteract the political influences of the "Jewish International which, with the complicity of Catholics, Protestants, and Communists, poses as the paladin of world Christian civilization."[71]

There, in that single sentence, is proof that there was no redeeming feature in Farinacci's character and personality. For, as will be seen presently, the *ras* of Cremona was not only the embodiment of totalitarian violence and arrogance, but he was also, through political opportunism rather than conviction, the Julius Streicher of Italy.

---

70. Police Report of December 10, 1942, ID–NA, T586, 031559–031560.
71. Farinacci to Hitler, March 4, 1943, *ibid.*, 026678–026683.

XIII

RACISM
COMES
TO ITALY

ANTI-SEMITISM, traditionally either an official policy or an admitted prejudice in countries with large numbers of Jews among their population, was never a problem in Italy, where the proportion of Jews to non-Jews was generally never more than about one per thousand.[1] There was, in some government and military circles, a veiled tendency toward anti-Semitism, so that, for instance, Jews were de facto excluded from the diplomatic career. But anti-Semitic postures and utterances were generally restricted, especially after the founding of the Kingdom of Italy in 1861 and the take-over of Rome from the Pope in 1870, to certain elements of the Catholic Church, primarily the Jesuits—who from time to time expounded on the "deicide guilt" of the Jews—and to a small proportion of writers and journalists who either flaunted their anti-Semitism out of deep conviction—as did Farinacci's friend and associate Giovanni Preziosi—or who used anti-Semitic slurs as part of their slander techniques. This Farinacci himself occasionally did.

Farinacci's sneering reference to some of Mussolini's collaborators as "the Jewish courtiers" in 1924, during the Matteotti affair, has been noted. The fact that *Aventine* leaders Claudio Treves and Emanuele Modigliani were Jewish was often odiously

1. According to the Census of Jews made in August 1938, there were at that time in Italy 47,252 Jews, of whom 12,799 were living in Rome, 10,219 in Milan, 6,085 in Trieste, 4,060 in Turin, and slightly more than 2,000 each in Leghorn, Florence, Genoa, and Venice, so that 90% of the total was concentrated in eight principal cities, with virtually none to be found in southern Italy. Total Italian population at the time was about 43 million.

underscored in the columns of Farinacci's *Cremona Nuova* and later in those of *Il Regime Fascista*. The Jewish faith of banker Giuseppe Toeplitz was also scornfully pointed out in Farinacci's campaign against the *Banca Commerciale*, in 1925. When Freemasonary came under attack and repression in 1926, the substantial number of Jews belonging to the disbanded fraternal organizations gave rise to a recrudescence of anti-Semitic language on the part of Farinacci and other sectarian Fascist journalists.

It was only after the rise to power of National Socialism in Germany, however, that Farinacci began to attack all Jews as a group, harping on such well-worn themes as the "Jewish international conspiracy," the "Jewish Bolshevik leadership," and the "Jewish financial octopus." "It is only natural," wrote Farinacci in one of his articles, "that we Fascist Catholics should demand that the smallest possible number of Jews be in positions affecting the life of the nation, and that [those few] be chosen taking into account [Jewish] numerical proportion."[2] Here again is an instance of Farinacci anticipating Mussolini, who had only recently stated that "Anti-Semitism does not exist in Italy . . . Italian Jews have always been good citizens, and have fought bravely as soldiers."[3] Mussolini would not resort to a policy of open anti-Semitism for several years more.[4] Not content with advocating the introduction in Italy of the *numerus clausus* as an official policy, Farinacci took up the cudgels again less than a year later, when a Piedmontese anti-Fascist was arrested while trying to cross the Swiss border into Italy with some anti-Fascist pamph-

2. *Il Regime Fascista* (Cremona), May 26, 1933.
3. Emil Ludwig, *Colloqui con Mussolini* (Milan: A. Mondadori Editore, 1932), pp. 71–73.
4. Despite his official pronouncements at this time, there are indications that Mussolini was always *in pectore* hostile to Jews. When the Royal Academy was created in 1929, for instance, its members did not include a single Jew. Mathematician Tullio Levi-Civita, a collaborator of Einstein and a member of the Papal *Accademia dei Lincei*, was repeatedly proposed for nomination to the Academy, but Mussolini, who had the last word on this as on all other state matters, always refused. Another Jew, famed archeologist Alessandro Della Seta, was also many times mentioned for the Royal Academy, but was never appointed to it.

lets. As a result, fifteen men and women were arrested, most of them Jewish and known for their Zionist activities.[5] To the initial attacks of *Il Regime Fascista* and other Fascist newspapers, many Italian Jews reacted with letters and public declarations of loyalty. But Farinacci brutally answered: "You must choose sides. Anyone who declares himself in favor of Zionism has no right to hold public posts or lucrative employment in our country."[6] Again he wrote, a few days later: "If Italian Jews want to prevent the growth in Italy of anti-Semitism . . . they must follow the advice we have given them: they must choose sides '"[7] The year 1934, however, marked the temporary alignment of Farinacci with Mussolini's directives, and it was not surprising, therefore, to see the worsened Italo-German relations reflected in some sharp attacks by Farinacci's newspaper against the Nazi racist doctrines.[8] In any event, Fascist Italy's relationship with Nazi Germany improved during the Ethiopian adventure and the subsequent intervention in Spain. This improvement, coupled with the alleged responsibility of the "Jewish International" for the League of Nations' application of "sanctions" against Italy after the attack on Ethiopia[9] and with the support of "Jewish Bolshevism" for the Spanish loyalists, soon brought Mussolini around to an unofficial but nonetheless clear policy of anti-Semitism, which predictably found its principal mouthpiece in Farinacci.

At the beginning of 1936, Farinacci's newspaper announced the irreducible opposition of Fascist Italy to "international Judaism."[10] In September, only a few weeks before the first trip to Germany of Foreign Minister Galeazzo Ciano and the subsequent

5. Renzo De Felice, *Storia degli ebrei italiani sotto il fascismo* (Turin: Giulio Einaudi, Editore, 1962), pp. 169–170.
6. *Il Regime Fascista* (Cremona), April 10, 1934.
7. *Ibid.*, April 18, 1934.
8. *Ibid.*, January 31, 1935.
9. Speaking in 1941 to his favorite biographer, Mussolini stated: "I first realized the hostility of Jews against Fascism when we began to put into effect our emergency economic policy [as a result of the 'sanctions']." (De Begnac, *Palazzo Venezia*, p. 643.)
10. *Il Regime Fascista* (Cremona) February 5, 1936.

speech of Mussolini announcing to the world the newly forged Rome-Berlin Axis,[11] Farinacci wrote: (We must admit that in Italy the Jews, who are a negligible minority, while they have schemed in a thousand ways to grab high posts in finance, banking, the schools, have not opposed our revolutionary march. Why, however, do they do nothing concrete to split their responsibility from that of all the other Jews of the world, the ones whose only goal is the triumph of the Jewish international? Why have they not yet risen against their coreligionists who are . . . destroyers of churches, sowers of hate, evil killers of christians?

We are sure that many will proclaim: we are Jewish Fascists. Not enough! They must prove with facts to be first Fascists, and then Jews.[12]

There were in fact loud protestations of loyalty on the part of Jewish leaders and organizations, but Farinacci retorted that "there is at Geneva a World Jewish Parliament where Italy too is well represented."[13] He declared: (It is true that the Duce has not felt till now the need to make distinctions of race or religion in Italy, but it is indeed some Italian Jews who make it a point to set themselves apart from Italians of other faiths, by participating in campaigns supporting Zionism and in meetings of the international Jewish Congress.[14]

As has been aptly stated, "[Farinacci's] 'till now' was the first signal of the impending racial campaign."[15]

By this time, Vita Italiana, the rabidly anti-Semitic monthly founded originally by Giovanni Preziosi, was being printed at Cremona. It represented itself openly as the "Monthly Magazine of Il Regime Fascista," with Farinacci holding a financial interest in it. In the columns of both his newspaper and the magazine, Farinacci continued his libelous campaign. Mussolini, through his Minister of Press and Propaganda, urged him to concentrate his

11. Elizabeth Wiskemann, The Rome-Berlin Axis, new revised edition (London: Collins Clear-Type Press, 1966), pp. 88–89.

12. Il Regime Fascista (Cremona), September 12, 1936.

13. Ibid., September 20, 1936.

14. Ibid., September 24, 1936.

15. De Felice, Storia degli ebrei italiani, p. 243.

attacks on "the eternal collusion between Jews and Communism."[16]

April of 1937 saw the publication of a book entitled *Gli Ebrei in Italia* (The Jews in Italy), in which the author, the well-known Fascist writer Paolo Orano, a good friend of both Farinacci and Preziosi, rehashed all the old anti-Semitic myths about Jews and concluded that it was incompatible for Jews to be good Italians and good Fascists. Public reaction was clamorous but twofold. On one hand, the Fascist press, led not only by Farinacci's publications but also by Mussolini's own newspaper, *Il Popolo d'Italia*, reviewed the book in glowing terms and gave its poisonous contents wide circulation. On the other hand, the mass of the Italian people, intrinsically immune to anti-Semitism and well acquainted through personal experience with the true background and behavior of Italian Jews, remained incredulous and unmoved by the Fascist anti-Semitic propaganda.

It was undoubtedly because of this failure of public opinion to react favorably to the anti-Semitic clamors of the Fascist press, and of the resulting need to arouse stronger public feeling or to find a different approach to the same ends, that no official measures against Jews were taken at this time. The Fascist leadership, however, having decided to embark on a definite anti-Semitic policy, probably intended by Mussolini as a pledge to Hitler,[17] took several steps in that direction. During the first half of September 1937, Farinacci led a fifty-man delegation to the Nazi Congress at Nuremberg to absorb racist doctrines and techniques at the fountainhead. At the end of the same month, Mussolini went to Germany on his first state visit, and, while in Munich on September 29 and 30, he discussed racial problems thoroughly with Hitler.[18] In October, Preziosi and Farinacci published a new edition of that hoary paragon of apocryphal anti-Semitic literature, *The Protocols of the Wise Men of Zion*. Mussolini and Ciano could thus well boast on November 6 to Nazi Foreign

16. Dino Alfieri to Farinacci, October 6, 1936, ID–NA, T586, 026569.
17. Tamaro, *Venti anni*, II, 305–306.
18. De Felice, *Storia degli ebrei italiani*, p. 291.

Minister Joachim von Ribbentrop, in Rome for the signature of the Anti-Comintern Pact: "We are pushing with great decision and growing intensity an anti-Semitic campaign, under the guidance of a man quite popular in Italy, the Hon. Farinacci."[19]

With the beginning of 1938, in fact, Farinacci's attacks against the Jews became an almost daily feature, repeating ad nauseam the old slurs and accusations, warning against the "dangers" created by the immigration into Italy of Jews escaping from Central Europe, and manufacturing tendentious statistics. In an article which singled out Trieste as a stronghold of Judaism, for instance, Farinacci wrote: ([Making due proportions between the 250,000 Catholics and the 4,000 Jews, we must conclude that the latter hold nine-tenths (900 to 1000) of the posts which control the intellectual, economic, financial, and syndical life of Trieste. But Trieste is not an exception. We have exact data about other Italian cities. And at the proper time we will publish names, surnames, and details of positions held.[20]

With the release on February 16 of a communique from the Foreign Ministry which denied foreign rumors of the imminent introduction in Italy of an anti-Semitic policy but reserved to the Fascist government the right "to control the activities of recent Jewish immigrants and to take steps so that the part played by Jews in the life of the nation should not be disproportionate to their numerical importance,"[21] the handwriting on the wall was unmistakably clear. Farinacci lost no time in again openly advocating that the quota system in all aspects of public and professional life become official government policy.[22]

Official action, however, still lagged, while the Fascist leadership searched for a way to sweeten or somehow disguise for the Italian people the distasteful pill of anti-Semitism. The Nazi hierarchy found Fascist hesitation irritating but was well aware of Farinacci's efforts, as shown by a letter written by a Nazi jour-

19. Galeazzo Ciano, L'Europa verso la catastrofe (Milan: A. Mondadori Editore, 1948), p. 220.

20. Il Regime Fascista (Cremona), January 24, 1938.

21. Informazione Diplomatica No. 14. Quoted in De Felice, Storia degli Ebrei Italiani, pp. 321–322.

22. Il Regime Fascista (Cremona), March 8, 1938.

nalist, Ludwig Pauler, to congratulate the *ras* of Cremona for the award of the Grand Cross of the German Eagle. "Even if the official policy of Fascism, for tactical reasons, has not yet solved the Jewish problem with the desired clarity," wrote Pauler, "nevertheless Germany will never forget your heroic struggle against the world plague of Judaism."[23] In any event, possibly as a result of further talks between Mussolini and Hitler during the latter's state visit to Italy at the beginning of May, the Fascist government finally decided that the best way to align Italy with Germany's racist policy was to camouflage anti-Semitism with pseudoscientific racial theories. Accordingly, on July 14, 1938, the press throughout Italy published a so-called "Manifesto of Racist Scientists," unsigned, but said to have been drafted by a number of Italian university professors,[24] postulating the existence of a "pure Italian race . . . of Aryan origin" and flatly stating that "It [was] time for Italians to proclaim themselves frankly racist." Jews were only mentioned in one of the ten paragraphs of the "Manifesto," under the heading: "Jews do not belong to the Italian race," followed by the mild (if untrue) accusation that Jews were the only people who had never become "assimilated" in Italy.[25] The Fascist press, however, led by Farinacci and Preziosi, immediately began to acclaim the "Manifesto," concentrating on its implicit anti-Semitic sense and multiplying its attacks on Jews and Jewish institutions. The Catholic press, instead, taking its cue from the semiofficial *L'Osservatore Romano*, was generally unfavorable in its editorial comments on the new racist attitude of the Fascist government, provoking sharp attacks by Farinacci against *L'Osservatore* and the Vatican hierarchy.[26]

And when the Pope himself, concerned especially with the

23. L. Pauler to Farinacci, May 8, 1938, ICSA, Farinacci Fund, 1938 Correspondence, Folder 71.

24. On July 26, a communique of the Secretary General of the Fascist Party, lavishing praise on the "Manifesto," identified its authors as nine virtually unknown instructors and assistant professors of anthropology and zoology at various Italian universities, and Professor Nicola Pende, holder of the chair of pathology at the University of Rome.

25. *Manifesto degli Scienziati Razzisti*, reproduced as Document 15 in De Felice, *Storia degli ebrei italiani*, pp. 611–612.

26. *Il Regime Fascista* (Cremona), July 19, 21, 22, 24, 1938.

consequences of a Nazi-like type of racial policy on mixed marriages, made a speech on July 28, pointing out that racism was alien to Italian traditions and deploring Italy's imitation of Germany, Farinacci wrote Mussolini: ❮*While I try ably to attack the Vatican's behavior, I keep in touch with some cardinals . . . who make no mistery of their opposition to . . . the speechifying of . . . the senile Pope.*

From some of them I have learned that . . . the [Vatican] Secretariat of State has made the speech even sharper . . . and that the Pope has been told that the Fascist racial campaign will bring about divorce, the annulment of marriages between Jews and Catholics, and the sterilization of Jews. . . .

This morning the Pope has asked to be shown pages 72 to 75 of Ludwig's book on Mussolini.[27] *I don't have the book handy, but I think it would be wise to prevent an eventual attack.*

The right-thinking circles in the Vatican feel sure that a few governmental measures (e.g., confiscation of Catholic newspapers or diocesan or parish bulletins) would cause a prompt backtracking, because Monsignor Pizzardo [Secretary of State of the Holy See] has terror of a clash between party members and the members of Azione Cattolica.

Dear President, is it true that the Pope's mother is [sic] a Jewess? If it were true, we could really have fun.[28]

While the ras of Cremona concentrated his barbs on the clerical opposition, the Foreign Ministry issued another communique which dispelled any possible doubt about the real aim of the racist "Manifesto." "To discriminate," the communique stated, "does not mean to persecute. . . . The Fascist government has no plans to persecute Jews as such. . . . There are 44,000 Jews in Italy . . . a proportion of one Jew for every thousand inhabitants. It is clear that from now on the participation of Jews to the over-all life of the state must be, and it will be, limited to that percentage."[29] The same day, Farinacci sent Mussolini a brief

27. Ludwig, *Colloqui con Mussolini.*
28. Farinacci to Mussolini, August 3, 1938, ID–NA, T586, 033900–033908.
29. *Informazione Diplomatica No. 18,* August 5, 1938. Quoted in De Felice, *Storia degli ebrei italiani,* p. 327.

note which plainly showed his anti-Semitic furor to be sparked by cynicism rather than misguided conviction. "To tell you the truth," wrote Farinacci, "the racial question, from an anthropological standpoint, has never convinced me. The problem is an exquisitely political one. . . . On the philosophical and scientific level, one can always argue; but in the field of politics, when there are reasons of state involved, one acts to win."[30]

Another example of Farinacci's cynicism and Mussolini's opportunism is contained in a letter written by the *ras* of Cremona to the *Duce* more than a month before the appearance of the "Manifesto." Having been urgently advised by the Ministry of Press and Propaganda to fire a Jewish secretary employed in his law office in Milan, Farinacci wrote Mussolini that the woman was a long-time Fascist and that he would prefer to ease her out later, adding: "I am fully agreeable even to exterminate all Jews, but before we reach the humble and innocent ones we must hit the powerful ones, especially those who are still in sensitive posts." The original letter in Mussolini's files, incidentally, bears a handwritten notation by his private secretary with the *Duce's* decision: "Tell Farinacci that it's in his interest to unload Miss Foa. If this leaked out in Germany, he would undoubtedly greatly lose face. One cannot pose as the paladin of anti-Semitism and keep a Jewish secretary hanging around. Let him give her even fifty thousand lire and get rid of her."[31]

All through the summer, Farinacci kept up a barrage of editorials in which he insisted that anti-Semitism was a basic tenet of Catholicism from earliest times, and that Fascist Italy was now simply putting into practice the commandments of church doctrine. To support his thesis, the *ras* of Cremona reprinted ample excerpts from a series of articles published by the Jesuit magazine *Civiltá Cattolica* in 1890, and went as far as entitling one of his printed harangues "A Lesson of Catholicism to the Catholics."[32]

At the beginning of September 1938, the Council of Ministers decreed the first official measures of the racial campaign in Italy,

30. Farinacci to Mussolini, August 5, 1938, ID–NA, T586, 033909.
31. Farinacci to Mussolini, June 6, 1938, *ibid.*, 034066–034068.
32. *Il Regime Fascista* (Cremona), August 28, 1938.

namely, the expulsion of all foreign Jews, including those who had acquired Italian citizenship since 1919, and the exclusion of Jewish children from all public schools. The shocked and generally disapproving reaction of the Italian people to this decree caused Farinacci to lead the Fascist press in denouncing such "bourgeois sentimentality," threateningly equating "Jew-pitying" with anti-Fascism, and sneering at "honorary Jews."[33] A month later, the Grand Council met to review the development of the racial campaign to date and to formulate a legislative program which would give formal approval to the virtual exclusion of Jews from the economic and professional life of the country, as well as from any cultural and political activities. While some of the participants, notably Balbo and Federzoni, tried to soften the proposed measures, Farinacci took the most intransigent position and argued vehemently against any relaxation in the concerted attack against the civil rights and the very existence of Italian Jews, backed in his uncompromising stance by Mussolini and the quasi totality of Grand Council members.

Acting once more as the standard bearer of sectarian intransigence, as in the days of the Matteotti crisis and of his party Secretaryship, the *ras* of Cremona then took the lead in neutralizing the growing opposition of church authorities to the new racist laws. On November 7, before the Fascist Cultural Institute in Milan, Farinacci gave a lecture entitled "The Church and the Jews," which was widely reported and acclaimed by the Fascist press. It gave the Vatican a clear warning not to interfere with the Fascist racial campaign. After quoting abundantly from the Scriptures and the Patristic literature, calling particularly on St. Jerome, St. John Chrisostom, and St. Paul to support his thesis that the Catholic Church was the original source and supporter of anti-Semitism, Farinacci bluntly asked: *What has happened to make the official Church become today philo-Semitic rather than anti-Semitic? . . . Why do communists, freemasons, democrats, all the avowed enemies of the Church, praise her today and offer to help her? To use her against Fascism. . . . We would hate to see the Church abandon its basic educational mission, in order*

33. *Ibid.*, September 7, 1938.

to interfere in political questions which are the exclusive province of Fascism.[34]

The threat was obvious, and the Vatican chose henceforth to refrain from public attacks on anti-Semitism. Not content, the *ras* of Cremona pressured a number of churchmen to endorse the Fascist racist policies, hoping in this way to influence the still unconvinced Catholic masses. The Bishop of Cremona, in a pastoral letter on January 6, 1939, supported the right of the state "to limit or suppress the economic, social, and moral influence of the Jews, when noxious to the tranquillity and welfare of the nation."[35] And the noted philosopher and *Rettore* of the Sacred Heart University in Milan, Father Agostino Gemelli, took the occasion of a celebration at the University of Bologna on January 9 to launch into a tirade against "the deicide people" worthy of the most rabid Nazi propagandist.[36]

Farinacci's relationship with the Nazi hierarchy became closer and closer as a result of his part in Italy's racial campaign, and his newspaper published anti-Semitic articles by some of them, notably Julius Streicher.[37]

During most of 1939, while the new Italian laws and regulations against Jews were being put into effect by the various ministries and government agencies, Farinacci and the other Fascist journalists continued to play up the old anti-Semitic themes. Soon after Hitler's invasion of Poland, they trumpeted a new one, the "war guilt" of the Jews.[38] On February 20, 1940, in fact, Farinacci lec-

34. R. Farinacci, *La Chiesa e gli ebrei* (Cremona: Societa Editoriale Cremona Nuova, 1938), p. 15.

35. *Il Regime Fascista* (Cremona), January 7, 1939.

36. *Ibid.*, January 10, 1939. Two months later, incidentally, Farinacci suggested to Mussolini that Father Gemelli be made a member of the Italian Academy, pointing out that Gemelli, besides being well liked by the German leadership, was in line to be made a Cardinal, and that "it would be very useful to have a man truly our own near the successor of St. Peter." (Farinacci to Mussolini, March 19, 1939, ID–NA, T586, 033912.)

37. *Il Regime Fascista* (Cremona) January 21, 1939.

38. In 1942, the Ministry of Popular Culture (formerly Press and Propaganda) issued a pamphlet which claimed the war had been decided at Cap d'Antibes on August 3, 1939, by Chief Rabbi Stephen Wise of New York together with Henry Morgenthau and Bernard Baruch. (De Felice, *Storia degli ebrei italiani*, p. 435.)

tured at the University of Naples on the theme, "How Israel Prepared the War." Shortly after Mussolini decided that he needed a few Italian casualties to gain a seat at the peace table and brought Italy into the war on the side of Germany, the *ras* of Cremona editorialized: "It's time to make an end of the Jews! They, who never again will have the honor to bear arms, today are only preoccupied with making money by the shovelful at the expense of the fighters and of embattled Italy. Can we go on like this? These are the traitors of the Motherland, the eternal agitators, those who have caused the war knowing they would not have to fight!"[39]

As Italy's involvement in the war became unexpectedly wider and deeper, Farinacci's attention was drawn more and more to military matters, about which he relentlessly goaded Mussolini —by letter, through his newspaper, and in person. The Jews, however, were not entirely forgotten, as Farinacci found time to instigate a rash of anti-Semitic incidents at Trieste in October 1941[40] and to resume briefly his attacks against the Vatican when the Catholic Church took a more decided stand against the Nazi atrocities in the summer of 1942.[41] Nor was he above complaining to Mussolini of such petty matters as the relative comfort in which "confined" foreign Jews were allowed to live at Asti, in Piedmont, receiving from the *Duce's* office the assurance that those Jews would soon be removed to concentration camps in central Italy.[42]

No account of Farinacci's part in the Fascist racial campaign would be complete without mention of one of its most sordid aspects. The racial laws provided for the exemption from restrictive measures of Jews falling within certain categories, such as the families of war dead or decorated war veterans, Catholic offspring of mixed marriages, or individuals who had "especially well merited from the nation," a purposely vague definition which opened the way for special treatment of those who could pay for

39. *Il Regime Fascista* (Cremona), May 25, 1940.
40. De Felice, *Storia degli ebrei italiani*, p. 453–454.
41. Police Report of August 11, 1942, ID–NA, T586, 033990.
42. Mussolini's private secretary to Farinacci, January 2, 1943, *ibid.*, 031575.

it. A lucrative traffic soon sprang up, as some of the functionaries charged with certifying the exemption began extorting large sums from both Jews who were entitled to it and others who were not but nevertheless tried to obtain it. A number of high Fascist officeholders also joined the racket, using their influence to obtain the exemption for those Jews who were willing and able to buy it. It was widely rumored that Farinacci was among them, and while no documentary evidence has been found to prove the charge, some support for it can be based not only on his notorious greed and lack of scruples, but also on the reports of Mussolini's usually accurate police informers.[43]

Whether or not Farinacci was involved in the exemption traffic, he was undoubtedly responsible to a large extent for the adoption in Italy of the racist measures which eventually led to the deportation and death of many thousands of Jews after the Germans had taken control in Italy, following the fall of Mussolini and the signing of an armistice between the new Badoglio government and the Allies in September 1943. No more trenchant judgment can be expressed than that contained in the words of an Italian Jew who was both an oldtime anti-Fascist and a survivor of a German concentration camp. "Never as now," he wrote, describing the horrors of life in the Nazi hell, "did I see so clearly the close connection between my first sentence and the first beatings which had humiliated my person in 1923 during the first Fascist reaction, and the horrible world in which I now found myself. Consciously or not, the Fascists had been the originators of the death camps."[44]

43. Police Report of January 29, 1942, *ibid.*, 033994.
44. Piero Caleffi, *Si fa presto a dire fame* (Milan: Ediz. Avanti, 1955), p. 135.

XIV

THE
INGLORIOUS
END

THE MILITARY crisis which confronted Fascist Italy in the spring of 1943 was matched by a political crisis of equal magnitude. While the Axis armies in North Africa retreated under the combined onslaught of British and American forces and Allied bombing of the Italian peninsula increased in frequency and intensity, the Italian people grew increasingly tired and disaffected with "Mussolini's war" and with Fascism itself. A number of military and government leaders as well as members of the royal family became convinced of the need to detach Italy from the suicidal German alliance and to put an end to Mussolini's dictatorship.[1]

Farinacci, both through personal observation and from his many contacts in Fascist circles throughout Italy, was well aware of the situation. When strikes broke out among industrial workers in Piedmont and Lombardy at the end of March, he wrote Mussolini complaining that the authorities had been "incapable either to prevent or to suppress [the strikes]" and had thus "destroyed the principle of the authority of the Regime." "The few arrests don't count," he continued. "We should have had the courage to make an example of a few." The *ras* of Cremona then urged the *Duce* to concentrate on weeding out some men in high places and not to take always upon himself the responsibility for other

---

1. The definitive account of the many and involved maneuvers which culminated in Mussolini's fall from power on July 25, 1943, will be found in Gianfranco Bianchi's *25 Luglio—crollo di un regime* (Milan: V. Mursia & Co., 1966).

people's mistakes. As usual, Farinacci blamed the army leadership for the disastrous conduct of the war[2] and accused the few
survivors of the Italian Expeditionary Corps repatriated from
Russia of spreading anti-German propaganda. As to the party,
Farinacci defined it as "absent and impotent." He added: *The
unbelievable is happening. Everywhere, on the streetcars, in the
cafés, in the theatres and cinemas, in the [air-raid] shelters, on the
trains, people criticize and inveigh against the regime, and slander
not just this or that hierarch, but the Duce himself. And the
worst is that the police keep quiet, as if they could no longer take
action. . . . We are going towards bad times which the military
events might render even more anguished. We must defend our
revolution with all our strength. . . . Therefore, dear President,
why don't you call [a meeting of] the Grand Council? Let each
one unburden himself, and tell you what he thinks. And let each
one be heartened by your words.*[3]

The crisis facing Fascism at this time was indeed as serious as
the one caused by the Matteotti Affair, and, just as in 1924, an
intransigent Farinacci was trying to spur a hesitant Mussolini into
repressive action. Twenty years of uncontested hegemony, however, had rendered Mussolini impervious to reasoned suggestion.
Only two months before, the Italian dictator had effected the
last of his frequent "changings of the guard" by suddenly re-
shuffling all but one of the cabinet members in his government,[4]
and he took no notice of Farinacci's urging. The ras of Cremona,
in any event, was not limiting his pressure to Mussolini; he was
counting more and more on the Germans to help Italy out of its
predicament, without realizing that Hitler's Reich, stunned by
the defeat of Stalingrad, struggling to contain the mounting
Russian offensive, and reeling under the blows of Allied bombing,
was in no condition to render effective help to its Axis partner.

2. At the end of January, Farinacci's friend, Marshal Ugo Cavallero, had
been replaced as Chief of the General Staff by General Vittorio Ambrosio.

3. Farinacci to Mussolini, April 1, 1943, ID–NA, T586, 026542–026545.

4. Most notably, Galeazzo Ciano had been removed after seven years from
the Foreign Ministry and sent as Ambassador to the Vatican, while Dino
Grandi had left the Ministry of Justice but had continued as president of the
Chamber of Fasci and Corporations.

Shortly after Mussolini's return from his meeting with Hitler at Klessheim in April 1943, a police informer reported that Farinacci was boasting to his friends that he had caused the dismissal of the anti-Nazi Chief of Police Carmine Senise and the introduction of several yet unannounced reforms. The report added: ([*The Duce, according to Farinacci, has received orders from Hitler to make these changes, because he, Farinacci, has sent to Germany a report on the Italian situation showing the need for immediate action. He says that the best thing would be to change Mussolini too, and that he had pointed this out in Germany, but for the moment the Germans, although in agreement with his ideas, did not see fit to arrive at this extreme solution. But if things do not change in the direction wanted by Farinacci, the Germans will demand the removal of Mussolini.*][5]

In view of Hitler's insistence, six months later, on placing Mussolini at the head of the puppet Italian Social Republic, it would appear that Farinacci's claims of having the Fuehrer's ear were largely unfounded. Yet there is no doubt that he had close ties with Himmler and Goebbels, and that, at least as far as the Nazi Propaganda Minister was concerned, an eventual succession of Farinacci to Mussolini was not only possible, but would have been welcome.[6] In Rome, Farinacci was a frequent visitor to the German embassy, where he passed on to the Ambassador, Hans Georg von Mackensen, information and suggestions for transmittal to Berlin, as he also did with Himmler's confidential deputy in Rome, the deceptively suave SS Colonel Eugen Dollmann.[7]

5. Police Report of April 16, 1943, ID–NA, T586, 031577.
6. *The Goebbels Diaries*, p. 403.
7. That Farinacci's cynicism extended to his feelings towards the Nazi leaders emerges from a note he sent to Mussolini in April 1943, referring to his own letter to Hitler of a month earlier in which he had attacked the Vatican and pointing out that "one of the men in Berlin who urged me most strongly to express those thoughts to the Fuehrer was Baron Weisstzecker (sic), Foreign Undersecretary, who now has been sent as ambassador of the Reich to the Holy See." "As I told you before," Farinacci concluded, "I am more than ever convinced that the Germans are strong in war, but in politics they are still novices." (Farinacci to Mussolini, April 23, 1943, ID–NA, T586, 031581.)

As each passing week brought more catastrophic news from all war fronts, Italian morale sank to unprecedented depths. With the final debacle of the Axis forces in North Africa and the fall of Tunis early in May, the fact that the war was hopelessly lost and that Italy itself would be the next Allied objective became clear to every Italian, from the king to the man in the streets. To every Italian, that is, except Mussolini and Farinacci. The sixty-year-old dictator, spending every spare moment in the love nest he had built for pretty Claretta Petacci, placed great faith in Hitler's increasingly frequent assurances of the imminent deployment of secret weapons which would turn the tide. He was, furthermore, blindly confident that his "lucky star" which had brought him through adversities and perils to the pinnacle of power would never abandon him. Farinacci, more realistically, saw that Italy was on the verge of collapse. Nevertheless, even Farinacci felt that victory could still be achieved by a truly revolutionary Fascist government which he would help organize and perhaps lead. To gain victory, however, Farinacci believed that the armed forces of both Italy and Germany must be placed under a unified German command, blame for the war should be shifted from Fascism to the monarchy and the king's generals, and the Italian people must be convinced or coerced into making a superhuman effort to work and fight for victory.

Farinacci made no mystery of his views in his frequent contacts with the German Ambassador, Hans von Mackensen, and with SS Colonel Eugen Dollmann. At the same time, he continued to press Mussolini both with criticism of his military policies and with pessimistic reports on the internal situation.[8]

One month after the fall of Tunis, the island fortress of Pantelleria surrendered after a heavy Allied bombardment, but Mussolini, meeting with Farinacci a few days later, declared himself convinced that if the Allies next attacked Sicily they would be bloodily repulsed by the Italian defenders. To Farinacci's remark that General Ambrosio and the rest of the General Staff were "a gang of traitors," the Duce is said to have replied: "Dear

8. Memorandum by Mussolini's private secretary, May 18, 1943, *ibid.*, 031585.

Farinacci, you always see treason everywhere. You should really get cured of this persecution mania."[9]

Undaunted as ever, on June 27 Farinacci went again to see Mussolini and informed him of the existence of a conspiracy led by Grandi, Badoglio, Ambrosio, and the Minister of the Royal Household, Duke Pietro Acquarone, but once more the *Duce* dismissed him as a perennial alarmist. Nor did Farinacci's warning carry more weight with Germany's Ambassador Mackensen, to whom he reported the same information two days later, adding the names of Bottai and Federzoni to the roster of conspirators.[10]

As the fateful month of July opened, the internal Italian situation became, in the words of no less well informed a person than the chief of Mussolini's secret police, "verging on desperation, because of food shortages and hardships due to bombing of the cities . . . while it [was] increasingly rumored that . . . great political changes would bring the war to an end."[11]

On July 10, 1943, with a massive amphibious operation, the Allies landed in Sicily. At once it was apparent that, in spite of Mussolini's boast that they would be stopped "at the water's edge," the island would be quickly overrun and the Italian peninsula itself would soon be invaded.

At this point, Farinacci made his move. As one of several Fascist leaders chosen by Party Secretary Carlo Scorza to address rallies in various cities in a last-ditch effort to bolster popular morale, the *ras* of Cremona asked that a meeting of all selected speakers be held at party headquarters in Rome to discuss strategy. When the Fascist leaders met, Farinacci launched instead into a

9. Bianchi, *25 Luglio*, p. 367. A series of articles published in Rome's daily *Il Tempo* after the war's end was said to have been drawn from a diary attributed to Farinacci. While the diary was subsequently held to be apocryphal, a number of independently confirmed details show that the author of the diary was well acquainted with Farinacci and that many parts of the diary's contents can be accepted as reliable accounts.

10. *Ibid.*, p. 371. As later events were to prove, instead, and as conclusively detailed in Bianchi's masterful reconstruction, Farinacci's information was substantially correct, for it was the coalition of Grandi and Bottai with the General Staff and the Royal Household which brought about the crisis of the Fascist regime and the fall of Mussolini on July 25.

11. Guido Leto, *OVRA, fascismo, antifascismo* (Bologna: Cappelli, 1952), p. 89.

harangue against Mussolini's vacillation and misrule, concluding: "Mussolini must be set aside."[12] After a heated discussion in which most of the participants concurred in the view that Mussolini should be asked to consult and co-operate with the rest of the Fascist leadership, it was decided to seek an interview with the *Duce*. That very afternoon, the same Fascist chieftains and several others hastily summoned met again at party headquarters, and Farinacci again took the lead in reviewing the critical situation, assailing the General Staff and proposing to ask that the Grand Council be convened, "so that each one could take his share of responsibility." The group, from which Grandi and Ciano were conspicuously absent, then proceeded to Mussolini's study in the *Palazzo Venezia*. Farinacci, at Mussolini's request, took the floor. As he himself related the encounter, *(I began by stressing that the situation was serious because we could not trust the General Staff and especially General Ambrosio, who a few days earlier had told me that the war was lost and that in fifteen days we would have to "close up shop." I asked Mussolini to allow all those present to share with him full responsibility, and therefore to summon the Grand Council.*[13]

Mussolini interrupted Farinacci often with sarcastic remarks. After Farinacci, other leaders spoke in the same vein but in a less aggressive tone. After former Party Secretary Giuriati had calmly stated that a series of reforms was imperative "because the institutions do not function and the laws are not obeyed," Mussolini announced his decision: "Very well, I shall summon the Grand Council. In the enemy camp they will say that it meets to discuss surrender, but I will summon it!"[14] Thus, by forcing Mussolini to convene the Grand Council, Farinacci unwittingly laid the stage for Dino Grandi's own move, while he himself performed on that stage "as a clumsy bear."[15]

12. Giuseppe Bottai, *Vent'anni e un giorno* (Milan: Garzanti, 1949), p. 277.
13. Farinacci's deposition at the 1944 Verona trial of Ciano, De Bono, and the other Grand Council members accused of treason. Quoted in Domenico Mayer, *La Verità sul processo di Verona* (Milan: Arnoldo Mondadori Editore, 1945), pp. 62–63.
14. Bianchi, *25 Luglio*, pp. 401–402.
15. *The Goebbels Diaries*, p. 407.

During the next few days, Mussolini held a brief and inconclusive meeting with Hitler near Feltre, in the Dolomites, while Grandi and King Victor Emmanuel's emissaries perfected their plan of action. Farinacci again vainly tried to warn Mussolini. According to the *Duce* himself, in fact, Farinacci on the morning of July 21 showed him a note from Marshal Ugo Cavallero which said: "Dear Farinacci, be ever more alert. Grandi and company are conspiring to overthrow Mussolini, but in any event their game will be upset because the Royal Household, with Acquarone, is making its own plans and will fool them all." In reply, Mussolini told Farinacci: *Keep calm and don't worry. I tell you that with regard to the king I'm perfectly safe. I saw him just this morning, and he, with an affectionate, almost fatherly smile, patted me on the shoulder and said: "Dear Mussolini, these are bad times for you, but I want you to know that I am your friend. And if, to make an absurd hypothesis, everybody should forsake you, I would be the last one to do so. I know how much Italy and the dynasty owe you."*[16]

Furious at Mussolini's attitude, Farinacci that same afternoon went to the German embassy to try to alert Ambassador Mackensen to the impending crisis. There, he was so outspoken against Mussolini that the naive Nazi diplomat asked him to abstain from further criticism of the *Duce*. Farinacci, however, who was accompanied by Marshal Cavallero, went right on inveighing against Mussolini's methods of government and insistently asking that the Germans take the initiative in setting up a unified military command. The German ambassador apparently formed the erroneous opinion that Farinacci commanded a strong following among Grand Council members and would be able to force Mussolini to effect military and administrative reforms which would facilitate German control of Italy. Consequently, he did not fully transmit to Berlin Farinacci's sense of urgency.[17]

The urgency nevertheless existed, for while the Fascist bosses were confronting Mussolini on July 16, a joint statement by

16. *Mussolini*, XXXI, 204.

17. Mackensen's telegram, July 22, 1943, German Foreign Office Archives. Quoted in F. W. Deakin, *The Brutal Friendship* (Garden City, N.Y.: Doubleday & Company, Inc., 1966), pp. 422–424.

American President Franklin Roosevelt and British Prime Minister Winston Churchill had warned Italy that it must overthrow Fascism in order to survive. While Hitler and Mussolini were meeting at Feltre on July 19, Rome had been bombed for the first time by the American Air Force. And while Mussolini was reassuring Farinacci and Ambassador Mackensen was discounting his warning, on July 21, 1943, Allied troops had entered Sicily's largest city, Palermo. In this charged atmosphere, Dino Grandi, who had been conferring at Bologna with Federzoni, returned to Rome and began canvassing the other members of the Grand Council to obtain their support for the resolution which he proposed to present at the Grand Council meeting called for the afternoon of Saturday, July 24.

The resolution, whose approval by a large majority in the Grand Council was to prove the catalyst in Mussolini's downfall, had been carefully drafted by Grandi and Giuseppe Bottai. The gist of it was that King Victor Emmanuel, who on June 10, 1940, had delegated to Mussolini the supreme command of the Italian armed forces, should be asked by Mussolini "to resume, together with the active command of all land, sea, and air forces, in accordance with Article 5 of the Constitution, that supreme initiative of decision belonging to him."[18] Clothed in the most flowery and deferential language, the resolution in fact opened the door to a move by the king to bring about drastic changes in the government along strictly constitutional lines, including, as later actually happened, the dismissal of Mussolini. At this stage, however, it was presented merely as a patriotic reaffirmation of faith in the Motherland and its institutions, which could galvanize the nation and help bring it out of its present predicament. All through the day of July 23, Grandi met, now with one, now with another of the Grand Council members, either in his office at the Chamber of Fasci and Corporations, or at party headquarters a few blocks away. In the office of Carlo Scorza, Secretary General of the party, in the presence of Ciano, Bottai, and Federzoni, Grandi discussed at length his proposed resolution, endeavoring to convince the Secretary General to support it. At

18. Bianchi, 25 Luglio, pp. 481–482.

one point, Farinacci arrived, and was shown the text with assurances that its sole purpose was to reorganize the country politically and militarily in order to continue the war. The *ras* of Cremona was ostensibly in agreement, but, as Bottai noted in his diary, the conspirators "all sensed the meaning and limits of his approval, which was understood as solidarity *jusqu'au bout* with the Germans."[19]

Since the previous day, Farinacci, in fact, had drafted, together with Marshal Cavallero, a resolution of his own, in which he suggested that King Victor Emmanuel resume only the military command and that the government structure be revamped. He insisted that it was "the sacred duty of all Italians to defend to the very end the holy soil of the Motherland, standing fast in keeping faith to the alliance concluded [with Germany]."[20] On the basis of subsequent events, it is not difficult to deduce that Farinacci's plan was to force the dismissal of Ambrosio, to have him replaced as Chief of the General Staff by Cavallero, and to convince Mussolini that he should dismiss or arrest the dissident oligarchs and form an intransigently pro-German government which would include Farinacci, possibly as Minister of the Interior. In any event, Farinacci did not inform his colleagues of his intention to present his own resolution. Grandi's resolution had by now been circulated to most of the Grand Council members, and was even brought by Party Secretary Scorza to Mussolini who "read it through and returned it with the comment that it was cowardly and quite inadmissible."[21] Scorza, at Mussolini's suggestion, then drafted a third resolution, which simply expressed the conviction that "the new situation created by war events must be met with new means and methods" and called for "reforms and innovations in the government, in the High Command, in the domestic life of the country, which . . . could bring victory to the united efforts of the Italian people."[22]

The next afternoon, as the Grand Council members began to arrive in the great council hall of the *Palazzo Venezia*, Grandi

19. Bottai, Vent 'anni, p. 291.
20. Bianchi, 25 Luglio, pp. 499–500.
21. Mussolini, The Fall of Mussolini, p. 53.
22. Bianchi, 25 Luglio, pp. 517–518.

collected their signatures to a typed copy of his resolution. Soon he had the expected total of nineteen, which included those of the two surviving *Quadrumvirs*, Emilio De Bono and Cesare De Vecchi, of Mussolini's son-in-law, Galeazzo Ciano, and even that of the Fascist ambassador to Berlin, Dino Alfieri. Farinacci moved from group to group of the assembled Fascist leaders, trying to sway some of them into subscribing to his version, but he met with no success. Promptly at five o'clock, Mussolini entered, accompanied by Party Secretary Scorza, and the curtain rose on the last act of the Fascist regime.[23]

For over an hour, the *Duce*, who appeared to be tired and suffering from his chronic duodenal ulcers, spoke monotonously, without any trace of his usual charismatic oratorical style. He reviewed the circumstances of his assumption of the supreme command and the highlights of three years of war, going into great detail. While he rambled on, Scorza and Farinacci, who were well aware of the political and military reforms which Mussolini had promised them he would announce at the Grand Council,[24] looked at each other, wondering if the *Duce* would reassert his leadership and take control of the situation.

But Mussolini droned on in a seemingly interminable lecture, without mentioning any reforms. At last, he concluded: "This is the time to close ranks and accept full responsibility. . . . I believe the Grand Council must face this problem: war or peace? Resistance or capitulation? . . . From this Grand Council should come the word which the nation awaits." But he added: *"Pacta sunt servanda"* (Alliances must be respected).[25]

The next speaker, Emilio De Bono, merely questioned the physical capability of the armed forces to continue the war. Farinacci took this opportunity to request that General Ambrosio

23. Carlo Scorza was the last Secretary General of the Fascist party. At war's end, he managed to escape to Argentina and has just recently published what is perhaps the most accurate and detailed account of the last Grand Council meeting: Carlo Scorza, *La notte del Gran Consiglio* (Milan: Aldo Palazzi Editore, 1968).

24. Scorza (p. 37) quotes Farinacci as having told him the day before: "If he [Mussolini] doesn't announce the reforms at the Grand Council, he ruins us."

25. Bianchi, *25 Luglio*, pp. 466–475; Scorza, *La notte*, pp. 25–37.

be called in to report on this matter. The *ras* of Cremona obviously then intended to assail Ambrosio and demand that he be replaced by Cavallero; Mussolini, however, said Ambrosio's presence was not necessary, as he himself was fully conversant with all military details. After the other *Quadrumvir*, De Vecchi, had briefly stressed the need of reforms within the party and within the army, Farinacci's old "revisionist" enemy, Giuseppe Bottai, analyzed the causes of the present fracture between the people and the party and of the disastrous course of the war and concluded: "The war has gone badly because Mussolini, having isolated himself from us, has been unable either to command or to make himself obeyed by the old world of the General Staff."[26]

With Bottai having first raised the question of Mussolini's responsibility for the political and military debacle facing Italy, it was then the turn of Grandi. In a long but brilliant oratorical display, Grandi was lavish in his praise of the *Duce* and his protestations of undying loyalty and devotion, stressing, when expounding on his motion and its avowed purpose, that it was "unfair that the monarchy, after having accepted from the regime all it could offer . . . should keep aside now that the fortunes of war are unfavorable, as if to indicate, by its attitude, a denial of responsibility." Grandi went on to suggest that the sole purpose of his proposed resolution was to give Mussolini an opportunity to approach Victor Emmanuel with the request that the King act as a unifying force for all Italians, this request coming from the supreme body of Fascism rather than from the *Duce* himself. Grandi then attacked the dictatorship which, he stressed, was not to be blamed on Mussolini, but on the bosses and bureaucrats who had acted without the *Duce's* knowledge and had often nullified the beneficial laws he had enacted. "We are all tied to the same rock, O *Duce* " Grandi cried histrionically at the end. "Listen to this cry of anguish surging from the hearts of your faithful; give us the chance to share with you all responsibilities; to win together, or sink together!"[27]

Ciano's speech, which followed, was a calm and concise review

26. Scorza, *La notte*, pp. 43–45.
27. *Ibid.*, pp. 46–63.

of the relationship between Italy and Germany, aimed at proving that Hitler's regime had been time and again unfair and overbearing towards its Axis partner. After citing specific instances of bad faith in Germany's dealings with Italy, the former Foreign Minister discussed the alternatives posed by Mussolini at the conclusion of his speech and plainly stated that if Mussolini and the Grand Council should decide to put an end to Italy's suffering by withdrawing from the war, no one could accuse Italy of having betrayed Germany, for the opposite was in fact true.[28]

Next on the list of those who had asked for the floor was Farinacci, who had been fidgeting and doodling while awaiting his turn. Now he rose to address the Grand Council. First, Farinacci read his own proposed resolution: (The Grand Council of Fascism, considering the domestic and international situation and the [Italian] political and military conduct towards the [Rome-Berlin] Axis:

turns its proud and grateful thoughts to the heroic Italian and [German] allied armed forces, united in a common effort and sacrifice for the defense of European civilization, to the population of invaded Sicily, more than ever dear to the hearts of all other Italians, to the working masses of industry and agriculture, who with their labors strengthen the embattled Motherland, to the Blackshirts and Fascists of all Italy who close their ranks with unchanged faith in the Regime;

affirms that it is the sacred duty of all Italians to defend to the very end the holy soil of the Motherland, standing fast in keeping faith to the alliance concluded [with Germany];

declares that to that end it is necessary and urgent that all functions of the state revert completely to their original form, assigning to the king, to the Grand Council, to the government, to the Parliament, to the party, and to the corporations, the tasks and the responsibilities fixed by our Constitution and by our laws;

invites the head of the government to ask His Majesty the King, to whom the hearts of the entire nation turn with faithful

28. Ibid., pp. 65–71.

confidence, to consent to resume the active command of all the armed forces, thus showing to the whole world that the people fight as one at his orders, for the deliverance and the dignity of Italy.[29]

Farinacci then launched into a broad review of the situation of the party and of the Fascist regime, describing as causes of the present disaster the aloof attitude of Mussolini towards the rank and file, the traitorous behavior of the General Staff, the animosity of the population towards the German ally, and the internal defeatism. "The party," he shouted, "has no longer any close relationship with the nation, not because the nation has left us, but because we ourselves, by the policy of appointments from above, have broken our bonds with the people." Turning to address Mussolini himself, the ras of Cremona continued: We did many beautiful things together, but then we let them go to hell or even destroyed them ourselves, because we pitted ourselves one against the other. It was the rule, after each "changing of the guard," that the new arrival should throw out all that his predecessor had accomplished. And this happened largely by your will, O Duce, or because of a secret political plan of yours.

Let me once more open my soul to you with the usual frankness. . . . You see, Duce, you never trusted us oldtimers completely. One by one, you sent us away from you, when all we asked was to serve our country and the Regime. . . . While you, unfortunately, have often appointed the least prepared, the least intelligent, and even the least faithful, just because they always answered "yes" to your every word, and swore—but falsely—that you were infallible.[30]

Having made clear his feelings towards Mussolini, Farinacci renewed his assurances of loyalty and solidarity if the Duce would only put into effect "new measures which would show that a lesson [had] been learned and that different criteria [would] be used in the future." Then Farinacci turned his ire on the leaders of the "peace" faction, Grandi, Bottai, and Ciano, pointing out that he alone was justified in moving criticisms to the party and

29. Bianchi, 25 Luglio, p. 500.
30. Scorza, p. 73.

even to Mussolini, without fear of being accused of having waited for a crisis in order to speak up. "The Duce is my witness," Farinacci said, while Mussolini nodded in agreement, ([that I never concealed from him my thoughts, orally or in writing. But I cannot repress my amazement in hearing the same criticisms spoken tonight by those who have remained without interruption in high posts in the government, the same ones who never said a word in my support when my attitude of mother-in-law of the Regime, as Mussolini jokingly called me, was being openly chastised in the highest circles.[31]

The *ras* of Cremona then replied to Ciano's indictment of the Germans with an impassioned defense of the Nazi alliance and with a scornful reproach of the attacks now being made on it by the same Fascist leaders who for many years had pretended to admire and support Hitler's regime. "While German soldiers are dying alongside our own," Farinacci shouted, "this spectacle of slander and contempt for Germany is far from decent!" Regaining his calm, Farinacci continued, pointing out that, with the Germans, it was necessary to speak frankly, as men and not as courtiers, and he hinted at the possible consequences of a withdrawal from the German alliance.

"In any event," he concluded, "whatever may be the decision which the Grand Council will take tonight, namely, 'resistance or peace,' I ask that you weigh carefully all the grave events which will derive from choosing either one or the other horn of the terrible dilemma posed by the *Duce*."[32] At the end of Farinacci's harangue, Mussolini spoke again to refute briefly some of the accusations made against the party and the regime by the first speakers. After a brief adjournment, the meeting, which had already lasted almost eight hours, was resumed to allow the remaining members to express their views. When each speaker except Scorza had addressed the assembly, Mussolini took the floor and analyzed the alternatives presented by the Grandi resolution. He pointed out that the king might refuse to resume the supreme command and that, in that case, a deep fracture

31. *Ibid.*, p. 75.
32. *Ibid.*, p. 76.

would be created between the Grand Council and the Crown. If, on the other hand, the king accepted the offer, he would almost certainly also want to resume political control. "Gentlemen," the Duce said, "be careful. The Grandi resolution may put the survival of the regime in jeopardy. Have you considered this possibility? Gentlemen, have you considered that a delicate personal problem will also arise, that of my own future? I am a man of sixty, and I know how these things go."[33]

Mussolini then had Scorza present his resolution, and the Party Secretary spoke at length, vainly trying to sway some of the supporters of the Grandi text into switching sides. Finally, however, the ailing dictator inexplicably called for a vote on the various resolutions in order of submission, and when the one offered by Grandi was approved by nineteen members, with seven others voting against it and one abstaining, Mussolini rose and, facing the assembled Fascist chieftains for the last time, said calmly: "Gentlemen, with this resolution you have opened the crisis of the regime. The meeting is ended."[34]

Farinacci, when his name was called, refused to cast his ballot, stating that he reserved his vote for his own resolution. As he would later testify, *I wanted my resolution to be on record so that my proposal should be known, and above all so that it would be known that I, as a man of honor and as a faithful Fascist, could not renege twenty years of revolution and could not forget that we were bound to Germany by an unequivocal alliance, meaning that the war had to continue down to the extreme sacrifice. . . . I must add that even though the Grand Council meeting had ended in that manner, I was not in the least worried: Mussolini, forty-eight hours earlier, had assured me that the king would keep faith with him and would never forsake him. A coup d'etat, therefore, lacking the king's will, could not take place.*[35]

So unworried, in fact, was Farinacci, that, after a few hours' rest on that fateful Sunday morning in 1943, he drove to the beach at Ostia and spent most of the day relaxing there.

Mussolini, instead, having sought an audience with the king for

33. *Ibid.*, p. 124.
34. *Ibid.*, p. 149.
35. Farinacci's deposition at 1944 Verona Trial, Mayer, *La Verità*, p. 65.

that same afternoon, walked unsuspecting into the trap which Grandi and the wily monarch had prepared for him. Forced by the king to resign and immediately replaced as head of the government by Marshal Badoglio, the Duce was placed in protective custody and spirited away under police guard in a waiting ambulance, while orders were issued for the arrest of a number of Fascist hierarchs, first among them Farinacci.

As luck would have it, however, when Badoglio's police, now led by the reinstated Chief Senise, went to arrest Farinacci, the ras of Cremona had flown the coop. According to Scorza, when Mussolini failed to return from the audience at the royal villa, the Party Secretary became concerned and began to suspect foul play. Scorza then decided to gather a few of the Fascist bosses who had not voted against Mussolini the night before, and he called first Farinacci. Farinacci, who had just returned from the seashore, balked at first, claiming that he was already undressed, but Scorza insisted and sent a car to bring him to party headquarters.[36]

By the time Farinacci arrived, however, Scorza had left in search of Mussolini, and the ras of Cremona, after expressing concern and the opinion that some plot was under way, walked to the Foreign Ministry around the corner in search of news.[37] There he found Undersecretary Giuseppe Bastianini and Dino Alfieri, Ambassador to Germany, who informed him that something ominous was under way, because all telephone communications between the ministries and the various Fascist headquarters had been interrupted. With an air of unconcern, Farinacci quipped: "I guess I'll get myself a deck of cards; it's the only way to kill time in jail," and left.[38] Once alone, however, Farinacci lost no time in rushing to the German embassy. There, after being recognized and jostled by the crowd which was already milling in front of the embassy gate, he was admitted into the presence of German Ambassador Hans von Mackensen and SS Col. Eugen Dollmann. Colonel Dollmann, who had been informed

36. Scorza, La notte, pp. 204–205.
37. Bianchi, 25 Luglio, p. 597.
38. Dino Alfieri, Dictators Face to Face (London and New York: Elek, 1954), p. 301.

of the previous night's events, had just been thinking of Farinacci as a man who could lead the elite Italian militia M Division, armed and trained by the German SS, to take over Rome and re-establish Mussolini in power. He described Farinacci's arrival: ⟨There was nothing the matter with him, apart from a torn jacket and a few bruises, but the jacket was part of a civilian suit, which struck me as an unpromising sign. My fears were confirmed. Farinacci gave the ambassador a dignified lecture on his, Farinacci's, obligation to serve the cause of Fascism in Germany. Since he was anxious to commend himself to Hitler as future head of the Italian government, he asked to be conducted to Field Marshal Kesselring, with all possible haste. He did not mention the Duce, and I was reminded that there had never been much love lost between the two men. Farinacci, too, declared his intention of leaving the embassy attired as a German airman.[39]

It was in fact in the uniform of a Luftwaffe officer that Farinacci that same night was driven to the nearby headquarters of Field Marshal Albert Kesselring at Frascati, from where, at his insistent request, the next morning he was flown to Munich.

The Italian people abandoned themselves to delirious outbursts of joy for the end of the Fascist regime, only to have their enthusiasm immediately dampened by Badoglio's proclamation that the war would continue and the German alliance would be faithfully upheld. Hitler and his henchmen correctly assumed that the new Italian government could not be trusted, and they began to plan steps to gain control of the Italian military and political situation, including in their plans the *ras* of Cremona. Farinacci was by now on his way to Hitler's headquarters at Rastenburg, in East Prussia. "The Fuehrer," wrote Goebbels in his diary on July 27, ⟨intends to use Farinacci in setting up an Italian countergovernment. This countergovernment is to be in power and supported by us as long as we can't get hold of the Duce. . . . I had a number of broadcasting stations in southern France changed over into illegal stations. . . . Farinacci might

39. Eugen Dollmann, *The Interpreter* (London: Hutchinson & Co., Ltd., 1967), p. 233.

use these broadcasting stations to address the Italian public in case he proves serviceable for our purposes. But we shall first have to wait and see what attitude Farinacci assumes.[40]

On July 27, 1943, Farinacci reached Hitler's headquarters, and after being first interviewed by Ribbentrop, he was received by the Fuehrer. There, according to Goebbels, whose diary provides the only known account of Farinacci's movements during these crucial days, "he behaved very unwisely." The Nazi propaganda chief wrote: [The Fuehrer expected he [Farinacci] would express his profound regret at developments and at least stand unreservedly by the Duce. This, however, he did not do. His report to the Fuehrer consisted mainly in severe criticism of the personality and conduct of the Duce. As he described events, the Duce was violently attacked by Ciano, Grandi, and several other defeatists during the session of the Fascist Grand Council. Farinacci, as I have already pointed out, found fault with him more from the viewpoint of Fascist ideology . . . It looks to me as though that clumsy fool Farinacci had been coaxed into taking part in a knavish plot of the Italian aristocracy and Freemasonry and now, of course, does not want to admit his guilt, even though it was involuntary. From the Fuehrer's talk with Farinacci, it is evident that this man cannot be used by us on any grand scale. Nevertheless we are making sure of keeping control of him. The Fuehrer handed him over to Himmler to look after for the present. Farinacci is a completely broken man. It is gradually dawning on him that he managed to put his foot in it.[41]

Obviously, in his eagerness to replace Mussolini as the head of Fascism, Farinacci had misjudged the morbidly close ties between

40. *The Goebbels Diaries*, p. 409. The initial reports received from Doll-mann and Mackensen had already given the German leaders a fairly accurate picture of the situation, including Farinacci's part in the Grand Council meeting, so that Goebbels, as early as July 26, could write: "Unfortunately Farinacci was also involved. . . . He had been prevailed upon to criticize Mussolini but wanted to give the whole attack a Fascist trend. He failed to prevail and thereby did great harm to the Fascist cause," while Hitler the next day felt that "Farinacci . . . possibly with the best of will and the noblest of intentions, had played a role that proved fatal." (*Ibid.*, pp. 406–407).

41. *Ibid.*, pp. 413–414.

the German and the Italian dictators, and he had overestimated his own standing with the Nazi leaders, who were quick to change their views about him to align them with Hitler's. The next day, Goebbels had a long talk with Hitler and was confirmed in his judgment, for he found the Fuehrer "tremendously disappointed in Farinacci. He [Hitler] expected to see an enthusiastic follower of the *Duce* and in reality met a broken man, who tries to slander the *Duce* by criticizing him in a tearful voice. With a fellow like that you naturally can't do much."[42]

What the Nazi leaders did do with Farinacci was to allow him and Giovanni Preziosi, founder of *Vita Italiana* who had also managed to escape to Germany, to broadcast from Radio Munich a series of messages to the Italian people extolling German armed might and urging resistance against the Allied "invaders." A few other Fascist leaders had also managed to reach Germany, among them Mussolini's oldest son, Vittorio; Renato Ricci, an old-time *squadrista*, the original leader of the Fascist youth organizations, who had been Minister of Corporations until the previous February; and Alessandro Pavolini, also dismissed in the February 1943 "changing of the guard" from his post as Minister of Popular Culture, and then made editor of the Rome daily, *Il Messaggero*.

When, on September 8, 1943, the announcement came of an armistice between the Badoglio government and the Allies who had landed successfully that same day at Salerno, south of Naples,[43] the Nazi leadership immediately considered the formation of a puppet Fascist government in Italy. While they considered a new policy, the Wehrmacht proceeded to disarm all Italian military units within reach and to occupy all major Italian cities. During the night of September 8, 1943, at Himmler's urging, Farinacci and the other exiled Italian oligarchs broadcast a proclamation to Italy announcing that a new Italian National Fascist government would be formed.[44] With King Victor

42. *Ibid.*, p. 417.

43. On September 3, British troops had already crossed the Messina Strait and had landed at the tip of the Italian peninsula, near Reggio Calabria.

44. Attilio Tamaro, *Due anni di storia, 1943–1945* (Rome: Tosi, 1948), I, 448.

Emmanuel and his government fleeing Rome to escape capture, the Italian capital was soon once more in the hands of Fascists, who now had the backing of Kesselring's troops. Before Farinacci and the others, however, could obtain Hitler's permission to join a resurgent Fascist leadership in Italy, Mussolini was rescued on September 12 from his mountaintop detention compound by a German paratroop raid, and he was immediately flown to Germany. There, after a comradely reunion with Hitler, he met with the small group of Fascist exiles. To their urging that he immediately form a new Fascist government, the *Duce* demurred; and it was only after several days of talks and meetings with Hitler that Mussolini agreed to constitute the Italian Social Republic, which, under German tutelage, would eventually establish its seat of government on the shores of Lake Garda, in Lombardy, where it would carry on a precarious existence until the final debacle, less than twenty months later.[45]

Farinacci, according to the apocryphal diary attributed to him, proposed that Mussolini be president and he prime minister of the new republic, a scheme to which the *Duce* at first seemed to agree, only to change his mind suddenly and to refuse Farinacci even the ministry of the interior or the secretaryship of the new Republican Fascist party, for either of which the *ras* of Cremona would have settled. There is no documentary evidence of these negotiations; but that the perennial conflict between the two men resulted in Farinacci's exclusion from the infant puppet government and his withdrawal from public life is shown by a brief handwritten note which Farinacci addressed on September 21, 1943, to the *Duce* at Mussolini's temporary residence in Bavaria. "Dear President," Farinacci wrote, "please grant me a last interview, before I clarify my loyal and unequivocal position with the German comrades. Last night I reflected deeply about everything, and have decided my line of conduct: just to save my family from the inevitable catastrophe. Yes, dear president, your latest

---

45. The definitive work on this period is F. W. Deakin, *The Six Hundred Days of Mussolini*, revised edition (Garden City, N.Y.: Doubleday & Company, Inc., 1966).

policies leave your old and faithful comrades without any hope."[46] Whether such a meeting took place—and, if so, what was said— is unknown. A week later, however, Farinacci's *Il Regime Fascista*, which had not been published since July 25—a lapse of some two months—reappeared on the streets of Cremona under a banner headline: *Eccomi di ritorno!* (I am back). During the night, riding in a Luftwaffe command car and escorted by two armed German motorcyclists, Farinacci had arrived in Cremona; and, after quickly rallying those of his supporters who had just come out of hiding, he had retaken possession of his newspaper and home. Farinacci's first editorial sounded as if he would at once begin a reign of terror to seek revenge on all the many who had promptly turned against Fascism on the previous July 25.[47] But no reprisals were made, and even Farinacci's old enemy Guido Miglioli, who had returned to Cremona a few weeks earlier, was allowed to remain without being molested.

The remaining period of Farinacci's life, in fact, was relatively colorless and anticlimactic. Rejected both by Mussolini and by the Germans for any post of national responsibility, and yet not liable to punishment for any treasonable activity, he resumed his role of a strictly local chieftain. Actually, he ruled the city and province of Cremona on behalf of the Germans, who, according to wide-spread rumors, paid him a monthly subsidy of 150,000 lire. Farinacci's newspaper was published daily, carrying pro-German news and editorials as well as the edicts of the German military commanders. From time to time, he published appeals for a return to Fascist intransigence, coupled with veiled attacks on the pseudosocialist doctrines of Mussolini's puppet government. Some of Farinacci's energies were absorbed in financing and trying to control a political movement started early in 1944 by an excommunicated priest, Father Tullio Calcagno, who advocated a return to evangelical purity mixed with Fascist social theories in the form of a schism within the Catholic church. The movement, *Crociata Italica* (Italian Crusade), published a weekly magazine by the same name which was printed on Farinacci's

46. Farinacci to Mussolini, September 21, 1943, ID–NA, T586, 031539.
47. *Il Regime Fascista* (Cremona), September 28, 1943.

presses in Cremona.[48] Farinacci at one time pointedly reminded Father Calcagno that the magazine was "published to back up discreetly *Il Regime Fascista's* campaign against the policies of the Vatican and of the great mass of the clergy who act against the interests of the Motherland."[49]

Even more of Farinacci's time and efforts were spent in legal maneuvers and political wire-pulling aimed at regaining full control of his private patrimony. One of the first acts of the Badoglio puppet government had been to install a Special Commission to Investigate Illicit Enrichment and to place in the custody of government receivers all moneys, stocks, and real estate belonging to the fallen Fascist chieftains. Farinacci's newspaper, apartments and lands, and three and one-half million *lire* in government bonds had been confiscated at once. Learning of this action in his German exile, Farinacci had written the Commission a long, obsequious letter, intended to prove that his wealth had come from legitimate sources rather than from graft or political contributions[50] and listing in great detail the many legal matters he had handled during his career and the large fees he had collected. When Mussolini returned to northern Italy at the end of September, disillusioned and embittered over the Fascist leaders of whom the vast majority had forsaken him, he decided that the Commission should continue its work. The investigators ascertained that, from 1926 to 1943, Farinacci, on the basis of his own letter of the previous August, had earned at least twelve

48. Early in 1943, Farinacci and Giovanni Preziosi had quarrelled, and the latter had broken any connection between *Vita Italiana* and *Il Regime Fascista*. During the short life of the Social Republic, Preziosi acted as Propaganda Chief and again published his monthly, in which, sometimes, he attacked Farinacci. After printing the three motions presented at the last meeting of the Grand Council, for instance, and pointing out that Farinacci's motion also asked the king to relieve Mussolini of command, Preziosi once wrote: "If the nineteen Grand Council members who approved the Grandi motion have been considered traitors and as such sentenced to death, why was similar action not taken against Farinacci?" (*Vita Italiana* [September 1944], p. 97.)

49. Farinacci to Father Calcagno, November 17, 1944, ID–NA, T586, 030037–030039.

50. Farinacci to Special Commission, August 28, 1943, *ibid.*, 031406–031415.

million *lire*, but he had declared and paid income tax during the same period on much lower amounts, so that he had evaded taxes for more than three million *lire*. The *ras* of Cremona stormed and protested; but after several meetings, the Commission issued its verdict, which not only fined Farinacci three million *lire*, but decreed that the newspaper and its properties, having been financed by contributions rather than by Farinacci's own funds, did not belong to him, but to the state.[51]

Farinacci now attacked editorially the new Fascist Minister of Justice, Piero Pisenti, who had jurisdiction over the matter,[52] and appealed to Mussolini with a long and bitter letter accusing the commission of persecuting him.[53]

He then obtained an audience with the *Duce* and afterwards sent him a formal request for an executive pardon, accompanied by a covering letter in which he bewailed "the sacking of [his] Milan law office by the Badoglio riffraff and the loss of the house and lands in Rome." He claimed that all he had left were the government bonds held by the republican administration to guarantee payment of the three-million-*lire* fine levied against him for tax evasion, and asked that the fine be remitted and the bonds returned.[54] Mussolini, however, was adamant, and the original of Farinacci's formal request in Mussolini's archives bears the *Duce*'s handwritten notation dated October 8, 1944: "Have written a note to [Finance] Minister Pellegrini, asking him to handle the Farinacci case according to the laws and regulations applicable to all citizens."

Farinacci, although kept by the Germans as Gauleiter of Cremona, was truly *persona non grata* to the puppet Fascist Republican government. His low standing in the regime was revealed, a few months later, when a sadistic criminal who had led the Fascist Secret Police in Milan, the notorious Lieutenant Koch, was finally arrested by the Germans: Koch wrote Farinacci a letter which was censored and confiscated by Mussolini's

51. Decision of the Special Commission for the Confiscation by the State of Wealth of Unjustified Origin, June 15, 1944, *ibid.*, 031430–031463.

52. *Il Regime Fascista* (Cremona), June 26, 1944.

53. Farinacci to Mussolini, July 6, 1944, ID–NA, T586, 031483–031498.

54. Farinacci to Mussolini, September 6, 1944, *ibid.*, 031505–031508.

Minister of the Interior, Guido Buffarini Guidi. The *ras* of Cremona denounced this intrusion to Mussolini, complaining also of other arbitrary actions on the part of Buffarini Guidi,[55] but the letter remained unanswered and he received no satisfaction.

Aside from his personal affairs, however, all through the period of the Social Republic's short life, Farinacci periodically wrote Mussolini also about political matters, but his influence was nil, and in any event the Duce and his puppet regime were truly powerless. There is no evidence that Farinacci personally took part in the continuous campaign of repression and terror conducted by the Germans and by the neo-Fascist Black Brigades against the Italian partisans who fought against them in the mountains and in the valleys in ever-increasing numbers and with mounting intensity and success. He was, however, as brutally intransigent as ever. When Mussolini announced in the spring of 1944 that all partisans would be shot on the spot but promised an amnesty for those who turned in their arms before May 25, Farinacci objected to Mussolini's "softness" in granting a period of grace.[56]

To the end, Farinacci also remained intolerant of any deviation from what he considered pure totalitarian Fascism. When, in March 1945, a neo-Fascist writer, Edmondo Cione, managed to obtain Mussolini's permission to publish *L'Italia Libera*, a daily newspaper which promised to offer "constructive criticism," Farinacci, oblivious to the realities of the military and political situation, thundered editorially against the unorthodox initiative: ([At a time when we are readying our youth to fight on the Apennine front and on the home front against our enemies, be they foreigners or foreign agents, such sudden sentimentalities, such absurd generosities, such strange proposals, would seriously smack of defeatism. . . . What we need is war and a fight to the finish to redeem the integrity and the honor of our Motherland. . . . We have repeated again and again that the pre-requisite of our internal social policy must be war and victory.*[57]

55. Farinacci to Mussolini, January 4, 1945, *ibid.*, 031509.
56. Charles F. Delzell, *Mussolini's Enemies: The Italian Anti-Fascist Resistance* (Princeton, N.J.: Princeton University Press, 1961), p. 378.
57. *Il Regime Fascista* (Cremona), March 29, 1945.

In any event, whether because of Farinacci's attacks or through the realization that the end had arrived for Hitler's Germany and for its Fascist puppet, Cione's newspaper ceased publication after only thirteen issues.[58] Early in April 1945, the Allied forces which had wintered on the Gothic Line between Florence and Bologna launched their final offensive. By the middle of the month, the Allied breakthrough was accomplished. Within a few days, vast areas of northern Italy were controlled by armed partisan groups organized by the clandestine National Liberation Committees which had been formed by coalition of all anti-Fascist political parties soon after the German take-over in the fall of 1943. The end was plainly in sight. By the last week of April 1945, just as Mussolini, with his mistress and surviving ministers, was attempting to reach the much discussed but nonexistent "Alpine redoubt" in southern Germany where the remnants of the Wehrmacht were rumored to plan a last stand, Farinacci also decided to escape. Only two days earlier, on April 25, in the last issue of his newspaper, he had expressed confidence that Fascism would ultimately triumph; and in a defiant tirade against "the scum coming back to the surface"—referring to the partisans—he had warned that he would personally avenge any Fascist harmed by them in Cremona.[59] For all his bluster, however, Farinacci, towards noon on April 27, entered a limousine with his friend Marchioness Carla Medici del Vascello and a bodyguard and drove off along side roads, trying to reach the main highway linking Milan to the Stelvio Pass between Italy and Switzerland. Near the village of Beverate, southeast of Milan, the partisans had established a roadblock; and when Farinacci, who was driving, ignored their challenge and tried to speed away, the partisans opened fire. The bodyguard in the back seat was killed instantly; Marchioness Medici was fatally wounded. Farinacci, protected by luggage piled on the back seat, was unscathed, but he lost control of the car and was soon surrounded by the partisans who, recognizing him, loaded him on a truck under guard and took him to their headquarters in the nearby town of

---

58. Delzell, *Mussolini's Enemies*, p. 474.
59. *Il Regime Fascista* (Cremona), April 25, 1945.

Vimercate. Early the next morning, Farinacci was taken before a summary court composed of members of the various parties joined in the National Liberation Committee. Farinacci claimed to be innocent of any wrongdoing, pointing out that he had held no official posts in the Fascist regime since 1926. "If you were to take me to Cremona," he argued, "my beloved townsmen would let me go free." The representatives of the Christian-Democratic and the Liberal parties proposed that he be turned over to the Allies, but the majority of the court sentenced the *ras* of Cremona to death by shooting. Half an hour later, after having asked and received the assistance of a local priest, Roberto Farinacci was executed by a partisan firing squad.[60]

60. Eyewitness reports in Annibale Del Mare, *Brianza, cimitero di Fascisti*, quoted in *Il Meridiano* (Naples), December 8, 1958. Both Delzell (*Mussolini's Enemies*, p. 542) and Wiskemann (*The Rome-Berlin Axis*, p. 394), wrote that Farinacci's body was taken to Milan and there exposed to the populace on the Piazzale Loreto, together with the corpses of Mussolini, his mistress, and the other Fascist bosses who had been shot by the partisans at Dongo the day before. This version is not correct, for Farinacci was buried at once at Vimercate. It was not until 1956 that, after a series of legal battles with the municipal authorities, his daughter Adriana succeeded in removing his body to the family plot in Cremona.

BIBLIOGRAPHY

Alatri, Paolo. *L'antifascismo italiano*. 2nd edition. Palermo: Editori Riuniti, 1965.

——. *Le origini del Fascismo*. Rome: Editori Riuniti, 1956.

Alfieri, Dino. *Dictators Face to Face*. London and New York: Elek, 1954.

Aquarone, Alberto. *L'organizzazione dello stato totalitario*. Turin: G. Einaudi, 1965.

Arendt, Hannah. *The Origins of Totalitarianism*. New enlarged edition. New York: Harcourt Brace & World, 1966.

Badoglio, Pietro. *L'Italia nella seconda guerra mondiale (memorie e documenti)*. Milan: Mondadori, 1946.

Balbo, Italo. *Diario 1922*. Milan: A. Mondadori, 1932.

Bauer, Riccardo. *Fascismo e antifascismo (1936–1948)*. Milan: Feltrinelli, 1962.

Bianchi, Gianfranco. *25 luglio—crollo di un regime*. Milan: U. Mursia & C., 1966.

Bonomi, Ivanoe. *Leonida Bissolati e il movimento socialista in Italia*. Milan: Cogliati, 1929.

Bottai, Giuseppe. *Vent 'anni e un giorno: 24 luglio 1943*. Milan: Garzanti, 1949.

Cancogni, Manlio. *Storia dello squadrismo*. Milan: Longanesi & Co., 1959.

Canevari, Emilio. *Graziani mi ha detto*. Rome: Magi-Spinetti Editori, 1947.

——. *La guerra italiana—retroscena della disfatta*. Rome: Tosi Editore, 1949.

Carli, Mario. *Fascismo intransigente*. Florence: R. Bemporad e Figlio, 1926.

Cavallero, Carlo. *Il dramma del maresciallo Cavallero*. Milan: Mondadori, 1952.

Chabod, Federico. *L'Italia contemporanea 1918–1948*. Turin: Giulio Einaudi editore, 1961.

Ciano, Galeazzo. *Diary, 1937–1938*. Translated by Andreas Mayor. London: Methuen, 1952.

——. *L'Europa verso la catastrofe*. Milan: A. Mondadori, 1948.

——. *The Ciano Diaries, 1939–1943*. Edited by Hugh Gibson. Garden City, N.Y.: Doubleday & Co., Inc., 1946.

Cusin, Fabio. *Antistoria d'Italia*. Turin: Giulio Einaudi editore, 1948.

Deakin, F. W. *The Brutal Friendship: Mussolini, Hitler, and the Fall of Italian Fascism*. Revised edition. Garden City, N.Y.: Doubleday & Company, Inc., 1966.

——. *The Six Hundred Days of Mussolini*. Revised edition. Garden City, N.Y.: Doubleday & Company, Inc., 1966.

De Begnac, Ivon. *Palazzo Venezia, storia di un regime*. Rome: Editrice La Rocca, 1950.

De Felice, Renzo. *Mussolini il rivoluzionario*. Turin: Giulio Einaudi editore, 1965.

———. *Mussolini il fascista*. Turin: Giulio Einaudi editore, 1966–68.

———. *Storia degli ebrei italiani sotto il fascismo*. Turin: Giulio Einaudi editore, 1962.

Del Giudice, Mario. *Cronistoria del processo Matteotti*. Palermo: La Cartografica, 1955.

Delzell, Charles F. *Mussolini's Enemies: The Italian Anti-Fascist Resistance*. Princeton, N.J.: Princeton University Press, 1961.

Dollmann, Eugen. *The Interpreter*. Translated by J. Maxwell Brownjohn. London: Hutchinson & Co., Ltd., 1967.

Dumini, Amerigo. *Diciassette colpi*. Milan: Longanesi, 1951.

Farinacci, Roberto. *Andante mosso, 1924–25*. Milan: A. Mondadori, 1929.

———. *Da Vittorio Veneto a Piazza San Sepolcro*. Milan: A. Mondadori, 1933.

———. *In difesa di Dumini* (Summation speech at Chieti trial). Rome: Libreria dell'800, 1944.

———. *La Chiesa e gli Ebrei*. Cremona: Societa Editoriale "Cremona Nuova," 1938.

———. *Squadrismo. Dal mio diario della vigilia, 1919–1922*. Rome: Edizioni Ardita, 1933.

———. *Storia della Rivoluzione Fascista*. Cremona: Societa Editoriale "Cremona Nuova," 1939.

———. *Un periodo aureo del Partito Nazionale Fascista* (Collected Speeches, 1925–26). Foligno: Campitelli Editore, 1927.

Gobetti, Piero. *Matteotti*. Rome: Libreria dell'800, 1944.

[Goebbels, Paul Joseph]. *The Goebbels Diaries: 1942–1943*. Edited and translated by Louis P. Lochner. Garden City, N.Y.: Doubleday & Co., Inc., 1948.

Graziani, Rodolfo. *Ho difeso la patria*. Cernusco sul Naviglio: Garzanti, 1948.

Guariglia, Raffaele. *Ricordi 1922–1946*. Naples: Edizioni Scientifiche Italiane, 1950.

Hibbert, Christopher. *Benito Mussolini, a Biography*. London: Longmans, Green & Co., Ltd., 1962.

Italian Central State Archives, Rome: Bissolati Fund, Farinacci Fund, *Mostra della Rivoluzione Fascista* Fund.

Keene, Frances, editor. *Neither Liberty nor Bread*. New York and London: Harper & Brothers, 1940.

Kirkpatrick, Sir Ivone. *Mussolini, a Study in Power*. New York: Hawthorn Books, 1964.

Leto, Guido. *OVRA, fascismo, antifascismo*. Rocca San Casciano: Cappelli, 1952.

———. *Polizia segreta in Italia*. Rome: Vito Bianco Editore, 1961.

Ludwig, Emil. *Colloqui con Mussolini*. Milan: A. Mondadori, 1932.

Mack Smith, Denis. *Italy: A Modern History*. Ann Arbor, Mich.: University of Michigan Press, 1959.

Matteotti, Giacomo. *The Fascisti Exposed*. Translated by E. W. Diekes. London: Independent Labour Party Publication Dept., 1924.

Mayer, Domenico. *La verità sul processo di Verona*. Milan: A. Mondadori, 1945.

Megaro, Gaudens. *Mussolini in the Making*. Boston and New York: Houghton Mifflin Company, 1938.

Miglioli, Guido. *Con Roma e con Mosca, quarant 'anni di battaglie*. Milan: Garzanti, 1945.

Mussolini, Benito. *Opera Omnia*. Edited by Edoardo and Duilio Susmel. Florence: La Fenice, 1951–63.

———. *The Fall of Mussolini*. Edited by Max Ascoli, translated by Frances Frenaye. New York: Farrar, Straus and Company, 1948.

Mussolini, Rachele, in collaboration with Michael Chinigo. *My Life with Mussolini*. London: Robert Hale Ltd., 1959.

Nenni, Pietro. *Vent 'anni di Fascismo*. Milan: Edizioni Avanti, 1964.

Nolte, Ernst. *Three Faces of Fascism. Action Francaise, Italian Fascism, National Socialism*. Translated by Leila Vennewitz. New York: Holt, Rinehart & Winston, 1965.

Pantaleo, Paolo. *Il fascismo cremonese*. Cremona: Societa Editoriale "Cremona Nuova," 1931.

Pausa, Giampaolo. *Guerra partigiana tra Genova e il Po*. Bari: Editori Laterza, 1967.

Pini, Giorgio, and Duilio Susmel. *Mussolini, l'uomo e l'opera*. Florence: La Fenice, 1953–55.

Preti, Luigi. *Le lotte agrarie nella valle padana*. Turin: Einaudi editori, 1955.

Preziosi, Giovanni. *Giudaismo, bolscevismo, plutocrazia, massoneria*. Milan: Mondadori, 1941.

Repaci, Antonino. *Fascismo, vecchio e nuovo*. Turin: Bottega d'Erasmo, 1954.

Ricchezza, Antonio. *La resistenza dietro le quinte*. Milan: Giovanni De Vecchi, Editore, 1967.

Rintelen, Enno von. *Mussolini l'alleato: ricordi dell' addetto militare tedesco a Roma, 1936–1943*. Translated by Cesare Alfieri. 2nd edition. Rome: Corso, 1952.

Rocca, Massimo. *Come il Fascismo divenne una dittatura*. Milan: Edizioni Librarie Italiane, 1952.

Rossi, Cesare. *Il delitto Matteotti*. Milan: Casa Editrice Ceschina, 1965.

———. *Mussolini com'era*. Rome: Ruffolo Editore, 1947.

———. *Personaggi d'ieri e di oggi*. Milan: Casa Editrice Ceschina, 1960.

———. *Trentatre vicende Mussoliniane*. Milan: Casa Editrice Ceschina, 1958.

Rossini, Giuseppe. *Il delitto Matteotti tra il Viminale e l'Aventino*. Bologna: Il Mulino, 1948.

Salvatorelli, Luigi. *Nazionalfascismo*. Turin: Piero Gobetti, 1923.
Salvatorelli, Luigi, and Giovanni Mira. *Storia d'Italia nel periodo fascista*. Revised edition. Turin: Giulio Einaudi editore, 1964.
Salvemini, Gaetano. *The Fascist Dictatorship in Italy*. New York: Henry Holt & Company, 1927.
———. *Mussolini diplomatico, 1922–32*. Bari: Gius. Laterza & Figli, 1948.
Santarelli, Enzo. *Storia del movimento e del regime fascista*. Rome: Editori Riuniti, 1967.
Scorza, Carlo. *La notte del Gran Consiglio*. Milan: Palazzi, Editore, 1968.
Senise, Carmine. *Quand'ero Capo della Polizia*. Rome: Ruffolo Editore, 1946.
Silvestri, Carlo. *Matteotti, Mussolini, e il dramma italiano*. Rome: Ruffolo, 1947.
Spagnuolo, G. *Ceka fascista e delitto Matteotti*. Rome: Ruffolo, 1947.
Susmel, Edoardo. *Mussolini e il suo tempo*. Milan: Garzanti, 1950.
Tamaro, Attilio. *Venti anni di storia, 1922–1942*. Rome: Editrice Tiber, 1953.
———. *Due anni di storia, 1943–1945*. Rome: Tosi Editore, 1948.
Tasca, Angelo. *Nascita e avvento del Fascismo: L'Italia dal 1918 al 1922*. 2nd edition. Florence: La Nuova Italia, 1963.
Toscano, Mario. *La politica estera italiana dal 1914 al 1943*. Turin: ERI, 1963.
———. *The Diplomatic Origins of the Pact of Steel*. Revised Edition. Baltimore, Md.: The Johns Hopkins Press, 1967.
U.S. National Archives, Washington, D.C.: Italian Documents, Microfilm Collection T586, Frames 1 to 113,217.
Vivarelli, Roberto. *Il dopoguerra in Italia e l'avvento del Fascismo (1918–1922)*. Naples: Istituto Italiano per gli Studi Storici, 1967.
Wiskemann, Elizabeth. *The Rome-Berlin Axis: A Study of the Relations between Hitler and Mussolini*. New revised edition. London: Collins Clear-Type Press, 1966.

INDEX